ESSENTIAL ACADEMIC SKILLS

SECOND EDITION

ESSENTIAL ACADEMIC SKILLS

Kathy Turner   Brenda Krenus
Lynette Ireland   Leigh Pointon

OXFORD
UNIVERSITY PRESS
AUSTRALIA & NEW ZEALAND

OXFORD
UNIVERSITY PRESS

Oxford University Press is a department of the University of Oxford.

It furthers the University's objective of excellence in research, scholarship, and education by publishing worldwide. Oxford is a registered trademark of Oxford University Press in the UK and in certain other countries.

Published in Australia by
Oxford University Press
253 Normanby Road, South Melbourne, Victoria 3205, Australia

© Kathy Turner, Lynette Ireland, Brenda Krenus and Leigh Pointon 2011

The moral rights of the authors have been asserted.

First published 2008
Revised edition published 2009
Second edition published 2011
Reprinted 2012 (twice), 2015 (D)

National Library of Australia Cataloguing-in-Publication data

Essential academic skills / Kathy Turner ... [et al.].
2nd ed.

9780195576054 (pbk.)

Includes bibliographical references and index.

Study skills.
Education, Higher.

Turner, Kathy.

378.170281

Edited by Bruce Gillespie
Typeset by diacriTech, Chennai, India
Proofread by James Anderson
Indexed by Heather Carlile
Printed and bound in Australia by Ligare Book Printers, Pty Ltd

Links to third party websites are provided by Oxford in good faith and for information only. Oxford disclaims any responsibility for the materials contained in any third party website referenced in this work.

CONTENTS

GUIDED TOUR

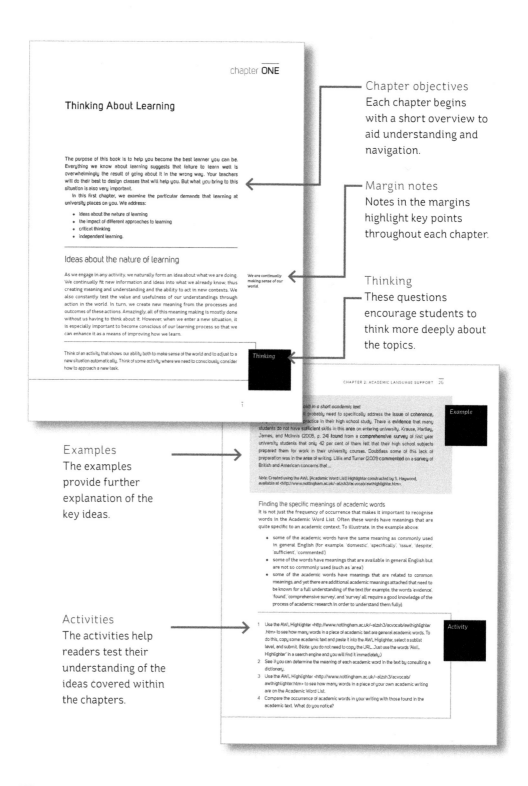

Chapter objectives
Each chapter begins with a short overview to aid understanding and navigation.

Margin notes
Notes in the margins highlight key points throughout each chapter.

Thinking
These questions encourage students to think more deeply about the topics.

Examples
The examples provide further explanation of the key ideas.

Activities
The activities help readers test their understanding of the ideas covered within the chapters.

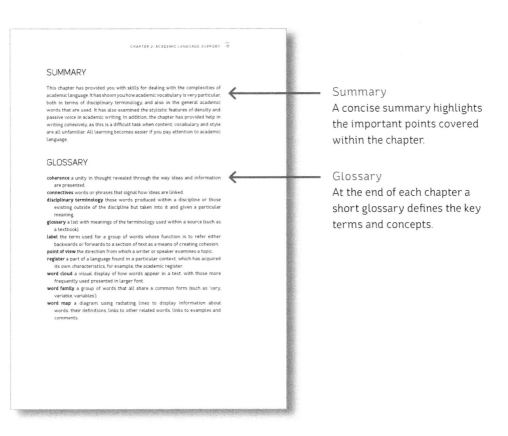

SUMMARY

This chapter has provided you with skills for dealing with the complexities of academic language. It has shown you how academic vocabulary is very particular, both in terms of disciplinary terminology, and also in the general academic words that are used. It has also examined the stylistic features of density and passive voice in academic writing. In addition, the chapter has provided help in writing cohesively, as this is a difficult task when content, vocabulary and style are all unfamiliar. All learning becomes easier if you pay attention to academic language.

GLOSSARY

coherence a unity in thought revealed through the way ideas and information are presented.

connectives words or phrases that signal how ideas are linked.

disciplinary terminology those words produced within a discipline or those existing outside of the discipline but taken into it and given a particular meaning.

glossary a list with meanings of the terminology used within a source (such as a textbook).

label the term used for a group of words whose function is to refer either backwards or forwards to a section of text as a means of creating cohesion.

point of view the direction from which a writer or speaker examines a topic.

register a part of a language found in a particular context, which has acquired its own characteristics, for example, the academic register.

word cloud a visual display of how words appear in a text, with those more frequently used presented in larger font.

word family a group of words that all share a common form (such as 'vary, variable, variables').

word map a diagram using radiating lines to display information about words: their definitions, links to other related words, links to examples and comments.

Summary
A concise summary highlights the important points covered within the chapter.

Glossary
At the end of each chapter a short glossary defines the key terms and concepts.

Online resources
There are further resources available for students available at the website. Please go to <www.oup.com.au/orc/turner2e> for more details.

CONTRIBUTORS

Kathy Turner has a PhD from the University of Queensland. She has lectured at Griffith University in Industrial Relations and published in the areas of Industrial Relations and Labour Process Theory. She is presently working at the Queensland Institute of Business and Technology, where she has developed and teaches courses on academic skills to both undergraduate and postgraduate students.

Lynette Ireland holds a degree in teaching, a postgraduate qualification in applied linguistics (ESL) and a Masters in Social Science. She is currently undertaking her PhD, encompassing thinking in learning. Her lecturing includes courses such as Academic Writing, Australian Indigenous Languages and Cultures, Cultural Diversity and Critical Literacy and Text Analysis. She has a broad array of experience in all levels and types of teaching, particularly in Indigenous contexts in both Queensland and the Northern Territory. She has also held various managerial positions in the private and the public sectors, as well as being experienced in curriculum design and community consultation in the areas of development, training and legislation. She is currently employed at James Cook University, where she lectures in the Tertiary Access Course, the Bachelor of Education and the Bachelor of Arts.

Brenda Rose Krenus has a Bachelor of Arts (The University of Melbourne), a Bachelor of Education (Secondary, The University of Melbourne), Master of Education (Monash University), Master of Education (The University of Melbourne), and is completing a PhD (Monash University). Brenda has held senior academic and academic management positions in public and corporate tertiary educational environments, including Director of the Graduate Program in English as an International Language for the Faculty of Education, The University of Melbourne. She has also held positions as assessment and quality-assurance coordinator and examiner for local and offshore programs; coordinator and lecturer in a range of 'mainstream', language and alternative pathways programs; developer of teacher education and other programs; senior project manager; writer of educational materials; and an instructional designer and supervising editor. She recently worked as a Senior Adviser, Strategic Initiatives, to the Deputy Vice-Chancellor (Academic) at RMIT. Currently, she is working at the University of Melbourne as Postgraduate Programs Manager, Education and Training.

Leigh Pointon has a Bachelor of Commerce (Hons) from Griffith University and a Graduate Certificate in Higher Education from the Queensland University of Technology. She has delivered courses in Industrial Relations, Human Resource Management, and Employment Relations within the Griffith University Bachelor of Commerce, Employment Relations and Business Communication within the Queensland Institute of Business and Technology Diploma of Commerce, and Government, Business and Society within the Queensland University of Technology Bachelor of Business. More recently Leigh has held educational leadership roles, and is currently the Academic Director of the Queensland Institute of Business and Technology, where she is responsible for managing delivery of nine academic programs.

ACKNOWLEDGMENTS

We are very grateful to all our students. Their eagerness to learn, bravery in asking questions and determination to understand have forced us to consider what it is we do and how we do it. We have been led to explain the steps in what we have taken for granted. In the process, we have enriched our understanding of the essential skills required for learning at university. We hope our learning can feed back into the learning of new students, and make the task of adjusting to university life easier and more exciting.

Many of our colleagues have contributed to the book. We are grateful especially to Margaret Buckridge, whose contribution to Chapter 1 was invaluable. The following have also contributed to the production of this book: Cameron Allen, Michael Browne, Tiiti Gill, William Lawrence, Judith O'Byrne, Leanne O'Neill and Mary-Anne Smith, as well as Therese Egan and the Academic Services team at Griffith University Library. Thank you.

The staff at Oxford University Press in Melbourne have been wonderful. We would especially like to thank our editors for each of the editions of *Essential Academic Skills* for their encouragement, support and expertise: Lucy McLoughlin, Karen Hildebrandt and Jessica Hambridge. We would also like to acknowledge, in particular, Tim Campbell and Estelle Tang, as well as Chris Wyness and Bruce Gillespie for their patience and care in editing the successive editions of this book; Heather Carlile, who created such intuitive and useful indexes for the revised and second editions; and Regine Abos for the design of both the cover and book for this edition.

Finally, as always, this book could not have been written without the support of our families. Thank you.

chapter ONE

Thinking About Learning

The purpose of this book is to help you become the best learner you can be. Everything we know about learning suggests that failure to learn well is overwhelmingly the result of going about it in the wrong way. Your teachers will do their best to design classes that will help you. But what *you* bring to this situation is also very important.

In this first chapter, we examine the particular demands that learning at university places on you. We address:

- ideas about the nature of learning
- the impact of different approaches to learning
- critical thinking
- independent learning.

Ideas about the nature of learning

As we engage in any activity, we naturally form an idea about what we are doing. We continually fit new information and ideas into what we already know, thus creating meaning and understanding and the ability to act in new contexts. We also constantly test the value and usefulness of our understandings through action in the world. In turn, we create new meaning from the processes and outcomes of these actions. Amazingly, all of this meaning making is mostly done without us having to think about it. However, when we enter a new situation, it is especially important to become conscious of our learning process so that we can enhance it as a means of improving how we learn.

We are continually making sense of our world.

Think of an activity that shows our ability both to make sense of the world and to adjust to a new situation automatically. Think of some activity where we need to consciously consider how to approach a new task.

Thinking

You have been involved in learning for a long time. As a natural result of this, you will have formed an idea of what learning is. Your **conception (idea) of learning** has been a useful one. It has enabled you to graduate from high school or university and brought you to your present study program. In the following activity, we are asking you to think about what your idea of learning is.

Activity

Ideas about learning

Complete the following statement to show what learning means to you.

When I say that I have learned something, I mean that I

_____

_____

_____

_____

_____

_____

Which statement below is *nearest* to your idea of learning?

a Learning is when I add to my knowledge.

b Learning is when I have successfully memorised something.

c Learning is when I know something and can use that knowledge in a new context.

d Learning is when I have understood something (it makes sense to me).

e Learning is when I understand things differently.

f Learning is when I am changed as a person because of what I have learned.

Note: Adapted from an activity designed by M. Buckridge, personal communication, January 2006.

All of the statements above are typical understandings of learning. They have been listed as the six conceptions of learning by Marton, Dall'Alba and Beaty (1993, pp. 283–284):

1 Increasing one's knowledge

2 Memorising and reproducing

3 Applying

4 Understanding

5 Seeing something in a different way

6 Changing as a person.

There are two good reasons for becoming aware of what we think learning is about:

- what we think learning is, is closely linked to the strategies and approaches we use to learn
- by becoming aware of what we think, we can change our approaches if new tasks require a new kind of learning.

As you can see from Table 1.1, different learning strategies are usually associated with different ideas about learning.

Students with different conceptions of learning tend to use different strategies to learn.

Table 1.1 Different learning strategies associated with different conceptions of learning

Conception	Learning strategies
Learning means:	If you think about learning this way, these are the things you would probably do in order to learn:
1 Increasing my knowledge	• Make a note of something • Highlight it in a text book • Listen to something, or read it, without taking further action
2 Memorising and reproducing	• Develop a mnemonic (a rhyme, an association) • Make a list of similar things • Say it or write it over and over • Test yourself or get others to test you
3 Applying	• Practise applying it, initially in simple ways • Look for examples • Work on projects that require this new knowledge • Use formulae to solve problems or do calculations • Practise using the knowledge in short answers or essays
4 Understanding	• Think about the new knowledge actively in relation to what you already know • Consider how the new knowledge relates to what you know (is it similar or different?) • Write about it in your own words to clarify it for yourself • Break it into parts and work out how the parts connect with each other • Talk about it • Find additional information about it • Draw a concept map or mind map or other diagram connecting it with other related knowledge • Engage in debates • Look for ideas and information that might show it is wrong or inadequate
5 Seeing something in a different way	• Think actively about the implications in relation to your own experience • Find out about what this means for others • Consider whether this makes a difference to everyday taken-for-granted ways of thinking • Look for how this changes other things you know
6 Changing as a person	• Change your ways of behaving and/or understanding because of what you now know • See yourself and your relationship to others differently

Note: Adapted from a table developed by M. Buckridge, personal communication, January 2006.

Activity

Strategies involved in learning

1 Examine Table 1.1. Tick all the strategies you have ever used for learning. (If you don't understand what is meant by a particular activity, do not tick it, as it means you have not done it.)

2 Go back to your initial conception of learning. Match it up with the main strategies associated with it.
   a Have you ticked all these strategies?
   b Have you ticked other strategies not included in your conception of learning?
   c Consider all the strategies you have ticked. Which ones do you find *most useful* for learning? Underline these.
   d Are the underlined strategies associated with your conception of learning?
   e Are there any strategies you have *never* used?

3 Discuss the following questions with the student sitting next to you:
   a Why might there be a difference between one person's learning conception and the strategies in which he or she has been engaged while learning?
   b Why might there be a difference in learning conceptions between people?

4 Tell the tutorial the main ideas you discovered about learning conceptions and learning strategies.

You have probably noticed that there is some relationship between learning conception and the strategies employed in order to learn. One reason for the close association is probably that both are linked to the motivation or intention a student has in learning.

Intention shapes how we learn.

Students whose main intention is just to pass a course tend to employ strategies that (in their own estimation) allow them to accumulate as much information as possible in the shortest time. They use the strategies associated with learning conceptions 1 and 2, and perhaps also 3. Their general aim is to reproduce the content in the course.

On the other hand, students whose intention to learn is based on their own interest in the content of a course favour those strategies that enhance understanding. They are likely to use strategies associated with the learning conceptions 4, 5 and 6. Their overall aim is to find meaning.

Thinking

Are your learning strategies linked to your aim in studying? Think of particular courses.

Approaches to learning

In order to succeed at university, students need to upgrade their approaches to learning. Marton and Saljo (1984) developed a **theory** of learning, and named two broad approaches: surface and deep. These describe patterns in the intention the student has in learning and the strategies employed as a means of fulfilling that intention. The aim of university education is to help students reach a deep approach to learning.

Students with a **surface approach to learning** are not interested in the content, but in some extrinsic factor (outside of the task). They may, for example, be aiming just to pass in order to obtain employment, or they may be studying because their parents expect it. As a result of a lack of interest and motivation, these students do not aim to understand the content, but to reproduce it. They learn as if they were filing information in a computer. Each new file is given a name and a place. However, the files are not linked. Such students also have a poor search function. While they can easily retrieve a particular file, they find it difficult or impossible to think about ideas that occur in different files.

A student with a surface approach to learning aims to learn by accumulating separate items of information.

Some students consistently employ a surface approach in their learning. However, most students act in a much more strategic manner, using it only occasionally, when the task demands it.

Thinking about a surface approach to learning

1   What happens when you ask a person who has a surface approach to learning *why* something occurs? Why do you get this response?
2   Can you think of anything you have learned with a surface approach? How did you learn it?
3   How long do you find you can retain (keep) information you have learned with a surface approach?

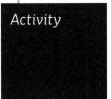

Activity

Students who have a **deep approach to learning** are quite the opposite. Such students have an intrinsic (linked to the task itself) motivation or intention. They want to find meaning in the content by:

- looking for connections between ideas
- looking at the way ideas and information are organised
- examining how their new knowledge fits in with what they already know
- critically assessing ideas and information.

A student with a deep approach to learning aims to create meaning by emphasising connections.

The term deep approach is usually reserved for speaking about students' intentions and strategies within an educational context. However, to reveal the importance of the deep approach in creating meaning, understanding and enjoyment, it is useful to think of it in terms of learning outside of an educational setting.

A student with a deep approach to learning is like a well-informed spectator at a sporting event. Such a spectator not only recognises each player, but also notices how he or she adds to or detracts from the game as a whole; and assesses what is happening in the game in terms of what has occurred in other games. These skills enable the spectator to understand what is so exciting, interesting or poor about the particular event being watched. A student needs to employ these same skills when learning at university.

Activity

Recognising when we have a deep approach to knowledge

1   Find someone else in the tutorial who shares a similar interest to you (such as football, cricket, soccer, table tennis, gymnastics, heavy metal music, travel, or surfing).
2   Take one particular instance (such as a particular player, band or beach). Describe what makes it memorable (or important).
3   Review with your partner how you described it:
    a   Did you make *connections* between aspects of the person or thing you described?
    b   Did you make *connections* to other similar persons or things?
    c   Did you make some judgment of the person or thing?
4   Do you consider you have a deep approach to learning about the topic you have discussed?

Whether a student has the desire or intention to learn in a surface or deep manner depends upon both the student and his or her educational environment. Clearly students have certain preferences for how they learn. The educational setting also encourages students to take a particular approach to knowledge. If a course is structured to provide a vast quantity of information, and if the assessment is aimed at testing how well students can memorise, then students are led into taking a surface approach to their learning. On the other hand, if a course aims to show how ideas and information are connected, and if the assessment tests and encourages students to show how ideas are linked, then students are encouraged to approach learning in a deep manner.

All university courses require a deep approach to learning.

Every university course aims, to some extent, to encourage deep learning. While many courses require some memorising, this is always expected to be carried out within the context of a general understanding of the content.

Although there is much variation in how particular courses are presented, the underlying aim is to encourage deep learning by:

- leading students to see how ideas and information are linked
- encouraging students to become curious and interested in the content
- enabling students to participate in discussion on course topics
- developing students' ability to display their knowledge of the course through assessment that tests not just knowledge of information and ideas, but also how students have thought about and integrated (put together) these.

Thinking about past experience

Activity

Find someone who has come from the same country or the same kind of schooling as yourself.

1 Together, examine the bullet-point list of ways that a university uses to encourage deep learning.

2 Think of how you learned previously (for example, in high school, or in the university in your home country). Were you encouraged to engage in deep learning? Explain your answer.

It is important to reassess our conception of learning as we enter new contexts. In particular, it is necessary to give thoughtful consideration to what kind of learning is expected at university. Domestic and overseas students who have succeeded at school by focusing on memorising separate pieces of information will find they have to transform how they learn in order to be successful at university. Moreover, all students, no matter what their preference is for an approach to learning, need to upgrade their learning skills to cope with the more demanding context at university.

Specific features of learning at university

Critical thinking

Part of the deep approach to learning is the ability to critically assess ideas and information. Indeed, **critical thinking** is one of the most highly prized qualities at university. Although there is debate about its meaning, it can be seen as involving:

- the ability to judge the credibility of a claim and the adequacy of an argument
- the ability to recognise and judge the effect of the social and/or power context on the production and use of knowledge.

Critical thinking traditionally involves considering the credibility of claims and the adequacy of arguments.

The traditional interpretation of critical thinking stresses the skills required in judging the credibility of a claim and the adequacy of an argument. It is based on the belief that claims may not be well supported by evidence, and arguments may not be well made. It involves (Facione, 1990, pp. 12–16) skills in:

- interpretation (finding the meaning of a claim or argument)
- analysis (breaking the argument into parts in order to see the relationship between parts and to the argument as a whole; and recognising assumptions)
- evaluation (judging the credibility of each claim and the degree of confidence that a person could have in the argument as a whole)
- inference (identifying ways to produce evidence in support of a claim; considering opposing views and formulating one's own view)
- explanation (providing reasons for your own conclusions)
- self-examination (reflecting about your own processes of thinking).

Probably in high school or in ESL classes you have engaged in critical thinking in relation to non-academic texts such as news items or political speeches. These are often constructed as arguments in the form of a series of claims leading to, or explaining, a conclusion. They are often adversarial as they are constructed as an argument made against another point of view. They are also likely to be emotive, appealing to the reader's feelings rather than being addressed to their thinking ability.

Activity

Critical thinking in relation to a non-academic text

Read the following text taken directly from the World Nuclear Association website <www. world-nuclear.org/education/intro.htm>:

Nuclear power produces wastes which are contained and managed … The main wastes produced by 'burning' uranium in a nuclear reactor are very hot and radioactive, placing them among the most unpleasant wastes from modern industry. However, these 'high-level' nuclear wastes are modest [i.e. small] in quantity. Handling and storing them safely is quite straightforward, they simply need to be shielded from human exposure, and cooled. Shielding can be by water, concrete, steel or other dense material, cooling is by air or water.

About 30 kg of spent fuel [waste] arises each year in generating enough electricity for about 1000 people in the western world …

One characteristic of all radioactive wastes which distinguishes them from the very [much] larger amount of other industrial wastes is that their radioactivity progressively decays and diminishes.

1   Interpretation:
    a   Make sure you have understood the text.
    b   The word 'simply' [sentence 4] is emotive. Why does the author use it?

2   Analysis:
    a   There are two statements (or claims) made to support the conclusion that 'nuclear
       power produces wastes which are contained and managed'. Underline these.
    b   What is the assumption that is made, but not written, in the claim 'they simply
       need to be shielded from human exposure'?

3   Evaluation:
    a   What evidence is produced to show that: 'these "high-level" nuclear wastes are
       modest in quantity'?
    b   Is this sufficient evidence to draw the conclusion that such wastes can be
       'contained and managed'? Give reasons for your answer.

4   Inference:
    Describe what evidence you would look for if you wanted to show that nuclear wastes
    are effectively 'shielded from human exposure'?

5   Explanation:
    Explain why you think this is a good argument for the safety of nuclear waste, or a
    weak argument.

Although the meaning of 'critical thinking' at university is related to the general idea outlined above, it is not the same. The material at university is complex and non-emotive, quite different from, for example, news items or political speeches. More importantly, the concept of argument is not the same in academic and non-academic contexts. At university, an **argument** is generally not made to support just one side of a debate, as for example, in politics; nor does it merely outline advantages and/or disadvantages of some idea. Typically, it is not adversarial. An argument in a university context generally means the stating and supporting of a position in such a way that an understanding of a topic is displayed. It often also means the presentation of new knowledge with evidence to support it. As well, university work has its own rigorous styles for the presentation of arguments and evidence. Hence, the meaning of 'critical thinking' at university is quite specific to that context.

University work has its own style of critical thinking.

This book teaches you how to engage in critical thinking at university in relation to:

- understanding (interpreting), analysing and evaluating what you listen to (Chapter 3) and what you read (Chapter 4)
- recognising, creating and presenting academic arguments (Chapter 6 especially, but also Chapters 7, 8, 12 and 13)

- recognising and using academic evidence (Chapters 5 and 6)
- evaluating the status of claims within research (Chapters 12 and 13)
- assessing the quality of inference (the support for conclusions) in research reports (Chapters 12 and 13).

Critical thinking includes considering the social and power context of knowledge.

The second way in which critical thinking can be done is to consider the social and power context in which knowledge occurs. The traditional form of critical thinking considers some of these aspects of knowledge, although usually not in any depth. By using a separate category for the social and power context it allows a greater focus to be given to these features. Consider:

- who has produced the knowledge
- who has funded (paid for) the research
- what the impact of the knowledge is.

Knowledge is always produced in a social and power context, and this may lead to problems in credibility. For example, a company or government or institution that performs its own research may create a biased result. As well, any knowledge produced within a social context that sees one group of people as not being equal to those who are researching them may be inadequate or even incorrect. This can be seen in the work of some Western university academics who made misleading claims about Aboriginal people or international students, just because they were working within a culture that holds assumptions about these people.

It is equally important to consider the funding for the research. For example, if a pharmaceutical company funds (pays for) someone to conduct research into one of the company's own drugs, it is reasonable to consider the results may be biased.

A deeper level of critique considers not just the social and power context of how knowledge is produced, but also the effect of the way knowledge is used. Some knowledge can be harmful. It is thus wise to ask a series of questions about knowledge in terms of its effect and use. Burbules and Berk (1999) advocated asking questions such as:

- How does this research benefit some people and not others?
- How is the knowledge generated by the research being used?
- Who is using the knowledge generated by the research?

The process may lead to a more complete analysis of the research on which the knowledge is based as a means of judging its credibility. It may leave the questioner with a moral or ethical decision about the best way to act.

Critical thinking is a skill that is developed over a long period of time and through constant practice and development. The aim is to produce an attitude to knowledge and skills in thinking about it that you can use in your work and your life.

Critical thinking at university

Here is an academic argument. It is an extract from Wong (2004, p. 154).

One of the issues that relates to Asian international students' perceptions about the quality of higher education is with regards to the difficulties and problems they face while studying in an Australian university ... interviews were carried out with nine Asian international students to gain insights into their difficulties and learning experiences. Based on these interviews, the three main difficulties highlighted by Asian international students are: different learning styles, cultural barriers and language problems ...

1   How is Wong's (2004) argument different from the argument given in Activity: Critical thinking in a non-academic text? Think of as many differences as you can.
2   What type of evidence does Wong use to support his argument?
3   What further evidence do you think Wong supplies about the types of students who were interviewed?
4   Do you think that it helps the credibility of the argument that the research was conducted by a person who is likely to be of Asian origin (Wong)? Explain your answer.

Independent learning

Learning well at university means being able to learn independently. Teaching and assessment are set up to place the responsibility of learning on you. Most of the time in each week is 'free', as lectures and tutorials only take up a small number of hours. Teachers at university are not as likely as high school teachers are to check regularly on how much you have learned, or even if you have understood. Most significantly, perhaps, in many subjects, you have to learn by producing your own knowledge beyond that presented in lectures in textbooks. Your assignments, which can be a significant percentage of your final mark, usually require that you find information, organise it, and produce an outcome entirely on your own or within a group of your fellow students.

Independent learning skills are essential for success at university. They also will enable you to deal intelligently with new situations as they arise in your future work and life.

Independent learning means to take responsibility for your own learning. It requires that you:

Independent learning means taking responsibility for your own learning.

- develop the academic skills needed for independent learning
- organise your time well
- reflect about what you know and how you learn
- seek help when required.

Developing academic skills for independent learning

Academic skills are independent learning skills.

All academic skills are built around the concept that when you learn you do not just memorise what is given to you in lectures and textbooks. You create your own learning. As Biggs (1991, p. 2) remarked, 'it is the learner who constructs knowledge'. This occurs not just in the processes of understanding the content of lectures, tutorials and textbooks, but also in finding other information and organising it to display your own understanding of a topic. This book teaches you the extensive independent learning skills involved in most university work:

- how to learn in a lecture and tutorial context (Chapter 3)
- how to find ideas and information by reading beyond the textbook (Chapter 4)
- how to organise your own thinking about a topic area through the production of an argument (Chapter 6)
- how to present your knowledge in a range of formats that show your own assessment and understanding (Chapters 5, 6, 7, 8 and 10)
- how to learn within a group context (Chapter 9)
- how to do your own research as a means of producing new knowledge (Chapters 12 and 13).

Organising time

It is crucial to organise time while studying at university because of the demanding context in which you are learning. Some work is regular, so is easy to plan for. Each week you need to attend and prepare for lectures and tutorials and learn their content. However, the greatest part of university work is irregular, with significant peaks occurring around mid semester and at the end of semester. This requires good planning. For example, you must estimate times for the production of assignments and learning for examinations. You have to engage in the difficult task of taking into account all the factors involved. In the case of assignments, it is essential to plan for accessing sources, reading, production, checking, seeking help, printing and travel. For examinations, you need to consider the time required for the learning of complex material, solving problems, seeking help and practising answers.

Allocate possibly 30 or more hours in total for each assignment. You will need additional time if your reading speed is slow, or English is not your first language, or the assignment is particularly long, or it is the first time you are doing such an assignment, or if it is a group assignment. For examinations, it is best to set up regular revision each week, with additional intense learning time in the days or weeks immediately before the examination.

Further complications that require careful planning are caused by paid work and other life commitments. Most students are not only studying at university but are also engaged in paid employment. The combination can be difficult to manage. Indeed, McInnis and Hartley (2002, p. 37) found 41 per cent of students engaged in paid work reported that it 'gets in the way of their academic study'. As well, all students need to spend time attending to their own lives, ensuring they are adequately cared for and have enjoyment and exercise. Some students also have family responsibilities. Planning will help you to maintain, to a certain extent, a healthy balance of all your needs.

In general, a full-time university load should take up a total of approximately 45 hours per week, including contact hours. However, because of the irregular work load at university you may do less in some weeks and much more in others. Be prepared to be flexible.

When planning, be flexible and maximise the use of 'free' time in a semester.

To organise your time, try the following:

- choose lecture and tutorial times that fit in with your work and other commitments
- ensure paid work commitments are doable for the whole of the semester (not just in the first weeks)
- allocate time for your own life (such as housework, leisure, sport and socialising)
- allocate some time each week for the regular work at university (attendance at and preparation for lectures and tutorials and learning of content)
- map out on a semester timetable the due date for all set assignments and examinations, and other forms of assessment
- select times that suit you for any assignment where you have a choice in time (it is usually best to choose a time early in the semester)
- allocate times for the preparation of assignments and examination revision
- check if it is possible to fit in the preparation times for all assignments. If not, strategically move your preparation times for some assignments to an earlier, less busy period in your semester (for example, use the first weeks of a semester, or the mid-semester break)
- use mid-semester break week as an intense study period
- use the 'study break' (examination revision period) at the end of the semester as an intense study period
- continually monitor how your timetable is going and make changes where necessary.

Using reflection

One of the keys to successful independent learning is the ability to reflect on both the knowledge that you are learning and the processes involved. **Reflection** is a part of learning intelligently (see Chapter 7). The first step in reflection is to stop and consciously think about what is happening. You may discover areas of knowledge that need attention; for example, points you do not understand,

Reflect on what you are learning and how learning occurs.

formulas you do not know how to use or skills that you do not have; or you may be satisfied with what you have learned. As well, you may notice that your learning processes are not as good as they could be; or perhaps you assess them as efficient. The next step in reflection is to plan ways to improve your knowledge, understanding and skills, and enhance your learning processes; or to maintain and strengthen what is working well. Finally, you need to try out your plans. Obviously, reflection is a continual process. The aim is to deepen your learning and to make it more efficient.

Seeking help

Be aware of when you need help and of what support is available.

Universities realise that independent learning places great demands on students both academically and practically, so they provide a wide range of support. In order to make use of this you have to be aware of both your need for help and how to access it. Good time-management plans and reflection will allow you to notice when support is required.

You can receive free help with your academic work by:

- meeting your tutor or lecturer during their consultation times
- emailing your tutor to request a meeting time
- attending workshops (usually organised through the library) to learn skills in any aspect of the presentation of an assignment or on how to use computer software such as PowerPoint or EndNote
- making an appointment with a learning adviser or academic adviser for help with assessments or study
- reading the online documents that explain how to study at university, work on assignments or use computer software
- using the online training tutorials on how to study at university, work on assignments or use computer software
- using the library help desk or other facility (email or chat or phone) for help with searching for sources
- using the services provided for developing English skills and editing assignments
- using other services, such as PALs (peer-assisted learning).

Students also find that other problems and challenges in their life can create difficulties for their academic work. The university offers support in many of these non-academic areas. Students can receive free help from a large range of services, including:

- Indigenous student units
- disability support services
- financial support
- accommodation support

- career and employment support
- counselling (for help with personal issues and also study concerns)
- health (nurses and doctors).

As can be seen, quite extensive help is available. Two problems can occur. The first is that you are not aware of your need for help. The second is that you do not know where to find it. Make it a task for the first week of your first semester to find all the support that is available to you.

Be prepared: Find all the sources of help early in your first semester.

Finding the academic and general support available at your university

1   In groups of two or three students, find all the support available at your university. List:
    a   What is available
    b   Where to find it (such as in the library or online)
    c   How to access it (for example, how to make an appointment, or the phone number or email address to use).

Activity

Go to our website <www.oup.com.au/orc/turner2e> for more activities on the skills covered in this chapter.

Activity

SUMMARY

In this chapter we have explored the nature of learning at university. It calls for a deep approach to knowledge, and the ability to think critically and learn independently. By becoming more aware of what we think learning is, of what kind of learning is required and how learning occurs, we have the power to alter and develop how we learn, and so increase our chances of success.

This book has been written to help you learn at university. It provides you with the essential skills in listening, reading, writing, speaking and researching that are required in undertaking most university courses. In each chapter we show you, in a step-by-step manner, the basic skills needed to complete each learning task. More importantly, we consistently encourage and support you to stretch your skills in learning. Our aim is to help you become the best learner that you can be, for success both at university and in life.

GLOSSARY

argument the statement of a position together with the evidence for each point. It is constructed in such a way that an understanding of a topic is displayed.

conception of learning an idea of what we mean by learning.

critical thinking the consideration of the credibility of claims and the adequacy of arguments, as well as of the social and power contexts in which the knowledge is produced and used.

deep approach to learning the approach to learning where the learner seeks meaning by looking for connections and structures.

independent learning the taking on of the responsibility for learning by the learner.

reflection the technique that involves thinking about the effectiveness of processes and the adequacy of outcomes, and planning and acting as a means of improving the situation.

surface approach to learning the approach by which the learner seeks to remember information as a series of discrete or isolated facts.

theory a description and/or explanation of what occurs, which is supported by evidence and usually produced through a careful process of research.

chapter TWO

Academic Language Support

Academic language is likely to appear foreign to all students, even those whose first language is English. It has a distinctive range of vocabulary. It also uses particular styles of sentence structure that create a density of meaning. Academic language is thus very difficult, especially for new students. Yet it must be learned.

This chapter helps you acquire familiarity with academic language. It teaches you how to recognise its features and gives you some techniques for learning and using it. It also provides help in writing with coherence, as this is made much more difficult when the content, vocabulary and writing style are all new.

Two broad areas are covered in this chapter:

- the distinctiveness of academic style
- creating coherence.

The distinctiveness of academic language

All academic work, whether it is a textbook or a research article, or even a lecture, tends to be presented in a distinctive style, or **register**, that leads to problems for novice users.

The main features of the academic register are:

- use of disciplinary terminology
- dense use of general academic words
- academic style.

Disciplinary terminology

Every occupation or profession produces its own words or uses existing words in a particular manner as a means of creating efficient and precise communication. At university these words are known as **disciplinary terminology**, because each area of study has its own specialised vocabulary. To be successful you must become an adept at recognising, understanding and using these terms.

To become familiar with disciplinary terminology:

1   Recognise that unknown words may be disciplinary terminology.
2   Check to see if the meaning of an unknown term can be discovered by using clues within the text itself.
3   Check a textbook glossary or online disciplinary glossary for meanings.
4   Take steps to become confident in your use of the term.

The first step in finding the meaning of disciplinary terminology is to recognise it. Some disciplinary terminology is relatively close in appearance to commonly used words. Examples of such terms are: 'shares' in accounting and finance; or 'plan' in marketing. Although their meaning is not a problem, care has to be taken with these terms. They often do not have exactly the same meaning within a disciplinary context as they do in everyday communication.

Disciplinary terms may be built on everyday words or invented within a discipline.

Other terms have been invented purely for use in the discipline. Many in science and medicine are developed partially from a different language, for example Latin or Greek. Most disciplines employ acronyms and initialisms. These are abbreviations made up, at least partially, of the first letters of the words used to describe something in full; for example, 'email' for 'electronic mail' and 'CEO' for 'Chief Executive Officer'. Invention of another kind also occurs in all disciplines. This is often done by modifying a noun with one or more other words (nouns and/or adjectives) to create a new name for a concept with a specialised meaning. Examples include: 'financial statement' in accounting; 'heart disease' in medicine; and 'strategic marketing plan' in marketing. Clearly the meanings of these words must be sought within the discipline that invented them.

Look for textual clues for meanings of disciplinary terminology.

Sometimes the unknown terms will be defined within the text. Look for the following, which may mean the text itself will help you understand the meaning:

- words that indicate a definition (for example, 'to define', 'means' and possibly any of the following: 'can be understood as', 'refers to')
- words that indicate an alternative meaning may be being presented (for example, 'in other words', 'or', 'that is')
- words that indicate an example will be supplied (such as 'an example', 'an instance', 'a case in point')
- words that indicate a more complete explanation follows (for example, 'characterised by', 'to explain', 'to elaborate')
- formatting that may indicate that the meaning is being given (where the meaning may be provided in parentheses (brackets) or possibly in a footnote).

The purpose of this exercise is to show how textual clues (clues given by the way the text is written) can lead to a better understanding of the meaning of an unknown term.

In the following extracts disciplinary terminology and other technical terms have been underlined. Find the meaning of the term in the text.

1   The extract is from an article written by Payne and Monk-Turner (2006, p. 132).

> Group projects are becoming a central feature of many college courses. The growth in group projects parallels the increased use of <u>active learning strategies</u> which are often characterized as collaborative or co-operative learning strategies. <u>Collaborative learning</u> "refers to a variety of instructional practices that encourage students to work together as they apply course material to answer questions, solve problems, or create a project" (Colbeck et al., 2000: 60).

2   The extract is from an article by Jung (2003, p. 562).

> Organization of the text is often indicated by <u>discourse signaling cues</u>. These are metalinguistic devices that function as directional guides to signal how readers and listeners should interpret the incoming information (Tyler, 1994). They explicitly cue the organization of a discourse by (a) signaling relationships between ideas, (b) indicating the relative importance of ideas, and (c) evaluating the given ideas. Such discourse signaling cues (called cues hereafter) include <u>previews</u> (e.g. There are four stages of this culture shock), <u>summarizers</u> (e.g. To sum up so far), <u>emphasis markers</u> (e.g. This is the key), and <u>logical connectives</u> (e.g. and, or, first, and second).

Often texts will not contain definitions or explanations for all their disciplinary terminology. In that case, the best place to look for such meanings is within the discipline itself. A general dictionary will not be useful, because it only covers disciplinary terminology that has entered popular usage (for example, CEO may be an entry but 'strategic marketing plan' will not be one). The best place, and in most cases, the only place to find these meanings is in a relevant **glossary**. It will contain definitions of the terminology as it is used within a discipline. Almost all textbooks have glossaries. There are also electronic glossaries for many disciplines. To find these, type into a search engine your discipline name and the word 'glossary'. For example, for accounting, type: accounting glossary; for marketing, type: marketing glossary.

Use relevant glossaries to find meanings of disciplinary terminology.

Recognising disciplinary terminology in a textbook and a research article

There are two extracts below. Underline all words you think might be disciplinary terminology.

1   The extract is from a first year accounting textbook (Marriott, Edwards, & Mellett, 2004, p. 6). Even if you do not study accounting you should be able to recognise what might be disciplinary terminology.

> Financial statements prepared for managers contain much more detail. The explanation for this difference may be found in the types of decisions to be taken. Shareholders base their decision to sell shares, retain their investment or buy more shares mainly on the level of reported profits. Management, in contrast, is keenly interested in the costs and revenues that make up the profit figure.

2   This extract is from a research article (Ramsay, Barker, & Jones, 1999, p. 132).

> In terms of possible differences between the two groups, some previous research has indicated that academic staff perceive Asian students as rote, surface learners (e.g. Samuelowicz, 1987). Recent studies using the Biggs Study Process Questionnaire (SPQ), however, have found that Asian students actually make somewhat greater use of deep and achieving approaches to learning than Australian students (Niles, 1995).

Knowing disciplinary terminology means knowing the relevant content in your discipline.

Understanding the meaning of a discipline-specific term is much more than merely being able to repeat a definition. You must also know the range of content the term makes reference to. It is therefore imperative that you learn the relevant content in your textbook and lectures. You also need to be able 'to keep up' with the term; that is, to understand and use it in all appropriate circumstances. Attentively watching how it is used in your textbook will help. Notice what common words or grammatical patterns are associated with the term (for example, notice a pattern such as 'X has shares in Y'). Also recognise other concepts that are similar in wording (such as 'shareholder' or 'equity share').

Make the disciplinary terminology 'yours' by using it.

A disciplinary term is not understood fully until you can use it with confidence. To enhance growth in ability to use the word:

- keep a notebook for your discipline where you write definitions of terms, make comments on them and create visual images of them
- practise creating sentences using disciplinary terms
- use the terms in writing that you submit to others
- speak the terms to a friend or to a tutorial group.

Keeping a notebook for disciplinary terminology can be fun. The basic step is to notice discipline terms and record their definitions. You will enjoy this task and learn more if you extend how you work with these words. Aim to embed the terms deeply into your mind by linking them with other words, images, memories and knowledge. Add a few examples of sentences that use the disciplinary terms and record them. You can also create a **word cloud** of text and a **word map** of terms as means of learning disciplinary terminology.

A word cloud is a visual display of how frequently words appear in a text (see Figure 2.1 below), and so can help you gain an intuitive understanding of key terms. A free program, such as *Wordle* <www.wordle.net>, enables you to instantly create a word cloud of any text that can be copied and pasted or submitted electronically.

Figure 2.1 Word cloud for the section 'Disciplinary terminology'

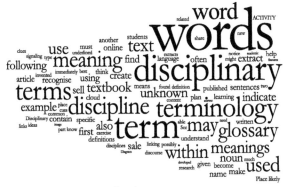

Note: Word cloud created using Wordle <www.wordle.net>.

A word map also aids learning of disciplinary terminology. Place the term on a page. Use lines radiating from any point to add information. Especially include definitions, other similar words and examples, and possibly comments. You can also include terms that are related to the one you are examining, although not the same. Indicate these by drawing a different type of line. See Figure 2.2. Use colour and images to enhance your learning experience.

As you become familiar with a term, begin to use it. Try this on your own first of all. For example, write a sentence containing the term or summarise a section of the textbook using it. The next stage of learning new terminology is to try it out in public. Include the term in written work that will be submitted to your tutor or lecturer. Speaking will probably be the most difficult task. Disciplinary terminology is unlikely to be in a dictionary, so you will not be able to listen to its pronunciation on an audio file or even see it phonetically written. To make matters worse, glossaries will not provide help with pronunciation. You must solely rely on listening to your lecturer, tutor or fellow classmates. If this is not sufficient to make you feel comfortable, see your tutor during consultation time and ask for help with pronunciation. Once you recognise how to pronounce it, try speaking the disciplinary term to a friend or in a study group. Finally, use the disciplinary term in a more formal context, such as a tutorial.

Figure 2.2 Word map for 'Disciplinary terminology'

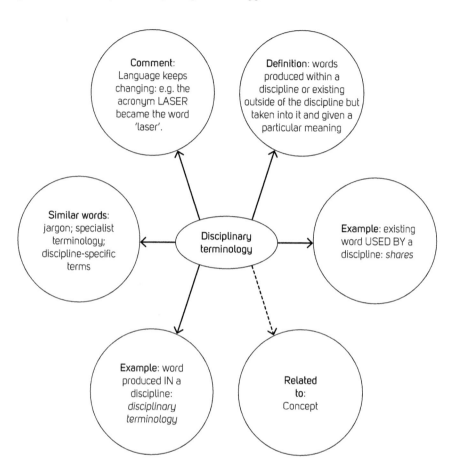

General academic words

Become familiar with the words commonly used in all academic work.

Clearly to understand and produce academic texts a large vocabulary suited to academic needs is required. As we have seen above, some of this vocabulary is peculiar to a discipline. However, there are, in addition, a significant range of words that are quite specific to the whole academic context.

The Academic Word List (AWL) is a useful collection of the most frequently occurring academic words. It lists 570 **word families** that are the most often found across a range of disciplines (from science to business), and which are not frequently used in general English (Coxhead, 2000). The AWL is divided into 10 sublists. The first, sublist 1, gives the 60 most frequently occurring words, and so on. To see which word families are included in the AWL you can search on the internet, as many academic language sites provide access to the lists. For students who enjoy language, examine the sublists at the Victoria

University of Wellington, New Zealand site, which gives the whole of each word family and especially indicates which of these words is the most frequently used in academic work: <www.victoria.ac.nz/lals/resources/academicwordlist/default.aspx>.

Although you may recognise many of the AWL words from your general knowledge of English, you still need to give focused attention to them as:

- they are frequently used in a whole range of academic contexts
- their meanings within an academic context are often quite specific to that context.

Some ways to become familiar with the words in the AWL is to:

- recognise clusters or groups of words that are used for similar purposes
- recognise the words as they are used in academic texts
- recognise that finding the meanings of the academic words is likely to involve knowing how they are used in an academic context.

Recognising meaning clusters in the academic word list

The sublists within the AWL are useful for indicating how frequently a word is used. However, just looking at a word in isolation does not help in learning it. One way of improving learning is to recognise clusters or groups of words that tend to be used for similar purposes. For example, many of the words in sublists 1 and 2 are technical words involved with the process of research: data, evidence, factors, method, per cent, procedure, research, significant, variable. Another cluster relates to theoretical discussion: theory, approach, structure, role, concept.

Finding a meaningful cluster of words within the AWL

Examine the AWL sublists 1 and 2.

1   List words that can be used to name parts of a thing.
2   List the most commonly occurring verbs.

Activity

Recognising and using the commonly occurring words for theoretical discussion

1   Examine the sentences below. Each sentence contains one or more of the most commonly occurring words for theoretical discussion. Use a dictionary and the sentences themselves to find a suitable meaning of each term in bold.

Activity

a 'This paper calls for a new **theory** of learner support in distance learning based on recent findings [results from research] in the fields [study areas]...' (Simpson, 2008, p. 159).

b 'At the base are what Richardson (1995) has described as two fundamentally distinct **approaches** to studying— ... a deep **approach**, and ... a surface **approach**' (Taillefer, 2005, p. 437).

c 'Because lecturers are in a position to mediate the transition [help students make the change] between school and university, this seems a fruitful [useful] **area** for action research' (Chanock, 2007, p. 275).

d 'Linton and colleagues (1994) draw attention to the role of text **structures** in signalling different attitudes in disciplines toward the discovery of knowledge' (Chanock, 2007, p. 276).

e 'While differences occur among Anglo-Saxon universities, the **concept** of 'reading a subject' remains fundamental' (Taillefer, 2005, p. 437).

2 Fill in the underlined blanks below with one of the words for theoretical discussion: theory, area, approach, structure, role, concept.

a 'A major gap in the previous _____ to the issue of language re-use, we believe, is an inadequate attention to the conventions of text/language re-use' (Flowerdew & Li, 2007, p. 442).

b 'Kolb's learning _____ sets out four distinctive learning styles' (Şirin & Güzel, 2006, p. 256).

c 'Staff views concerning the _____ of Blackboard in getting and keeping students engaged with the course were mixed' (Heaton-Shrestha, May, & Burke, 2009, p. 87).

d 'The _____ of plagiarism ... assumes a model of communication based on ... individuals who behave as originators of their own discourses [spoken or written communication]' (Scollon, 1995, p. 1).

e 'Academics themselves in these discipline _____ may lack the skills ... to provide support for students who need to develop their English language competence' (Benzie, 2010, p. 450).

Recognising academic words in texts

Another step in becoming familiar with the academic words is to recognise them when they occur. An example below shows the occurrence of academic words in a short piece of text. There are 14 words from the academic word list in just 102 words of text (13.7 per cent). In fact, it is typical that these words make up approximately 12 per cent of the words in business texts, and about 9 per cent of words in science texts (Coxhead, 2000, p. 222).

Academic words (in bold) in a short academic text

Domestic students will probably need to specifically address the **issue** of **coherence**, **despite** having some practice in their high school study. There is **evidence** that many students do not have **sufficient** skills in this **area** on entering university. Krause, Hartley, James, and McInnis (2005, p. 24) **found** from a **comprehensive survey** of first year university students that only 42 per cent of them felt that their high school subjects prepared them for work in their university courses. Doubtless some of this lack of preparation was in the **area** of writing. Lillis and Turner (2001) **commented** on a **survey** of British and American concerns that ...

Note: Created using the AWL [Academic Word List] Highlighter constructed by S. Haywood, available at <www.nottingham.ac.uk/~alzsh3/acvocab/awlhighlighter.htm>.

Finding the specific meanings of academic words

It is not just the frequency of occurrence that makes it important to recognise words in the Academic Word List. Often these words have meanings that are quite specific to an academic context. To illustrate, in the example above:

- some of the academic words have the same meaning as commonly used in general English (for example, 'domestic', 'specifically', 'issue', 'despite', 'sufficient', 'commented')
- some of the words have meanings that are available in general English but are not so commonly used (such as 'area')
- some of the academic words have meanings that are related to common meanings, and yet there are additional academic meanings attached that need to be known for a full understanding of the text (for example, the words 'evidence', 'found', 'comprehensive survey', and 'survey' all require a good knowledge of the process of academic research in order to understand them fully).

1   Use the AWL Highlighter <www.nottingham.ac.uk/~alzsh3/acvocab/awlhighlighter.htm> to see how many words in a piece of academic text are general academic words. To do this, copy some academic text and paste it into the AWL Higlighter, select a sublist level, and submit. (Note: you do not need to copy the URL. Just use the words 'AWL Highlighter' in a search engine and you will find it immediately.)

2   See if you can determine the meaning of each academic word in the text by consulting a dictionary.

3   Use the AWL Highlighter <www.nottingham.ac.uk/~alzsh3/acvocab/awlhighlighter .htm> to see how many words in a piece of your own academic writing are on the Academic Word List.

4   Compare the occurrence of academic words in your writing with those found in the academic text. What do you notice?

Aim to become an expert in using academic words. Create a special academic word project file or notepad in which you record information about academic words. Use the same techniques as you did for disciplinary terminology.

Academic style

As we have seen above, academic writing and speaking uses a significantly different range of words from those usually found in non-academic work. Further distinctive features of academic texts are the density of writing style and the type of sentence structure employed.

There is general recognition that academic writing is more complex than that found in non-academic texts. It has often been assumed that the complexity occurs because sentences are elaborated, by providing additional information in the form of clauses using connectives, such as 'because', 'but', 'when', 'which', 'who' or 'and'.

Academic writing is dense. It conveys a lot of information in a small number of words.

However, academic writing mainly uses other devices to elaborate or add information. Instead of using clauses that lengthen a sentence, academic writing tends to rely on devices that provide a lot of information in the shortest space. We will briefly examine how academic writing uses three of these devices, as outlined by Biber and Gray (1998, p. 6):

- adjectives
- nouns to add information to a noun
- prepositional phrases (groups of words beginning with words such as 'of', 'to', 'in') to add information to a noun.

Academic language also frequently uses the passive voice, where the structure is: object of the action—verb—agent of the action. For example: 'Ideas are conveyed in a precise manner by writers using academic language'. Such sentences are more difficult to understand than the commonly used active voice, which has a direct structure: agent of the action—verb—object of the action. For example: 'Writers use academic language to convey ideas in a precise manner'.

Example

Academic style

Dense

Extract from Smith, Campbell, and Brooker (1998, p. 328):

Hounsell (1984a, b), for instance, focusing on student understanding, identified three qualitatively different conceptions of an essay amongst history undergraduates: respectively, the essay as an argument, viewpoint or arrangement.

Passive voice

Extract from Turner and Williams (2007, p. 64)

It is not uncommon for these courses to be taught in a lecture format and to assess student knowledge through multiple-choice exams.

Students are likely to find both of the above examples difficult to read. The vocabulary is relatively simple. It is the academic style that is likely to create problems. The first example has a basic active voice structure: *Hounsell ... identified ... three conceptions of an essay*. However, there are complex ideas contained in it, and all of them are carried in dense writing where words are closely packed together. The second example is less dense, but it is equally complex, as the sentence uses passive voice.

The above techniques of academic writing have been developed for good reasons. Experts value such texts for their precision. However, new students will find them foreign, and reading them will be a major challenge. It helps understanding to unpack the meanings by rewording using an everyday sentence structure. In general this means to elaborate ideas by using clauses; and by rewriting in the active voice so that the agent that performs the action is given emphasis by placing it before the verb.

Table 2.1 Unpacking academic language

Academic language		General language	
	Example		Example
Use of groups of words beginning with an 'ing' word	*Hounsell, ..., focusing on*	Expand: Use connectives such as 'who' or 'which', and a verb	e.g. Hounsell who focused on ...
Adjectives, adverbs and nouns that add information to nouns	*Three qualitatively different conceptions*	Expand: Use verbs and clauses (groups of words usually with a verb and a connective such as 'which', 'who' and 'that') to add information	Three conceptions that are qualitatively different
Use of phrases beginning with a preposition (e.g 'of', 'on', 'in') to add information to a noun	*Among history undergraduates*	Expand: include a verb	Undergraduates who studied history
Use of academic words	*Conceptions of an essay*	Reword: use closest general English word	Ideas about an essay
Use of disciplinary terminology	*argument*	Consult meaning in a glossary	argument
Use of passive voice (the object of the action is given emphasis)	*It is not uncommon for these courses to be taught in a lecture format and to assess student knowledge through multiple-choice exams*	Reorganise: Use active voice (the agent of the action is given emphasis).	University teachers commonly use lectures to teach and multiple choice to assess student knowledge.

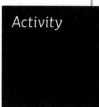

Activity

Unpacking academic texts

Extract From Gilquin and Paquot (2008, p. 42)

Read the following short extract:

Producing a text in a given genre [i.e. style] therefore requires what Lorenz (1999: 64) calls "text-type sensitivity".

Unpack the sentence above so that meaning is expressed in an everyday manner.

By taking the time to unpack dense sentences, you will not only make reading more meaningful, but you will also be teaching yourself how to write in an academic style. Thus careful reading of academic texts is important. It is never a matter of skimming the text, as often recommended in ESL courses and study guides. The academic style of writing demands full attention from all novice readers.

Creating coherence

Coherence is highly valued at university.

It is expected that academic writing be clear, coherent, structured and have an argument. All of these demands rest on your ability to create **coherence**; that is, to display a unity in thought revealed through the way ideas and information are presented. If you do not write with coherence you are likely to receive a low mark and such comments as: 'You do not have an argument'; 'There is no consistent point of view'; or 'Your ideas are jumbled and not well presented'.

However, it is difficult to write cohesively when so many of the features of academic language are unfamiliar. It is also difficult when you are required to maintain coherence over not just sentences but over paragraphs and even essays. This chapter teaches you some of the ways in which coherence is produced.

Coherence is achieved in four main ways:

- referring backwards to the 'thing' the text discusses by repeating its name in various ways
- referring backwards (or forwards) to a section of text by using a 'labelling' technique
- using the same point of view
- using connectives to produce links in meaning.

Continual reference to the same 'thing'

The basic form of coherence is established by speaking or writing about the same thing. This is done by:

- using the name of the 'thing'
- using pronouns to refer to the 'thing'
- using variations on the name of the 'thing'.

Repetition of the name of the 'thing' is the easiest way to show coherence in terms of what is being spoken or written about. Typically, though, some of these names would be replaced with pronouns (such as he, she, it, him, her, they, them, this and these). Another technique, and one that shows considerable sophistication, is to use variations on the name. For example, if you were writing about 'plagiarism', that term would be often used. However, you may also use variations that point to the same 'thing' (for example, 'presenting the work of others as if it were your own'), or a particular aspect of it (for example, 'copying text without giving acknowledgment') or use a term that names it while giving additional information (for example, 'this form of cheating'). The original name for the 'thing' is placed early in the text. Variations occur after that.

Repetition of the name of a 'thing' creates cohesion.

> ***Reference to the same 'thing'***
> Extract from Baik and Greig (2009, p. 402):
>
> *Although most Australian universities have responded by offering a range **of language and academic support programs**, the effectiveness of **these** has been questioned by numerous scholars (e.g. Durkin & Main, 2002; Hyland, 2002; Wingate, 2006) and research into the impact of **these programs** on student learning outcomes is limited.*
>
> *Full name of the 'thing'.*
>
> *Variation on the name of the 'thing'.*   *Pronoun used to refer to the 'thing'.*

Example

Recognising references to the same 'thing'
Read this extract from Jung (2003, p. 563) and answer the questions.

Vocabulary note: A cue is something that signals to someone to respond in a particular way. For example, a smile may be a cue to continue a conversation; whereas looking at a watch may be a cue to finish it.

> *In contrast to the extensive research on the role of cues in reading comprehension, relatively little research has been conducted on the role of cues in listening*

Activity

comprehension. Hron, Kurb-juhn, Mandl, and Schnotz (1985) attempted to determine whether the beneficial effects of cues observed in earlier reading research could also be found in L1 [using first language] listening comprehension. Compared to listeners who received the nonsignalled texts, listeners who received the signaled texts recalled significantly more main ideas and performed better on open-ended questions when tested.

The beneficial effects of cues on LI listening comprehension received further support in Rickards, Fajen, Sullivan, and Gillespie's (1997) study. The presence of signaling devices in the text led to a significant increase in the quantity of listeners' notes both overall and on the main ideas. Cues also helped listeners recall more information overall, as well as more important information from the text.

1 How many times has the word 'cue' or 'cues' been used?
2 What variations on 'cue' have been used?
3 Examine the first sentence: *'In contrast to the extensive research on **the role of cues** in reading comprehension, relatively little research has been conducted on the role of cues in listening comprehension'*. In what other ways could the underlined words have been written? Think of as many as possible.

Using the way references are made to the same 'thing' to help understand difficult texts.

Read the extract from Larcombe and Malkin (2008. p. 321), then answer the questions.

Law is a challenging course of study for almost all students and, in particular, for the one-third of our students for whom English is a second language. This is not only because of the linguistic demands of the coursework. As MacKinnon and Manathunga (2003) observe, students from 'non-dominant and diverse cultural and community literacies' carry an additional learning [burden] in higher education.

Examine the underlined phrase *'students from 'non-dominant and diverse cultural and community literacies'*. This is a difficult phrase to understand. To help:

1 Circle the name of the 'thing' in the text that is probably the same or close to this in meaning.
2 Replace the underlined phrase with the original name. Does it make reading easier?
3 Do you think the underlined phrase names exactly the same 'thing' as the original phrase? Explain your answer.

Using a labelling technique to refer backwards or forwards to a section of text

A typical way of producing cohesion is to refer backwards or forwards, not just to a 'thing', but to a whole section. This is achieved by the use of a group of words surrounding a noun (a nominal group) that names an entire section. Francis

(1994) calls such groups of words '**labels**'. A list of nouns commonly used as the central unit of a label and selected from those supplied by Francis (1994, pp. 89–92) is given below. The list has been divided into two types of labels. The first are those that refer to sections of the text that describe or explain an event, behaviour or process occurring outside of the text. The second column contains labelling nouns that name features of the language of a section of the text. It would be a very good idea to become familiar with these words. In particular, pay special attention to the words in the second column. They occur frequently in academic writing and speaking. They also have particular meanings within that context. See the section 'General academic vocabulary'.

Labels create cohesion by referring backwards or forwards to a whole section of text.

Table 2.2 Commonly used labelling nouns

Labelling nouns referring to a description or explanation of something occurring outside of the text	Labelling nouns referring to the type of language or its function within the text
Approach	Account
Aspect	Analysis
Case	Argument
Difficulty	Assumption
Fact	Belief
Outcome	Claim
Problem	Comment
Process	Conclusion
Reason	Criterion (criteria)
Result	Criticism
Strategy	Debate
Technique	Definition
	Description
	Distinction
	Example
	Explanation
	Formula
	Hypothesis
	Idea
	Point
	Position
	Theory

The simplest use of a label is to refer forward. Such a label names a section of text that follows, and helps the reader or listener understand the text in a particular manner. The general patterns for a forward label are:

- 'The' or 'a' + labelling noun (for example, 'The reasons …' or 'The argument …')
- 'The' or 'a' + additional information + labelling noun (for example, 'A generally accepted argument'; 'The two reasons').

A label can also refer backwards. This type of label creates cohesion by doing two things. It refers to a whole section of text that precedes the label by naming it, so holding it together as a single unit. It also produces the possibility of moving forwards. The typical patterns for labels that refer backwards are:

- 'this' or 'such' + the labelling noun (for example, 'This argument' or 'Such an analysis')
- 'this' or 'such' + additional information + labelling noun (for example, 'This early analysis' or 'Such a theoretical approach').

Example

Use of labels to refer forwards

Note: The labelling phrase is in bold. The section of the text it refers to is underlined.

Alternatively, however, you may want to emphasise **the point** that actual readers are unlikely to respond all in the same way, especially readers differing in gender, class, age, ethnicity or some other aspect of social identity.

There appears to be, then, no justification for **the claim** that manual and non-manual earnings are starting to overlap and becoming more comparable.

The argument presented here is that in the latter part of the twentieth century more and more capitalists have come to believe that their objective interests are best served through transnational practices, as evidenced by the phenomenal growth of the presence and influence of the TNCs …

Use of labels to refer backwards

The state, he claims, may sometimes fly in the face of the short-term economic interests of this class; but it will not damage their political interests, and in this way political order is maintained. As it stands, **this claim** raises more problems than it solves.

Knowing is a process, not a product. There are two steps in **this argument**. The first assumes that one can distinguish between process and content in a discipline …

Note: Examples generated using the Academic section of The British National Corpus (Davis, 2004–).

Recognising labelling

1   Examine the way the labels are included as part of the text in the example above.
    a   What word usually follows a labelling phrase that refers forwards?
    b   What type of sentence structure can be used with labelling nouns that refer backwards?

2   Read the following extract from Silva and Leki (2004, p. 6).

> *Rather than concerning itself so much with the creation of good texts this paradigm [way of understanding] focuses on creating good writers through reflection on the meanings that the writer wants to express. Although the consideration of audience is an important feature of this approach, it is the writers' intentions that hold centre stage.*

    a   Find the label in the extract above. Circle it.
    b   Underline the section of text it refers to.

3   Read the following extract from an article by Tang and Ng (1995, p. 106). Answer the questions below it.

> *Hartnett (1986) finds that poor writing can be improved when some connectives are taken out. With the absence of connectives readers can usually supply the links from their expectations and predictions from within the text. This kind of reconstruction [however] ... is neither reliable nor consistent in terms of communication.*

    a   Circle the label.
    b   Underline the section of text it refers to.

Using the same point of view

A different type of cohesive device is using the same **point of view**. This means to speak or write about a topic from a single perspective or single focus. We can say that having the same point of view means having the same topic.

Maintaining the same point of view creates coherence.

To produce the same point of view, two steps need to be taken:

- recognise what is the topic
- use techniques to continue the focus on the topic.

Recognising the topic

What is regarded as the topic depends on the unit of language we are considering. If it is a sentence, then it is usually the first 'thing' (person, animal, object, entity) named. The remainder of the sentence is typically a comment on the topic. Consider the following sentence: 'The United Nations is an international organisation founded in 1945 after the Second World War by 51 countries'. If we consider this as a single sentence, then the topic is 'The United Nations'. The basic comment is that it was 'founded … by 51 countries'. If the text is a paragraph, then the notion of topic is different (see Chapter 5). If the text is an essay, the idea of topic is different again (see Chapter 7).

Techniques for creating the same point of view

To create the same point of view means to create links between sentences in such a way that the topic is viewed from the same perspective. To create the same point of view in a series of sentences:

- construct each sentence so that it focuses on the same topic (the 'thing')
- construct sentences so they extend the comment that is being made about the topic.

The topic of a sentence is almost always placed at, or near, the beginning of a sentence. Thus the first manner of creating the same point of view is to have each sentence begin with the topic, or some variation of it, easily making for a single focus. This is a basic technique which you would be very familiar with.

The pattern is:

Topic^1 + comment^1

Topic^1 + comment^2

A more complex way of creating the same point of view is to link to the comment made on the topic. A basic sentence structure consists of a topic (the 'thing' being discussed) and a comment on that. To create this link successfully requires two moves. The first is to use some part of the comment in the previous sentence as the topic of the following sentence. The second step is to construct the comment on the new topic in such a way that it links back to the original topic.

The pattern is:

Topic^1 + comment^1

Topic^2 + comment^2

These techniques are used for creating the same point of view across sentences. They can also be used in creating cohesion between topic sentences of paragraphs. More complex cases of creating a single point of view occur when you consider cohesion within a paragraph (see Chapter 5) and when an argument is presented, as for example, in an essay (see Chapter 7).

Creating the same point of view across sentences

Constructing each sentence to focus on the same topic

1   The extract is from the United Nations Information Centre for Australia, New Zealand and the South Pacific. Words in bold show repetition of the same topic as a means of creating cohesion.

> **The United Nations** *is an international organisation founded in 1945 after the Second World War by 51 countries ... [T]he **Organisation** can take action on a wide range of issues, and provide a forum for its 192 member states to express their views ...*

2   Constructing a sentence to extend part of the comment made in the previous sentence

> The extract is from Handa (2007, The point of trepidation section, para. 1). Words underlined show how a comment can be extended as a means of creating cohesion.

> *Immigration and education are the only ways <u>for people from the developing world</u> to obtain a passage to the Western world. <u>They</u> are prepared to pay large amounts of money for these opportunities.*

Recognising the construction of the same point of view

Read the extract from Lea and Street (1998, Academic literacies section, para. 1) and answer the questions below.

> *Learning in higher education involves adapting to new ways of knowing: new ways of understanding, interpreting and organising knowledge. Academic literacy practices—reading and writing within disciplines—[are] central processes through which students learn new subjects and develop their knowledge about new areas of study. A practices approach to literacy takes account of the cultural and contextual component of writing and reading practices, and this in turn has important implications for an understanding of student learning. Educational research into student learning in higher education has tended to concentrate on ways in which students can be helped to adapt their practices to those of the university (Gibbs, 1994).*

1   What is the topic of the second sentence? Underline the words it refers back to in the previous sentence. Is it repeating the topic of the first sentence or repeating part of the comment in the first sentence?

2   What is the topic of the third sentence? Underline the words it refers back to in the previous sentence. Is it repeating the topic of the second sentence or repeating part of the comment in the second sentence?

3   What is the topic of the fourth sentence? Underline the words it refers back to in the previous sentence. Is it repeating the topic of the third sentence or repeating part of the comment in the third sentence?

Creating connection by using connectives

Connectives are words or phrases that signal how ideas are linked. They may link ideas within a sentence, and across sentences, paragraphs and even sections of a document. They allow a writer to display in a very clear manner a range of different types of connections between ideas, and so are essential to good writing and speaking at university.

The main types of relationships indicated by connectives are:

- addition (such as 'first', 'second', '…', 'also', 'moreover')
- example ('for example')
- clarification ('to explain', 'to clarify')
- order in time (dates in sequence, 'first', 'second', 'then')
- summary ('in conclusion')
- similarity (for example, 'in a similar way')
- adversative (for example, 'in contrast', 'on the other hand')
- concessive (for example, 'however', 'although', 'despite')
- situation–problem ('however')
- claim–counterclaim ('however')
- effect (for example, 'as a consequence')
- reason ('because').

Connectives are powerful language tools.

When connectives are used well, they are powerful language tools. They reveal the organisation of ideas in a simple and clear manner. When they are incorrectly used, however, connectives become a major source of confusion.

To use connectives well students need to:

- recognise the type of connection that exists between ideas
- understand how to use connectives.

Recognising the type of relationship between ideas

Because connectives convey a relationship between ideas, it is useful to consciously name the relationship. First, check to see if the second idea is just a continuation of the first. In this case, no connective is required. If, on the other hand, there is a relationship between two ideas, name it. This will point you in the direction of the correct connective.

Example

Recognising when no connective is required

Example	Relationship between sentences
The extract from Tang and Ng (1995, p. 105) *[Connectives] only express the cohesive relationships that already exist in the writer's thinking. They are indicators or visible signals of the relationship.*	Continuation of idea. No connective required. The pronoun 'they' is used as a cohesive device linking the sentences.

Care has to be taken with some of the relations indicated by connectives. Some are simple and do not pose a major problem for students (addition, example, clarification, summary, reason, consequence). Others are difficult to recognise, especially those that indicate a relationship between ideas that differ. Table 2.3 below outlines four different types of relationship involving ideas that differ: adversative, concessive, situation–problem, claim–counterclaim. These are very important relations in academic writing.

Table 2.3 Connectors used when ideas differ

Type of relationship	Example
Adversative (on the other hand) Claims the ideas both exist but that they are distinctly different. There is nothing surprising about the two coexisting	Students need to give serious attention to learning **disciplinary terminology**. On the other hand, they can have a relaxed attitude to learning new **SMS words**.
Concessive (however) Claims both ideas differ but also exist together. The existence of the two ideas together is somewhat surprising	Students need to give serious attention to learning disciplinary terminology. However, they may find ways of making it fun.
Situation–problem (however) Claims that some situation exists and indicates a problem in relation to it	[Situation] Students need to give serious attention to learning disciplinary terminology. However, [problem] many courses do not help students to do this.
Claim–counterclaim disputing the truth of the claim (however) Makes a claim and then provides a counterclaim that shows the first claim to be incorrect or inadequate	[Claim] Much writing about disciplinary terminology claims it is quickly learned as a natural process of studying course material. However, [counter-claim disputing the first claim] there is some evidence that not all students can master disciplinary terminology so easily.

Activity

Judging the type of relationship between ideas

1   In each of the examples below judge the type of relationship expressed between the two sentences. Choose from the following: continuation; example; adversative; consequence, concessive, situation–problem, claim–counterclaim.

a   Modified from Rose, Lui-Chivizhe, McKnight, and Smith (2003, p. 42):

Few of our students have had any previous experience of reading academic texts, let alone writing academic essays. Many have great difficulty independently reading set articles and completing written assignments.

b   Modified from Tang and Ng (1995, p. 112):

Some types of connectives are seldom used. Inferential, Transitional, and Summative connectives are not often used.

c   Modified from Biber and Gray (2010, p. 2):

These styles are efficient for expert readers, who can quickly extract large amounts of information from relatively short, condensed texts. They pose difficulties for novice readers.

d   Modified from Biber and Gray (2010, p. 7):

Thus, Figure 1 shows that complement clauses and adverbial clauses are much more frequent in conversation than in academic writing. Relative clauses are more frequent in academic writing than in conversation.

e   Modified from Crewe (1990, p. 324):

Student writers need a much greater awareness of the problem and much more rigorous training [in using connectives], which would oblige them to think through their argument before deciding on how it might be reinforced with logical connectives. In a developmental sequence in the use of connectives, this process would be paramount at every stage.

f   Modified from Hancioğlu, Neufeld, and Eldridge (2008, p. 465)

Much recent work (Charles, 2007 ...) has successfully focused on and identified linguistic variation between disciplines. Genres cut across subject fields, and [style] is defined ... by the conventions of the given genre.

2   Rewrite the sentences above using appropriate connectives (if required).

Understanding how to use connectives

Even when you have correctly judged the relationship between two ideas, care has to be taken with:

- the selection of the correct connective from those available for a particular relationship
- the way in which the sentences surrounding the connective are written.

Perhaps the major problem students have in selecting connectives is to choose correctly between 'on the other hand' and 'however'. When the wrong connective is selected the writing appears very strange and is confusing for the reader. It is easy to decide:

- 'on the other hand' is used only when two contrasting ideas are joined and when no other relationship exists between them
- 'however' is used most often, as it can play at least three roles (see above).

Be careful in choosing between the connectives: 'on the other hand' and 'however'.

Another problem in selection occurs when students assume that all connectives indicating a particular relation have the same meaning. They do not. For example, there are a number of possible connectives to convey a relation of addition. Each one is subtly different. See Table 2.4 below.

There are subtle and important differences between connectives that convey the same type of relation.

A further problem in selecting connectives is to overselect. Some students, particularly those who have studied ESL courses, feel they must use a connective between each sentence. The result is that the text becomes 'extremely contorted' (Crewe, 1990, p. 320). Use the following guidelines:

- connectives should not be used when a sentence merely continues an idea from a previous sentence
- the connectives 'first', 'second', and so on can often be omitted
- the connectives that convey complex relations must be used.

It is difficult to learn all the subtle differences between connectives, and so it is best to select one connective from each of the relationships and become familiar with its use. As you read you will naturally recognise and be able to use other connectives.

The second feature of connectives that must be attended to is the way sentences surrounding a connective need to be written. The connective alone cannot carry the relationship between two ideas. It is supported by other aspects of writing. See Table 2.4 below for the construction of sentences surrounding connectives of addition.

Table 2.4 Language structures to support connectives indicating addition of ideas

Type of connecting word	Example	Sentence structures
Addition: a list (first, second …) A list is used when the items belong together, but the writer does not wish to show any further relationship between each item	Students need to learn <u>two features</u> peculiar to academic writing. <u>First, they need</u> to recognise academic vocabulary. <u>Second, they must give attention</u> to the particular structure of academic writing. Optional: the connectives may be omitted	• The list is announced as the topic • Each item on the list is numbered using words • Each sentence in the list has the same (or similar) grammatical pattern

(continues)

Table 2.4 Language structures to support connectives indicating addition of ideas (*cont.*)

Type of connecting word	Example	Sentence structures
Addition: connection emphasised (as well, also) Used when the writer wants to place some emphasis on the fact that the ideas are connected	Students need to learn <u>two features</u> peculiar to academic writing. <u>They need</u> to recognise academic vocabulary. <u>As well, they must give attention</u> to the particular structure of academic writing.	• The topic is announced, but there is no need to number the features • A connective is used between the items • Sentence structures need to be similar
Addition: with emphasis on the last item (moreover) Use when the writer wants to show the items occur together, and that the last item has slightly more significance	Students need to learn <u>the features</u> peculiar to academic writing. <u>They need</u> to recognise academic vocabulary as it is quite specific to that context. <u>Moreover, they must give attention</u> to the particular structure of academic writing as it <u>is so</u> <u>distinctive</u>.	• The topic is announced (no indication is given of the number of features) • A connective is used between the items • The sentences carrying the two items have a similar structure • The greater significance of the second item can be carried in words as well as in the use of the connective

Activity

Writing connections

1   **First sentence:** An overuse of connectives leads to confusing writing.
    a   Add a sentence that adds another idea.
    b   Add a sentence that is adversative.
    c   Add a sentence that has a concessive relation to the first sentence.
    d   Add a sentence to display an effect.

2   **First sentence:** It is often claimed that an overuse of connectives leads to confusing writing.
    a   Add a sentence that provides a counterclaim.

Activity

Go to our website <www.oup.com.au/orc/turner2e> for more activities on the skills covered in this chapter.

SUMMARY

This chapter has provided you with skills for dealing with the complexities of academic language. It has shown you how academic vocabulary is very particular, both in terms of disciplinary terminology, and also in the general academic words that are used. It has also examined the stylistic features of density and passive voice in academic writing. In addition, the chapter has provided help in writing cohesively, as this is a difficult task when content, vocabulary and style are all unfamiliar. All learning becomes easier if you pay attention to academic language.

GLOSSARY

coherence a unity in thought revealed through the way ideas and information are presented.

connectives words or phrases that signal how ideas are linked.

disciplinary terminology those words produced within a discipline or those existing outside of the discipline but taken into it and given a particular meaning.

glossary a list with meanings of the terminology used within a source (such as a textbook).

label the term used for a group of words whose function is to refer either backwards or forwards to a section of text as a means of creating cohesion.

point of view the direction from which a writer or speaker examines a topic.

register a part of a language found in a particular context, which has acquired its own characteristics, for example, the academic register.

word cloud a visual display of how words appear in a text, with those more frequently used presented in larger font.

word family a group of words that all share a common form (such as 'vary, variable, variables').

word map a diagram using radiating lines to display information about words: their definitions, links to other related words, links to examples and comments.

chapter THREE

Listening and Participating

Listening is an important skill for success at university. Most of the information and ideas you learn will be presented first in a lecture. It is expected that you will be able to listen to these complex and unfamiliar ideas with little or no chance of asking questions or making comments.

Tutorials offer an opportunity to participate more fully in learning. A different set of listening skills is required, as you will be in the demanding context of a discussion with a group of twenty or more students. As well, you are expected to contribute.

Both lectures and tutorials require specialised strategies (plans) for listening so that you gain maximum benefit.

This chapter will help you to listen well by examining:

- the five processes involved in listening:
  - attending
  - perceiving
  - interpreting
  - remembering
  - responding
- strategies for listening in a lecture
- strategies for listening and participating in a tutorial.

Listening

There exists a common misconception that *listening* is the same as *hearing*. It is not. While hearing is a physical act, listening is a meaning-making activity.

Listening is a complex process essential to learning. It employs a range of skills to construct meaning from the verbal (or sound) signals that others send (such as words, sentences, groans and shouts) and the nonverbal (or physical) signals that accompany the message (such as facial expression and body movement).

Purdy (1996b) has defined listening as:

the active and dynamic process of attending, perceiving, interpreting, remembering and responding to the expressed (verbal and nonverbal) needs, concerns, and information offered by other human beings. (p. 8)

Listening is one of the first skills we learn. However, while we are taught how to read and write, and even perhaps how to speak in certain contexts, we are rarely taught how to listen. Hence, the development of our listening skills may not keep up with the changes in our life.

Listening to speech is a distinct form of communication, significantly different from reading and writing. Speech has many of its own **linguistic features**, making listening a specialised skill.

Table 3.1 General differences between the linguistic features of speech and writing

Speech	Writing
Uses 'idea units' (groups of words without complete verbs)	Uses complete sentences (with verbs)
Sounds words together (e.g. 'far away' is usually spoken as 'fa-ra-way')	Maintains the separation of each word
Uses **colloquial (speech) expressions** and words (e.g. 'His argument is full of holes')	Uses more formal expressions (e.g. 'His argument has many faults')
Includes many *hesitations*: • pauses • fillers, such as 'mmmm', 'ah', 'yeah', 'but' • repetitions, such as 'I'm going to tell you about' ... 'Mmm'... 'Anyway, today we will discuss the way that ...')	Aims for coherence and continuity

Listening for the linguistic features of speech

Activity

1   Your tutor, or one of the students, will talk to you for a few minutes on a non-academic topic that interests her or him. Listen to see if you can catch any of the linguistic features of speech.

(*Note*: the linguistic features of speaking are *not* mistakes—they are the techniques that make speaking alive, interesting and useful. If we are competent speakers, we use them.)

   a   *idea units* (incomplete sentences)
   b   sounding a number of words together as a single word
   c   colloquial words or expressions
   d   hesitations.

2   Discuss what you heard with the student sitting next to you.
3   Report your findings to the whole tutorial.

As well, listening, unlike reading, occurs in 'real time', and so requires particular abilities. If you do not understand something when reading you can reread it any number of times. You cannot continually review what you are listening to. There is a limit to the number of times we can ask a person to repeat what he or she has said, or to explain it more fully. Moreover, in some important contexts (such as a lecture) there is often no chance for clarification.

Listening is thus a skill that needs to be learned, particularly at university, where much of the information is conveyed in a spoken form in lectures and tutorials.

Listening well

Listening consists of five separate processes (Purdy, 1996b). They are:

- attending
- perceiving
- interpreting
- remembering
- responding.

Each of these can be developed to make listening more effective. Good listening skills lead to better learning and more confident **participation** in lectures and tutorials.

Attending

Hearing is basic to all listening. It may be affected by either a physical impairment, or by aspects of the environment. For example, a number of people speaking at the same time, other noise in the surroundings, or the listener being too far from the speaker, can create problems in hearing.

Attending to listening depends on the physical ability to hear, and the mental skill that enables a person to listen to what the speaker is saying.

Attending to listening also depends on the listener's mental preparedness. There are two interrelated aspects:

- motivation
- focus.

Motivation

Motivation is required in all learning contexts. Hui (2005) noted that in Chinese education it is expected that students show determination to learn. Diligence and persistence are viewed as desirable qualities in a student.

Moreover, according to Russell, Ainley and Frydenberg (in Ainley, 2004):

Motivation and engagement are essential for [all] student learning … Motivation is about energy and direction, the reasons for behaviour, why we do what we do. Engagement describes energy in action; the connection between person and activity. (para. 1)

Motivation can be used to enhance listening, and therefore also learning. Students can 'learn to listen, and listen to learn', as the title of Lebauer's book (1999) proclaimed. To create motivation to improve listening:

- State your *motivation* and *desire* to listen and participate effectively.
- Ensure that your *intent* is clear and your *expectations* are realistic and achievable.
- Clarify your *purpose* as to why you are listening, and understand the *relevance* of what you are doing.
- Be *dedicated*, as achievement of goals often requires perseverance.

By consciously choosing to be motivated and to engage in listening, you gain ownership of the process and take responsibility for yourself. This is an act of empowerment.

Focus

A consistent and directed *focus* is required for good listening. Many things can distract our attention: loud noises, our moods (feelings) and our own thoughts. It does not matter how the distraction originates; it is experienced as a distraction within our minds. Hence, focus requires attention to what is happening in our mind.

Focus requires attention to what is happening in our mind.

Usually our mind is full of thoughts and feelings. Some of these are directly linked to the particular topic we are engaged in; often they are not. The habit of our mind to continually 'talk' and 'feel' is called **inner speech**. It can create a hindrance to listening by being irrelevant to the topic, or negative.

Irrelevant inner speech occurs because we are distracted. It may occur because of something in our listening context (for example, we begin thinking about what the speaker is wearing, or the activity of students around us). Sometimes irrelevant thoughts are totally unrelated to what we are trying to listen to (we think of how we are feeling, or what the weekend was like). Sometimes we become so engaged in these thoughts that we are entirely unaware of what is being spoken.

Negative inner speech tends to occur because of a habit we have developed over a long period of time. We may, for example, react to difficult circumstances by falling into a negative thought pattern (see the following example). Negative inner speech is our mind repeating that pattern to us when we feel some task is difficult, such as listening to complex information in a lecture or listening in a demanding context (such as a tutorial).

Example

Negative inner speech

'This is too difficult for me. I'll never understand these theories.'

'I wonder how that girl in the front row always seems to know the right answer. She must be more intelligent than I am.'

'I won't bother answering his question. I know I will be wrong and then I'll end up looking like a fool.'

Thinking

Consider the above examples of inner speech. What do they all have in common? How might such inner speech affect a student's listening?

Activity

Recognising inner speech

Your lecturer or tutor will play a short excerpt from some spoken text to you (such as a presentation of a news event from the ABC: <www.abc.net.au> or from the BBC: <www.bbc.co.uk>).

1 You have a double task: listen to what is said in the most focused way possible *and* at the same time notice what you are thinking about, and how you feel.

2 After listening, discuss your experience with the student sitting next to you. Consider:

   a   What is the main idea in the spoken text?

   b   Did you catch your mind wandering off the topic you were listening to?

   c   Did you notice any inner speech (any thoughts not related to the topic)?

   d   Did you notice any feelings not related to the topic?

   e   When did the inner speech occur? Why?

   f   When did the feelings occur? Why?

   g   How did you attempt to refocus on listening?

Table 3.2 Acknowledging inner speech and refocusing

Type of inner speech	Action to refocus on listening
Irrelevant inner speech (short-term strategy)	• Recognise the thoughts • Refocus your mind on listening
Negative inner speech (short-term strategy)	• Recognise the thoughts • Encourage yourself (e.g. 'I will keep trying to listen ...') • Refocus
Negative inner speech (long-term strategy)	• Recognise the contexts that lead to negative inner speech • Remind yourself that negative inner speech is just a habit rather than a true reflection of who you are • Replace the negative view with a more positive and realistic one (e.g. change from seeing yourself as a 'failure' to viewing yourself as a 'learner') • Encourage yourself (e.g. think: 'I can get through this ...' or 'I'm pleased with how I did ...') • Expect success (but realise that it will take time, and that it may not be in the form you imagined) • As a different approach, you can ignore the negative thoughts, and shift your focus to success (Chu, 1992, p. 111).

We might also be able to positively use our ability to engage in inner speech to help focus while listening. Martoran and Kildahl (1989) claimed that all productive thinking is achieved in the form of *internal speech*, existing as either monologues (one 'voice') or dialogues (two or more 'voices'). If we experience such inner speech, we can use it to think about the topic as we listen (such as 'That's a good idea' or 'I don't think so').

Perceiving

Attending naturally leads us to perceive aspects of the listening–speaking relationship. When we listen we are not just focusing on the words but also placing them within a context. We are **perceiving** (noticing):

- how something is spoken (with what tone of voice, what emphasis or what choice of words)
- what nonverbal cues accompany it (such as a smile or a frown)

- the environment in which it is being spoken (in a tutorial, at work or as we sit at a dinner table at home)
- what is used to convey the message (such as a mobile phone text message, a television, a voice).

Perceiving aspects of the message, speaker and context

In each of the following, the same words are spoken. However, the context and/or the emphasis (shown by the word in **bold**) is different. What impact do these have on meaning?

1 '**You** can lose weight' spoken by a girl to her friend.
2 'You **can** lose weight' spoken by a doctor to a patient.
3 '**You** can lose weight' spoken to a girl, by someone she does not like.

Interpreting

Focus requires attention to what is happening in our mind.

Attending and perceiving make it possible to interpret speech—make it meaningful. We **interpret** what is spoken, how it is spoken and the context of speaking. Interpretation may or may not lead to understanding. It is possible that we are left with questions, or perhaps we are incorrect.

To interpret anything we link it to what we already know. This includes:

- our cultural knowledge of meanings in relation to speech, actions and nonverbal messages and context (developed by being a member of a particular culture)
- our personal patterns of meanings (developed from our own particular experience)
- our personal substantive knowledge (e.g. of words and grammar, information and ideas).

Our existing knowledge *colours* (gives a particular quality to) what we hear. Of course, we share a great deal in common with others, and hence we largely agree on our interpretations, otherwise we could not communicate. However, the interpretations of different people cannot match perfectly. In fact, we tend to 'experience, to some degree, what we *expect* to experience' (Purdy, 1996a, p. 25).

As part of the 'natural' process of interpreting, we constantly evaluate what we hear. We judge it in terms of its relevance to ourselves. We assess if we are interested in the information; whether it is useful, understandable or wrong.

Thinking about interpretation

Activity

1   How can interpretation lead to prejudice?
2   Have you ever experienced saying something that a listener cannot understand because the person does not have the relevant cultural knowledge? Explain what happened.
3   Have you ever experienced or noticed two people who cannot listen to each other because they have totally opposite interpretations? Describe the situation.
4   Have you ever experienced listening to something that is not interesting to you because you do not have the same basis of information as the speaker? Describe what happened.
5   When can we say we have understood something we have heard?

As a consequence of how we create meaning we are limited in our listening abilities by the type of information we are listening to (see Table 3.3). This point becomes very significant when we consider listening in lectures or tutorials.

Table 3.3 Typical reactions to different types of information

Type of information	'Natural' reaction
Information that is extremely well known	• Boredom • Stop listening
Some information known, some unknown	• Interest • Keep listening
Information mostly unfamiliar	• Cannot understand • Confusion • Stop listening

A complication arises when we consider that to listen well we also need to hear the speaker's point of view. Understandably, this is a very difficult task, as we naturally interpret from our own point of view. It requires quite an effort to try to *bracket* (set aside or not consider) our own understanding, so that we can really listen to another. This skill is particularly important in two contexts:

- an intercultural context, where we do not share the same cultural knowledge
- a stressful context, where it is likely that both the speaker and listener is interpreting in a quite different way.

Our aim in most listening contexts is to achieve a balance, that is, to bracket our store of knowledge so that we can listen to what the speaker says, and to use our knowledge to make sense of that. It is not an easy task, but well worth aiming for.

Remembering

Listening is useful if we can remember the information. Remembering allows us to store the information either for later use, or even for immediate response. The degree to which we remember anything spoken to us will probably depend on our abilities to attend and interpret. While we possess this skill to a certain extent, it also needs to be consciously developed.

Activity

Interpretation and memory: the game of 'Chinese whispers'
(Note to lecturer or tutor: see <www.oup.com.au/orc/turner2e> for some possible stories.)

1   Your lecturer or tutor will give you a piece of paper containing a short story.
2   Read the story a few times, then 'whisper' the story (*not* read it) to another student, who in turn must 'whisper' the story to yet another student. You may keep the chain of storytelling going for as long as you like.
3   The final person is to tell the class what story she or he was told.
4   The lecturer or tutor reads out the original story.
    a   What differences are there between the last and first stories?
    b   Why are there these differences?

Responding

Finally, interpreting leads automatically to some response. The response may be internal (we may just think what we would say in response). However, in almost all listening contexts there is an opportunity for some external response:

- nonverbal (such as a nod of recognition or a frown of puzzlement)
- **back-channelling cues** (short verbal utterances) that indicate how we are interpreting what is said (such as 'Mmmm, yes' or 'Mmmmm, no')
- verbal utterances (a question to clarify something, a comment on what was said or an idea or piece of information that extends the topic).

A response, whether verbal or nonverbal, provides **feedback** to the speaker. Feedback informs the speaker of what we have understood, what we think about it, what we need to know or how we'd like to carry the topic further. Mathony and Poulis (2004) perceive feedback as providing opportunities for students to practise their learning and make appropriate modifications to their interpretations.

All the processes involved in listening (attending, perceiving, interpreting, remembering and responding) lead to the understanding of what has been spoken. Complete understanding may not be possible, but the best chance for a practical, useful level of understanding in which both listener and speaker recognise they belong to the same listening–speaking community is given when the listening processes are engaged in fully.

The aim of listening is to understand what is said.

Listening

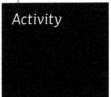

Activity

Your lecturer or tutor will play a short spoken text to you.

(Note to lecturer or tutor: you may like to choose a presentation of a news event from the ABC: <www.abc.net.au> or from the BBC: <www.bbc.co.uk>.)

Your task is to listen to what is said. After listening, discuss the excerpt with the student next to you. Consider:

1   What was the main message in the excerpt?
2   How many details can you remember? What helped you to remember?
3   Evaluate what you have heard:
    a   Would you say this was likely to be reliable information? Why?
    b   How does this link to anything you already know?
    c   Could this be useful information for you? Why or why not?

4   If you were able to speak to the presenter of the information:
    a   What question would you ask? or
    b   What comment would you make? or
    c   What further information would you add?

Listening in different contexts

Listening occurs in a wide range of contexts. In some situations listening is about *social interaction*. For example, in a conversation both people involved have equal rights to speak, and both take turns to speak. In other contexts there is almost no interaction and no overt (obvious) participation (as when listening to a lecture).

Each context requires adjustments to how we listen, both in terms of which processes are emphasised and how they are carried out.

Figure 3.1 Range of participation rights involved in various listening contexts

Listening well is crucial to your effectiveness as a university student. Around 50 per cent of your time at university is spent listening, and most of that is in the quite demanding contexts of the lecture or tutorial. The following sections examine the particular aspects of listening within these two contexts.

Listening strategies for a lecture

The most complex act of listening at university is that of listening to lectures. They are long, deal with difficult, unfamiliar subject matter, use technical terms, and usually there is no chance to ask questions or engage in discussion. They are not easy listening.

Develop strategies to overcome some of the difficulties in listening to a lecture. According to Rost (2001), 'listening strategies are conscious plans to deal with incoming speech, particularly when the listener knows that he or she must compensate for incomplete input or partial understanding' (p. 10).

Before the lecture

The unfamiliar content in a lecture creates a significant listening problem, as we need existing knowledge to help interpret what we hear. One strategy to aid listening is to make some of the lecture content familiar, before the lecture begins.

Prepare before the lecture to make the content familiar.

Prepare before a lecture:

- Read the course (or subject) outline to find the title of the lecture and how it fits in with other lectures.
- Print the lecture handout.
- Read the lecture handout.
- Try to find the meaning of any words you do not understand in the lecture handout.

- Use your textbook and examine:
  - the glossary (the list of technical words and their meanings)
  - the margin notes (small notes of key points separated out from the text and usually in the margin)
  - words written in bold.
- If you cannot find the meaning of a word, put a question mark on it to alert yourself to listen for its meaning during the lecture.
- Look at the structure of the lecture by noting how headings are organised.
- Read the relevant textbook chapter, or at least look at the headings and the key objectives, which are usually highlighted in some way at the beginning of the chapter.
- Read one or more of the recommended readings (this is ideal, but probably not possible until later years at university).

Activity

Preparing for a lecture

Below is a slide for a mini-lecture you will be listening to. Prepare for the mini-lecture:

1   Read the slide.
2   Find the meanings of any words you do not understand by using this textbook.
3   Put a question mark beside any word you still do not understand.
4   Examine the structure of the lecture by looking at the headings. (What do you notice about the headings? What does this tell you?)
5   Read a relevant section in this chapter.

Listening

- Aspects of spoken text that are different from written texts:
  1 Phonology
     - The 'correct' sounds of individual words are modified in speech through:
       - assimilation,
       - elision,
       - intrusion.
- Affect on comprehension for:
  - native listeners,
  - second language listeners.

(Buck, 2001)

Good preparation is a great aid to listening. It gives you confidence, hence minimises the distraction of negative inner speech. It makes the content familiar, and so helps understanding. It also focuses your attention on the topic and, hopefully, generates motivation and curiosity about it.

During the lecture
Attend to the listening environment
Lecture theatres, particularly for first year university courses, are often very large and can be noisy. In some of your courses you are likely to be attending a lecture with 300 or more students. Make sure you enhance your own listening within this context by choosing a seat where you can easily hear the lecture and see the slides. Arrive early and prepare for listening.

Ensure that you show respect for the lecturer and your fellow students by remaining quiet and attentive during the lecture. Some students feel they can leave at any time, and even speak, or do other activities. This is not appropriate behaviour. Universities offer a great deal of freedom to you, as you are seen to be responsible adults who are learning how to act independently and professionally. It is expected that you will act well during a lecture. It is equally expected that if you are not able to listen attentively, then you do not attend. The choice is yours.

There are likely to be a number of distractions that make listening difficult. Your lecturer may speak with an unfamiliar accent, or not speak clearly, or give the lecture too quickly. Your fellow students may create noise. You may find your mind wandering from the topic. Try to listen, despite these difficulties. Do not give up.

Listen to content
Understand the lecture by focusing on its structure.
When listening to a lecture aim for understanding of the content in a number of ways. First, listen for the way in which ideas and information are connected. To do this listen for the lecture structure. This will be given in:

- the headings
- the use of connectives.

Next listen for what the lecturer considers most important. Notice the way you are directed to significant content by:

- words and phrases used as *signposts*
- repetition
- stress (produced by using a slightly louder or slower voice)
- nonverbal communication (such as tapping the desk or pointing to the slide).

Typical signposts *indicating importance of content*

- Words indicating importance: crucial, significant, critical, imperative, important …
- Phrases announcing expectations: you must know; have to understand; should be able to …
- Statements emphasising importance: I cannot emphasise this enough. It would be useful to note this …
- Statements directly linking content to assessment: This will be on the exam. You may be tested on this …
- Repetition for emphasis: This happened because … X. As I said, the cause of this is X.

Example

You can also listen for supporting ideas. These are given in the structure of headings (they will be subheadings). They will also be indicated by the use of words, as described in the following example.

Words and phrases indicating supporting points are being presented

- To illustrate this point …
- For instance …
- As an example …
- That reminds me of a …
- Let me just highlight this by …
- To demonstrate …

Example

Take notes during a lecture to enhance understanding, evaluation and remembering, and as an initial response. Kahn (1998) contended that, 'note-taking from listening … should include not only what the speaker or writer said, but also a critical response to what was said or written. In short, you need to make notes as well as take notes' (p. 14).

Use note-taking to record in brief form:

- the main points; their relationships to each other; and the main supporting points (not needed if lecture slides are provided);
- explanations of terms or concepts that you do not understand;
- references made to sources of information (to books or articles you can read to gain more knowledge);
- your evaluation of ideas (indicate those you consider most important; are likely to be most useful; you don't understand fully, or don't agree with).

Note-taking enhances learning.

Usually lecturers provide well-organised slides of the main ideas and their supporting points. You can use these, and write notes beside the points. However, if slides are not supplied you will need to create more extensive notes.

A note-taking system helps create clarity and understanding. Research has consistently found that the use of a framework or structure improves overall note-taking effectiveness (Armbruster, 2000).

Below is an example of a note-taking structure designed to help you generate a good understanding of a lecture: by using interpretation, evaluation, remembering and responding.

Example

A note-taking system

Lecturer:
Date:
Topic:
Textbook (or other) reference:

Key points from the lecture
- Idea X
  - A point
  - B point

My comments
Do I: Understand? Agree? Need more clarification?
What are my questions?
Can I link the idea or information to something I know?
Can I use it?

Action:
Read *Author* (recommended in the lecture)
Talk to: ...
Discuss with ...

As note-taking needs to be brief, it is usual to:

- use symbols rather than words
- use abbreviated forms of words (as in text messaging)
- Use part sentences.

Some possible note-taking symbols

Symbol	Meaning
@	at
*	important
**	very important
✓	yes/right
×	no/not right
!	take note of this
!!	really need to know this
♂	male
♀	female
e.g.	example
re	about (concerning)
&	and
?	unsure of meaning
??	really do not understand
+	plus/more
−	minus/less
↑	increase
↓	decrease
=	equal
≠	not equal to
<	less than
>	greater than

Taking notes

Lecturer/tutor: there is additional information to accompany the slide in the resource kit for lecturers.

1   Your lecturer will present a mini-lecture from the slide you have already worked on, in Activity: Preparing for a lecture.

   a   Have the slide (with your preparation shown on it) in front of you.

   b   Listen to the lecture, taking appropriate notes (either on the slide or on a separate piece of paper).

2   After the mini-lecture, compare the notes you have taken with those of the person beside you. Consider:

   a   Did preparing for the lecture help you listen to it? How?

   b   What did you learn about note-taking?

After the lecture

As soon as possible after the lecture:

Review, revise, reflect to embed understanding and memory.

- *review your notes*: rewrite your notes, if needed, to make them clear and to fill in gaps in the information (even add colour, images and diagrams)
- *revise the content*: read the relevant course material and make additional notes; consider creating a concept map of the lecture (see Chapter 4)
- *reflect* on what you have learned and what you need to learn.

Activity

Concept map

1   Read about concept maps in Chapter 4.

2   Locate examples of concept mapping online.

3   Create a concept map for the mini-lecture in this chapter.

4   You may add pictures, colours, symbols and diagrams.

You can add to a concept map as you gain more knowledge on a topic.

Listening strategies for a tutorial

Listening in tutorials is more interactive than in lectures.

Tutorials are commonly used at university to help you engage more thoroughly with material delivered previously in a lecture. Tutorials typically give students an opportunity to participate in activities, either individually or with other students, to help expand and clarify understandings.

Listening skills for tutorials are much the same as those for lectures. In a tutorial, however, your listening skills and strategies are somewhat more **interactive**, and your social relationships extend beyond you and your lecturer to include other students in your class. Listening in tutorials is therefore largely about participation, and participation in tutorials usually involves *proactive* (planned) and *reactive* (unplanned) contributions to class and small group discussions and activities.

Offering ideas and opinions effectively or even asking questions can be challenging, especially for shy students or for students who lack confidence. In the next few pages there are a number of strategies, similar to those outlined previously, that are aimed specifically at listening and participating in tutorials. They will help you to deal with this challenging listening context.

Before the tutorial

In most cases your tutorials will be conducted after you have had an opportunity to experience the same topic in a lecture. If you have prepared well for your lecture, and followed the strategies outlined above to help you engage effectively with the lecture, you should be somewhat familiar with the topic by the time you commence your tutorial. You should therefore be able to use that knowledge to help you to listen during your tutorial.

Use the knowledge gained in the lecture to help you to listen during the tutorial.

Some preparation is needed before a tutorial:

- At a minimum, reread the lecture notes, the notes you made after your lecture and the notes you made after reading the required course material on the topic.
- If you have time, reread the required course material and any further reading that has been prescribed for the topic.
- For some tutorials you may be required to complete set exercises or activities. To make the most of the learning opportunities in your tutorial, and to help you listen well and participate, make sure you complete any required tasks set by your lecturer or outlined in your course materials.
- If you have difficulty with the activity, or have trouble understanding any aspect of the course material, prepare a question and make a note to ask for assistance in the tutorial.

Material covered in your tutorial may still be challenging. However, if you prepare you will find that you will be better able to contribute in class and, more importantly, be able to ask questions about topics or concepts you are unsure of. Having pre-read course material and/or attempted set exercises, you will be better able to focus your listening and target your questions.

Preparation can also help avoid negative inner speech that might lead to unnecessary distractions. By preparing specific questions about areas you are unsure of you can reduce feelings of uncertainty and therefore reduce unnecessary distractions.

During the tutorial

Listening environment

Tutorial rooms are generally smaller than lecture theatres (for example, suitable for 25 to 30 students) and the seating arrangements can differ also. Depending on the course, seating in a tutorial can be arranged in a number of different ways. These can include:

- small clusters of desks suitable for small group discussion
- disconnected rows with desk space available for each student
- connected rows with a computer terminal for each student
- chairs only, able to be reorganised at short notice for various activities.

Your tutor may or may not be positioned at the front of the class, and she or he may stand or be seated.

The way you sit in a class has a significant impact on the way the class will be conducted. For example, when you are faced with clustered seating it usually means you will be engaging in group discussion and activity. You should therefore, at a minimum, prepare to listen and to participate with students seated in your immediate cluster.

The tutorial environment can be perceived as more informal than a lecture, and this can have an impact on students' behaviour when they enter the room and when they are seated. Experiences within tutorials are generally more interactive and more dynamic than lectures; however, they are aimed at achieving certain objectives. Therefore it is equally as important to show respect to your tutor and fellow students by remaining focused on the tasks at hand and engaging with the experiences in a motivated and purposeful way.

Stay focused; the dynamic environment of a tutorial can make listening more challenging.

Listening well can be quite difficult in a **dynamic and interactive environment**. When you undertake discussions in groups, noise levels can be a barrier to your ability to stay focused on what is being said by your tutor or by students within your own group. It may also be difficult to listen and participate in discussions if everyone is talking at the same time, or if one person is dominating the discussion.

Participation

Be aware of your communication behaviour and plan to contribute effectively.

To ensure the best learning outcomes for all students, it is important that all students in small group activities have an opportunity to listen well and participate in a discussion. It is also important for all students to feel comfortable listening and contributing in whole-of-class activities. Initially your involvement in tutorials might be in response to what is being said or asked by your tutor, or in response to what other students are contributing. When you develop more confidence, your contributions might be more proactive and based on your preparation before your tutorial.

Whether you are confident or shy, the following strategies might be useful in helping you to participate effectively or to encourage others to participate during tutorials.

Confident speakers	• Aim to minimise your responses for maximum impact
	• Decide to respond about three or four times in a tutorial
	• Wait patiently and respond at a time that enables you to make maximum impact (e.g. after many people have given their opinions, then you speak)
	• Encourage others to speak:
	  – if anyone looks as if he or she might want to speak, shift focus to that person (look at the person and wait for a response)
	  – say what you think, then ask generally what others think (don't ask a particular person to respond)
	  – listen carefully to everyone who says anything
	  – don't leap in and comment on what everyone says (wait for maximum impact)
	  – don't finish others' sentences.

Hesitant speakers	• Aim to contribute at least once or twice, and then increase your involvement as your confidence increases • Show interest and engagement by using nonverbal cues (e.g. nodding) • Show agreement through the use of verbal back-channelling cues (e.g. saying 'OK' or 'Yes') • Prepare a question before the tutorial and ask it at an appropriate time • Ask a question to clarify a point • Add information to what someone else has said; look for a cue and fit your contribution in by agreeing, then adding to or restating the idea or giving information (e.g. 'I agree … and it could also mean …') • Create a new idea; agree with someone, then add your idea (e.g. 'Mmmm … I also think …' or 'There is another issue …').

Activity

Learning to listen and participate

The aim of this exercise is to encourage everyone to participate. Your tutor will hand each of you two sticky notes.

1   When you contribute to the tutorial discussion, place a sticky note on the desk in front of you.
2   The topic you are to discuss is: 'The difficulty of speaking in tutorials'.
3   When the discussion is finished assess:
   a   What made it easy for you to contribute?
   b   How did you help others to contribute?

c   How did others help you to contribute?

d   If you could not contribute this time, what do you plan to do next time so that you can participate?

Clarifying understanding

In a tutorial, there are likely to be many interpretations of the same information. These different interpretations become apparent as students engage in discussion and respond to information provided by the tutor and other students. It is important to remember that our interpretations in tutorials are influenced by our prior experiences, which include the particular way we have understood the information from the lecture, or our reading of course materials, as well as our cultural and social context.

Listening in a tutorial is a two-way communication process.

If during a tutorial it becomes apparent that your own interpretation of information is different from others', or if you are unsure of your understanding of an issue, then you should attempt to clarify your own and others' understandings by asking questions. Unlike in a lecture, in a tutorial it is expected that the communication process will be two way. That is, when you listen and don't understand, or when you listen and hear contradictions, you do have a chance to respond immediately to check your interpretation. How should you respond?

Ask for more information	If you think that you need more information to help you to understand an issue or topic, ask the speaker (tutor or student) to provide more detail about what he or she said or thought. For example, you might say, 'I think I understand what you are saying, but can you give me some more information.'
Clarify interpretations	If you have heard more than one interpretation of an issue, or if you are unsure of your own understanding of what has been said, you can seek for clarification. You can do this by using your own words to restate your understanding of what the speaker has said, or by asking for more information about the part of the message that might have confused you. For example, you might say, 'Are you saying that ...?' or 'I understand what you mean by ... but can you tell me more?'

After the tutorial

If, after the tutorial, you are still uncertain or confused, reread your notes and if possible redo the exercises and activities. If your understanding does not improve, arrange a consultation with your tutor as soon as possible. This will give your tutor a chance to give your question his or her full attention. Do not wait too long to seek assistance. If you do you may fall behind and find it very difficult to catch up.

Go to our website <www.oup.com.au/orc/turner2e> for more activities on the skills covered in this chapter.

Activity

SUMMARY

In this chapter we have examined the five processes that constitute any listening: attending, perceiving, interpreting, remembering and responding. We have also looked at the particular strategies that need to be employed to enable listening in the demanding contexts of lectures and tutorials. Listening well produces a good understanding of course material presented in lectures and enables you to discuss it with your peers (classmates) in tutorials. As you engage in listening and participation you are making this new, quite complex knowledge 'your own'.

GLOSSARY

attending (in listening) to be motivated and focused in order to listen to a message that has been heard.

back-channelling cues brief verbal responses made to a speaker to show how a listener is interpreting the speaker, and also to indicate the listener does not want to make any further comment at that point.

colloquial expression groups of words carrying a meaning that is acceptable in speech but usually not in writing.

dynamic participative, active, energetic, changing.

feedback information given to a person, about how his or her ideas, information, images, music, etc., are received.

inner speech mental thoughts, often in the form of discussion or advice or comment.

interactive communication processes that are two way, i.e. involving more than one person.

interpreting to create meaning from what is presented by linking it to one's own store of knowledge.

linguistic features aspects of language.

participation (in class) being actively involved; not just being present; not just attending the class.

perceiving (in listening) noticing aspects of the speaker, the message and the context.

chapter FOUR

Reading in an Academic Context

The ability to read well gives you the means to succeed in your university courses. It also enables you to keep up with the changing knowledge in your chosen discipline, even after you have left university.

This chapter helps you to:

- appreciate why we read widely at university
- acquire skills in finding sources by learning how to:
  - recognise different types of sources
  - assess the suitability of sources
  - find sources
- acquire skills in reading, by learning how to:
  - prepare
  - understand
  - assess critically
  - write to produce new meaning
- use reading to help your writing skills.

Lectures and textbooks are extremely important. They provide basic information and guide you in your study. You need to learn this material well, both for success in your examinations, and as a foundation for your other assessments.

However, in most courses, you are also required to learn beyond lectures and textbooks. You will normally be set some assessment tasks, such as essays, reports, presentations and seminar papers, that require you to read widely.

Universities attach great importance to reading well, because knowledge changes and develops. As well, omissions and mistakes occur in even the best academic work, so extensive and careful reading is needed. Moreover, in some disciplines, there are competing theories (different ideas and explanations about what occurs and why) leading to different types of research and resulting in different, and even contradictory, ideas and information. If we can read well, we can assess these, and so use the information intelligently.

Skills in finding sources

Most of the information and ideas at university come from secondary sources.

Reading well begins with skills in finding sources. You need the ability to:

- recognise different types of sources
- select academically reputable sources
- find sources.

Recognising different sources

There are two general types of sources of knowledge: primary and secondary. Whether a source, such as a book, a conversation, images or a film, is primary or secondary depends on our relationship to it. A **primary source** is one with which we have a direct relationship. For example, if we ask someone questions about his or her study habits, then the answers are a primary source of knowledge for us. If our source of knowledge is indirect, then it is a **secondary source**. For example, if we find out about the study habits of students, not by asking them directly ourselves, but indirectly, by reading a book about this topic, then the book is a secondary source of information. Most of our knowledge at university comes through secondary sources.

Activity

Recognising primary and secondary sources

Which of the following are primary sources of information, and which are secondary sources?

1   A football match we are watching (to gain information about how the game is played).
2   A newspaper report of the football match (that we are using to find out how the game was played).
3   A newspaper report of the football match (that we are using to find out how newspapers write up sports events).

Thinking

Why would we make a distinction between primary and secondary sources of knowledge?

The main types of academic secondary sources are:

- books (authored and edited)
- journal articles (paper and electronic)
- conference papers
- websites.

Books: authored and edited

Books can be either authored or edited. An **authored book** is one where the entire book is written by the author(s). An **edited book**, on the other hand, has different authors for each chapter, and an editor or editors whose main task is to organise the authors. Authored and edited books have different title pages, tables of contents and chapter title pages (see Figures 4.1 and 4.2).

Figure 4.1 Title page and table of contents for an authored book

Recognising authored and edited books

Examine Figures 4.1 and 4.2 and note the differences between authored books and edited books in their:

1   Title pages
2   Tables of contents.

Activity

Figure 4.2 Title page and table of contents for an edited book

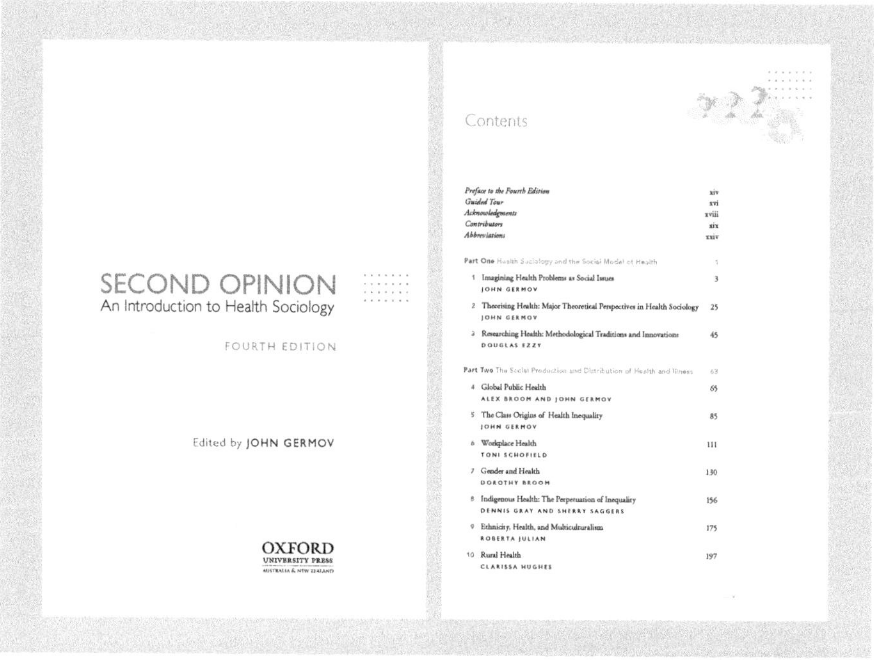

SECOND OPINION
An Introduction to Health Sociology

FOURTH EDITION

Edited by JOHN GERMOV

OXFORD
UNIVERSITY PRESS
AUSTRALIA & NEW ZEALAND

Contents

Journal articles: paper and electronic

Articles are quite short, usually about as long as a chapter in a book. They are accounts of research and/or analysis written by one or more authors and published in a **journal**.

An academic journal is a periodical (published on a regular basis). Each journal is devoted to an academic area of interest, indicated by its title (for example, *International Journal of Human Resource Management*, *Studies in Higher Education*). Every time the journal is published, its title remains the same. **Volume numbers** and **issue numbers** are used to specify any particular copy. The volume number indicates how many years the journal has been published at that date. The issue number designates the order of publication within a specific year.

While most articles are part of a journal, when they are accessed through **databases** they appear to exist on their own. In both cases, however, the title and author(s) of the article are shown on the first page, as is the title of the journal and its volume and issue numbers. Usually an article also displays a **Digital Object Identifier (DOI)**, which uniquely names it within the electronic environment.

Recognising features of an electronic copy of a journal article

The display screen result for an article from the Academic Search Premier database is given below.

> *Learning to use the Internet as a study tool: a review of available resources and exploration of students' priorities.*
>
> *By: Bond, Carol S.; Fevyer, David; Pitt, Chris. Health Information & Libraries Journal, Sep. 2006, Vol. 23, Issue 3, pp. 189–196, 8 p; doi: 10.1111/j.1471-1842.2006.00656.xa*

1   What is the title of the journal?
2   What is the title of the article?
3   In what year was the article published (printed in the journal)?
4   What is the volume number?
5   What is the issue number?
6   What is the DOI (Digital Object Identifier)?
7   What are the authors' names?

Conference papers

Conference papers are written documents presented, usually verbally, at a conference. Occasionally, the papers from a particular conference are published as a book. Sometimes, individual papers are available electronically, often through an academic database.

Websites

There is a vast amount of information available on the World Wide Web. While there is no difficulty in recognising a web source, it does create some problems when it is regarded as a secondary source of information for an academic assignment.

Assessing suitability of secondary sources

There are a vast number of secondary sources of information, from popular magazines to academic articles. You are required to read those that are quite well written and researched, so that the information and ideas you are considering have some value. Hence, another skill in finding sources is the ability to recognise what is a suitable secondary source for use in a university assignment.

A reputable source is one recognised as being produced within an academic community.

Reputable sources are those that are recognised as being 'good work' within the academic community. They meet the following criteria:

- the research reported in the source has been conducted in an acceptable manner and the results interpreted with care (see Chapters 12 and 13)
- the ideas and information contained in the source are situated within the relevant academic literature through the use of in-text citations (see Chapter 5)
- the source has been reviewed by other academics (also called 'refereed') and assessed as suitable for publication.

Assessing whether a secondary source is reputable is mostly easy. If a book or journal is held in the university library or is available through the library databases as a scholarly source, it is generally acceptable. Usually, lectures and textbooks are not regarded as suitable secondary sources for assignments, though they are essential for learning course content. Sources written for a general, rather than an academic audience, such as newspapers, magazines, encyclopaedias and general websites, are often not considered appropriate (see Table 4.1).

Websites may or may not be suitable. They need to be assessed. Use a web page as a source:

- if you are permitted to use web sources
- if it is produced within, or hosted by, a reputable organisation, such as a university, government department or large business
- if it is presented in an academic manner with in-text citations giving acknowledgment to the authors of the ideas and information used on the web page.

Table 4.1 Guide to suitability of different types of secondary sources for academic assignments

Secondary sources generally used	Secondary sources generally avoided
• Books in a university library • All articles in journals in a university library • All articles selected as 'scholarly' from an academic database • All conference papers in an academic database • All statistical and other information gathered from an academic database • Academically suitable web pages (if permitted)	• Newspapers • Magazines • Encyclopaedias • General reference books • Dictionaries (as sources of definitions) • Textbooks • Lecture notes • General web pages

There are exceptions to the rules above. In some courses you will not be able to use web pages; in some you must. In other courses, you may be permitted to use textbooks, or to refer to newspapers and magazines. In all cases be guided by your lecturers' requirements.

A reputable source is one that is recognised as having been produced, in a reasonable manner, within an academic community. It does *not* mean that the information and ideas are correct.

The information and ideas in a reputable source are not necessarily correct.

Finding sources

There are four steps to finding sources:

1   Find the content keywords and notice **limiting words**.
2   Read some basic background material on the general topic area.
3   Develop a search strategy.
4   Select sources.

Finding content keywords in the assignment task

You must establish the content areas to be addressed in your assignment. Begin by reading the question or task very carefully. Ask yourself: what parts of my course am I required to address in this assignment?

Focus on the content **keywords** in the assignment topic. Look for the words or meaningful clusters of words that direct you to content areas. As you are using keywords to find sources, select those that will enable you to find all the information so that you can assess it. Hence, when selecting keywords for a search, be guided by the following:

If the content area is not clear, speak to your tutor or seek out any other form of assessment help available to you.

- Select nouns that stand alone (for example, *examinations*)
- If two words are used to name something, select them. Show they belong together by using double inverted commas (for example, "university students")
- If two or more words occur together, but you are expected to make a judgment about the fact they describe (for example, *lower results*), select only the noun that indicates the general content (*results*)
- Select verbs if they name a specific relationship. For the purposes of finding sources, change the verb to a noun (for example, *achieve* is changed to *achievement*)
- If a verb indicates part of a relationship about which you are expected to make a judgment, change it to a noun that will indicate the general content area to be investigated (for example, change *underperform* to *performance*).

Example

Keywords (italicised)

Topic: *"Test anxiety"* causes *"university students"* to ~~underperform~~ in their *examinations*.
Discuss.

Note: performance

1   Use double inverted commas around "test anxiety" and "university students" to show
    that in both cases the whole phrase is a keyword.
2   As *underperform* is a verb and is negative, the keyword has been changed to a noun
    that will find all information in the general area of *performance*.

Some assignments include limiting words, for example, 'since Federation', which do not indicate new content but rather limit the focus of the existing content. They are not used in searching but are necessary in the selection process.

Activity

Finding content keywords and limiting words

Underline the content keywords in the following assignment topics. Make modifications to keywords as needed. Circle any limiting words.

1   University students find it difficult to read critically. Discuss.
2   Comment on the following statement: Girls do worse than boys in mathematics
    examinations.
3   Stress about examinations often leads to cheating. Comment.
4   Examine the impact of language courses on student success during the last decade.

Reading a basic background source

In order to search effectively you must know something about the content addressed by the assignment task. Lecture notes and textbook chapters are particularly helpful, as they give immediate access to theories, ideas and issues, as well as to appropriate terminology.

Probably you will not be able to use any of the background reading directly in your assignment. However, it is an excellent place to start, as it provides basic knowledge and makes both searching and further reading much simpler.

Developing a search strategy

The aim of searching is to produce a reading list of relevant sources for an assignment.

The aim of a search is to produce a list, called a **reading list**, of relevant sources that you may read for your assignment. A search strategy helps you achieve this. It contains plans for what, where and how to search.

- *What*: the production of a comprehensive and precise list of **search terms**
- *Where*: the plan for which collections of sources to search
- *How*: the knowledge of the most appropriate search technique to use.

Planning what to search for

To organise what has to be found, produce a comprehensive list of search terms:

Develop a list of search terms.

- keywords, and alternative terms
- relevant titles and authors.

Keywords are essential for searching. List them. However, as sources may use different terms from the keywords in the assignment task, produce a list of alternative keywords. For example, a source may not use 'performance' but instead use 'achievement' or 'GPA' (Grade Point Average). To find alternative keywords look in relevant:

- lecture notes
- chapters in a textbook
- articles or books on the topic
- a thesaurus attached to a database.

Once you have found one source that is suitable, use that to help find other sources. The author is likely to have written further on the topic, so use the author's name as a search term. The reference list will provide the titles of other useful sources. Find promising titles and use them as search terms.

Planning where to search

Planning where to search involves knowing what types of collections are available and which one best suits your information needs. The aim of all searching is to find suitable sources that can be accessed, either physically in the library, or online as a **full text**, that is, as a complete text rather than just a summary. These are available in a range of searchable collections:

Planning where to search means to match your information needs with the collections available for searching.

- the whole, or most, of the collection held in the library
- sections of the library collection, such as books, databases, ebooks or course material
- (free) web databases.

Libraries hold a significant range of sources in physical form, such as books, DVDs, films, music or paper copies of journals. They also provide access to other libraries, as well as to a vast range of online material available in databases, or in the form of ebooks or ejournals. Traditionally, each of these different types of collection has had to be searched separately.

Recently, though, some libraries have made it much easier to access everything the library holds or can provide access to. They have joined all collections together into one searchable set. If this is the case you do not need to make a decision about where to search.

If your library does not have the possibility of searching the entire collection, then plan where to search. There are two main possibilities. Select the library **catalogue** if you want to access books on general topic areas related to your assignment or you require other physical sources, such as DVDs or films, or possibly course material. If you need the most recent information or a very particular type of information, or statistics, company information or news, it is best to access this material via databases. These provide an index to the material available, and also usually give complete access to the full text electronically. As the library has subscribed to the databases, the material is freely available to you.

If you plan to search databases, you also need to check which databases to access. Typically, databases cover a specific disciplinary area. To make the selection process easier, libraries usually organise databases by subject area, and may also have developed sets or groups of databases relevant to your discipline. If such a set is available, choose it, as a single search only is required to access all databases in that group. If not, you need to search each database separately. Choose a suitable one from your subject area listing to begin the process.

A further search possibility is to use Google Scholar: <http://scholar.google.com>. It indexes the scholarly information on the internet. Choose this if you find that searching databases is not helping. Google Scholar makes searching simple. However, it often leads to sources that are not freely available. This is not a large problem, as the full text of such sources can be easily retrieved from a library database. See the section: 'Planning how to search'.

Knowing where to search is an essential skill at university. It would be useful to spend a day or two at the beginning of a semester becoming familiar with all the search possibilities at your library. If you are unsure where to search, ask a librarian.

Activity

Examining the searchable collections in your library

1   Can you search all, or many, collections in your library using a single search?
2   Does your library provide a list of databases for your disciplinary area (area of study)?
3   Does your library indicate the most useful databases in your discipline?
4   Can you do a 'cross-search'; that is, search a number of databases at the same time with the one search?
5   Can you search for course materials?

Planning how to search

All searching is based on:

- Boolean logic
- phrase searching.

Boolean logic uses the logical operators AND, OR, NOT to create a precise search that will best meet your information needs (see Table 4.2).

Table 4.2 Boolean logic

AND	Finds all documents containing *both* the keywords	*Example:* examination AND anxiety
OR	Finds all documents containing *either* keyword	*Example:* examination OR test
AND NOT or NOT	Finds documents containing the *first keyword* but *not the second*	*Example:* examination NOT medical

Phrase searching is used to find documents containing an exact phrase, making the search more efficient. Double inverted commas around the phrase holds it together as a single search term. For example, the phrase "university students" will find sources dealing with that precise topic, whereas a search of the separate terms 'university' and 'students' will produce a large number of irrelevant results.

Once the basis of all searching is understood, it is quite easy to learn how to use the techniques employed by different collections. The following types are examined:

Use different search techniques in different collections.

- a single search of the entire library
- a library catalogue search
- a library databases search
- a (free) web database search.

A single search of the whole library

A number of libraries have introduced a single search across all collections. It is called 'Summon' or 'LibrarySearch', or 'Library One Search', or some other similar name. It uses a Google type of search, with the possibility of selecting refinements to narrow the range of items found to those that are most suitable. Only two steps are required:

1 Perform an initial search using only a few significant keywords.
2 Refine the search by selecting from the refinement options.

Begin the search with only a few of the search terms. For example, for the topic 'Test anxiety causes university students to underperform in their examinations. Discuss', use only "test anxiety" and "university students". A complete list of keywords is not required, as it is best to utilise the refinement option to narrow the search. No logical operators are needed, but you must employ phrase searching if you wish any keywords to be kept together.

The initial search will produce a huge range of sources listed according to relevance, probably by the appearance of the keywords in the title. These need to be narrowed to a more workable range by using the refinement options. See Figure 4.3 below.

Figure 4.3 Searching the entire library

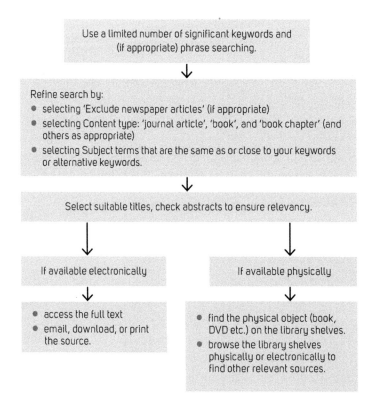

Once the list is as refined as possible, select suitable titles (see Table 4.3). In most cases you can view, download or email the full text immediately; or if the item is a physical object, such as a book or DVD, you can find it on the library shelves; or you may even be able to 'browse the shelf' electronically by clicking on the link supplied to find other relevant sources.

Some libraries have a different type of single search, sometimes called 'MultiSearch'. The search process is similar to that described above. However, an item may not be immediately accessible. You probably will have to click on an icon to activate software, such as SFX, which will then search for places where the full text is available. Follow any suggestion produced to find the full source.

Refining a search of the library by selecting subject terms

Activity

A search of the entire library for the topic 'Test anxiety causes university students to underperform in their examinations. Discuss' was conducted with the search terms: "test anxiety" and "university students".

Narrow the list of items found by using a refinement option. Which of the subject terms listed below would you select to help focus the research more on your topic? Choose three.

Subject terms: students (1582) ... college students (1540) ... children (1478) ... anxiety (1217) ... United States (1035) ... performance (900) ... colleges and universities (497).

Using the library catalogue

The main search functions in the library catalogue are: keyword, title, author, subject and course code. The keyword function is the one most likely to be used, at least initially; however, it has some limitations. Keyword searching is generally confined to words in titles, the **table of contents** pages of books, and summaries of contents. There is no ability to search within books or articles, or even to search for articles in journals.

Searching in the library involves both searching the catalogue and the library shelves (see Figure 4.4). Start with the most general keywords if you are using the basic search function. The advanced search function gives access to the Boolean operators 'AND', 'OR' or 'NOT'. Initially, use only the 'AND' operator and a few keywords. Once the initial search is performed, a tag cloud or a list consisting of subject terms generated by the library may be shown. If so, refine your search by selecting one of these terms.

Figure 4.4 Using a library catalogue

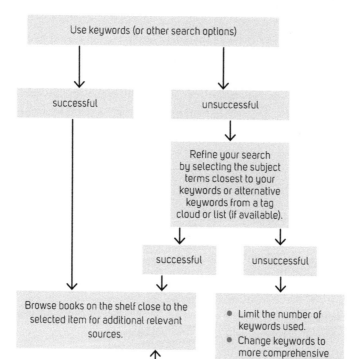

Your search may be unsuccessful, as either you have used too many keywords or the keywords are too specific for library searching. If so, limit the keywords to the most significant or change them to more comprehensive terms (for example, change *topic sentence* to *essay writing*) and search again. If you are uncertain how to do this, ask a librarian. Once a suitable title has been found, use the **call number** (the library number for the book) and locate the book on the shelves. Check quickly to see if it is relevant. If it is, examine the books nearby, as they are very likely to be on the same topic.

Activity

Searching skills for a library catalogue

Imagine you use the following keywords for a library catalogue search, but are not as successful as you would like to be. Provide a more comprehensive keyword for each of the following:

1   Writing paragraphs
2   First year university students

3   Multiple-choice tests
4   Brazilian students.

Searching databases

Once you have selected the relevant database or database set, begin with an advanced keyword search (unless you know the title or author). See Figure 4.5. Join keywords with 'AND' and use 'OR' to link in alternative keywords (for example, "test anxiety" AND "university students" AND performance OR achievement AND examinations). Ensure that only scholarly articles are retrieved by selecting that option. If most of the items on the first page of your search results are irrelevant, modify the search by using some different keywords. Databases often help by suggesting alternative subject headings. Experiment to find what works best. Once you select a source (see Table 4.3), you can usually find the full text immediately or follow an SFX link to a full text, then email 'full text' to yourself, or download it or print it.

Figure 4.5 Searching databases

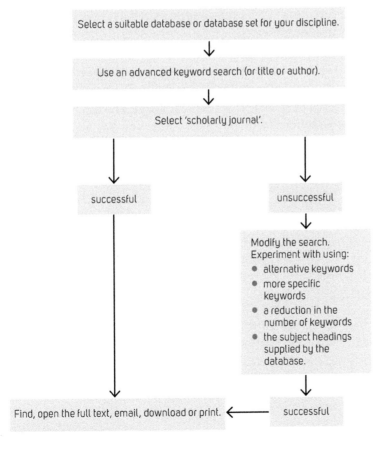

Most databases have links from any source to similar ones, either by the same authors, or on the same subject. Use these links to quickly build a reading list.

Activity

Searching databases

You are searching to find sources for the following assignment topic: *Anxiety* causes *university students* to underperform in their *examinations*. Discuss.

Find and select an Education database or database set. Explore how the advanced search function with appropriate keywords can be used to narrow the range of sources to those that are most useful. In each case, note how many sources are retrieved and also glance at the range of topics covered in the sources. What do you notice?

a   Use a basic search with the keyword : examinations.
b   Use an advanced search with the keywords: examinations AND "university students".
c   Use an advanced search with the keywords "test anxiety" AND "university students" AND performance OR achievement AND examinations.

Using Google Scholar

Google Scholar is one of the specialised searches available within Google. Select it for searching scholarly material. As it uses a Google search, use keywords without logical operators. Do use phrase searching if you want words to remain as a group. The process is easy, and will generate the titles of many relevant scholarly articles. Sometimes a full text version is available; most often you will be asked to pay for it. Don't be concerned. You can access the full text in one of the library databases by using the title as a search term. Note that some databases 'misread' punctuation. If that is the case, remove the punctuation before searching. See Figure 4.6 for a summary of how to search. Although using Google Scholar often requires two steps, it is an efficient means of finding relevant sources as the search is so simple.

Activity

Testing Google Scholar

You are searching for sources for the assignment topic: *Anxiety* causes *university students* to underperform in their *examinations*. Discuss.

Open Google Scholar and use the keywords: "anxiety", "university students", performance, examinations.

1   Open a relevant title. Have you free access to the full text of the article?
2   If you do not have the full text, copy the title and use that as your search statement in one of the specialised education databases, such as Academic Search Premier (EBSCO) or ProQuest Education Journals. Do you have access to the full text?

Figure 4.6 Using Google Scholar (or similar free database)

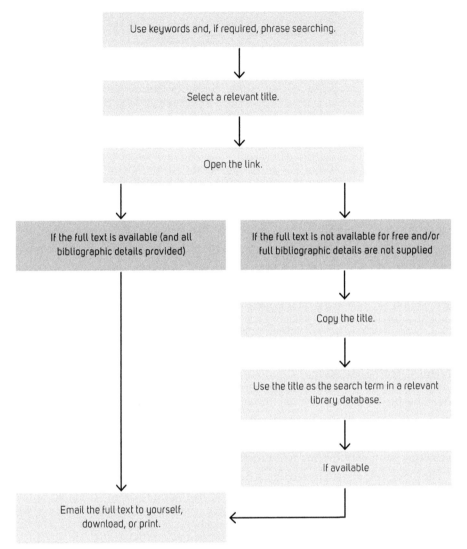

Selecting sources

The final task is to examine the list of sources produced by your search and select the most relevant. Pay attention to its coverage of content, including the focus provided by any limiting words in the assignment topic. Read the title. If it looks relevant, explore a little further. For a book, read the table of contents and examine the index; for an article, conference paper or report, read the Abstract or Executive summary and quickly check headings. See Table 4.3.

Table 4.3 What to read in a source to judge if it is likely to be useful

Source	What to read
Book	• Title • Table of contents • Index (list of contents at the back of a book)
Article in a journal, conference paper, report	• Title • Abstract or Executive summary (short summary placed before the introduction) • Headings

Reading well

Read over a number of weeks.

Once you have found your sources, it is time to read them. Do not rush the reading. It is best to start a few weeks, if not more, before your assignment is due. Read only one or two sources each day. This slower pace has two great advantages. The task is less daunting and, more importantly, you are giving your mind time to work on the ideas even when you are not actively thinking about them.

Reading in stages

Reading for an assignment has three stages. In the early stage of reading, the most relevant sources are read thoroughly. The aim is to learn about the topic. In the middle stage, as a firm basis of knowledge has been established, more precise selection from within sources is possible, and your reading is faster. In the final stage, your reading is directed by a desire to follow up on particular ideas and check on points. It is likely to be very precise and fast.

Figure 4.7 Reading stages

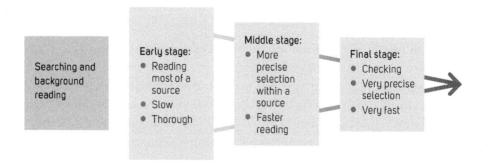

Reading processes

No matter what stage you are at, reading well requires attention to the four processes of reading: preparation, understanding, assessing critically and writing to produce new meaning. What changes between stages is the emphasis placed on each of the processes and the time needed to achieve a good outcome.

Reading well takes time, patience, curiosity and intelligence.

While each of the processes is listed separately, in practice they occur simultaneously. They are presented separately so that you can learn the skills.

Reading well involves four processes:

1 Preparing to read:
   - selecting what to read
   - getting to know the source
   - reading quickly to gain a general understanding of the content
   - checking meanings.

2 Reading for in-depth understanding:
   - reading to find the organisation of ideas and information
   - reading for rich details
   - recognising the status of the claims
   - reading to link to the assignment topic.

3 Reading to assess critically:
   - assessing the support for the argument within a source
   - situating the source within the general literature on the topic
   - assessing the social and power context of the source (possibly)
   - assessing the need to seek further sources.

4 Writing to create a new meaning:
   - margin notes
   - note taking
   - concept mapping.

Preparing to read

At all stages be clear about why you are reading. Constantly return to the assignment topic to remind yourself of your general aim. You will also have more specific aims in reading, which will differ depending on what stage of reading you are at. Remind yourself of these by asking questions, as outlined in Table 4.4.

Select what to read.

Once you have selected a source, or part of one, get to know it. Reread its title, headings and subheadings. These give quite a significant amount of information that helps your later in-depth reading. Also notice the type of academic content it contains, as this also helps prepare you for reading.

As you read, keep linking to your assignment topic.

Table 4.4 Making selections from within sources at different stages of reading

Reading stage	How to select	What to select
Early stage	Ask: *What are the most relevant sources for my topic?* Read: • title • headings and subheadings • introduction • abstract	An entire source
Middle stage	Ask: *What do I need to read in this source for my topic?* Read: • title • headings and subheadings	Relevant sections within a source
Final stage	Ask: *What precise information am I looking for?* Read: • title • headings and subheadings • topic sentences • indexes	Particular ideas or information within a source

Types of academic content are:

- a general overview of research (a summary of what has been discovered through research)
- a theoretical overview (a summary of ideas and theories)
- a company or government report (see Chapter 8)
- a research report (see Chapter 13).

In the early stage of reading, aim to gain a general understanding of the content.

Make sure you know the meanings of all the disciplinary terminology.

The next preparation stage is to read quickly through the chosen sections in the source. If you don't understand words or ideas, do not worry; keep reading. Reading quickly enables you to gain a general understanding of the source, even if your English is poor. You are starting to learn—without much effort.

The final stage of preparation is to find the meanings of any major words you do not know. If the words are **disciplinary terminology** it is very important to find their meanings (see Chapter 2).

If you do not know most words, then the source is too difficult for you to read. Ask for help, or set it aside, and perhaps return to it later.

Reading for in-depth understanding

Reading with a focus on in-depth understanding is mainly done in the early and middle stages of reading as they are the most complex. In the final stage, understanding is easier because you are searching for very specific ideas and information.

In-depth understanding is achieved by first recognising the big picture, or overall structure; then by examining the detail—exploring paragraph by paragraph—and finally, by stepping back to look at the big picture again.

To begin the process of in-depth understanding, select one section of a source and look at the big picture. Focus on the structure and content of the section by rereading the title of the source, then reading the headings and subheadings in the section you have chosen. If there are no headings, read the topic sentences. Ask yourself: 'What is this section about?'

Figure 4.8 Reading for in-depth understanding

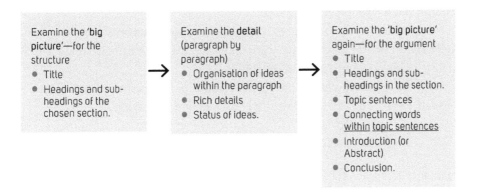

Next, move to the detail, at the level of individual paragraphs. Paragraphs in academic texts are likely to be much more complex than any you have read before. Therefore reading them requires careful work. At this stage of reading, never skim and scan as advised in, for example, ESL classes. Never rely only on topic sentences for information. Instead, read thoroughly and intelligently.

Why do you need to change how you read when it comes to academic texts?

Thinking

When using in-depth reading, give careful attention to:

- what the author is claiming, by examining the topic sentence and the way the ideas and information are linked within the paragraph
- the richness of the information
- the status of any claim within the paragraph.

The first step in intelligent reading is to notice how the author has linked ideas. Look carefully at the topic sentence, which is usually the first sentence.

In-depth reading is thorough and intelligent reading.

It should tell you the main idea in the paragraph. Ask: 'What is this paragraph about?' Then examine sentence by sentence, looking for how the main idea is explained and/or supported. Focus on the connecting words and other devices to aid recognition of how the ideas are organised (see Chapter 2).

The detail in a paragraph is also very important. It provides the rich information you require for the production of a good assignment. To find this, ask: 'What details have been supplied?'

Finally, check the author's relation to any idea presented. Notice who made any claim. Authors will usually supply an in-text citation, or acknowledgment, indicating the name of the person who originally presented an idea or piece of information. They also give some indication of their attitude to it. By examining the language, you can see if an author believes the claim to be true; or takes it to be tentative only; or does not accept the claim, but is merely presenting it in order to show why it is inadequate.

Reading at this level requires skill and patience. Academic texts are very dense. See Chapter 2 for some techniques you can use to help 'unpack' the writing to make it more understandable.

Continue reading paragraph by paragraph in this manner until you are finished. Expect to read the same material over and over again.

Activity

Reading a paragraph for in-depth understanding

1   Read the following extract (in *italics*) from p. 41 of an article by Rose, Lui-Chivizhe, McKnight and Smith, published in 2003. Answer the questions below it. The topic sentence is underlined.

> *In common with Indigenous [Aboriginal and Torres Strait Islander] university programs around Australia, a primary goal of the Koori Centre is to provide access to tertiary study for Indigenous Australians who have historically been excluded from higher education. Our students have made a commitment to come back to study, despite past experiences of schooling that were often painful and discouraging. As a result of these experiences, few Indigenous adults who are now re-entering education had successfully completed high school, and many were forced to leave with little more than primary schooling (see Australian Bureau of Statistics, 1996, pp. 1–2). This includes students in both our Tertiary Preparation and Diploma courses.*

   a   The topic sentence is the first sentence. What is the main idea presented?
   b   Circle any words or phrases that help connect ideas within the paragraph. What additional detail do these sentences provide?
   c   There is one in-text citation: an acknowledgment to the Australian Bureau of Statistics. What information does that source support? Is it good support? Explain your answer.

    d   What is the status of the claim 'many were forced to leave [school] with little more than primary education'? In other words, do the authors of this source agree with this claim, disagree with it, or wish to modify it?

2   Examine the following extract (in *italics*) by James Bell, published in 2003 (p. 157).

> *In 1991 over 38% of all college students were 25 years of age or older. In 1998 that number had increased to nearly 46% (Howard & Henney, 1998). Another study found that non-traditional [not school leavers] students make up approximately one-half of the undergraduates (Kinsella, 1998).* <u>*Clearly, the average age of college students has been increasing.*</u> *Even in foreign countries similar trends are being noticed.*

    a   The topic sentence has been underlined. What details have been supplied to support the claim in the topic sentence?

    b   Does Bell agree with the claim that 'in 1991 over 38% of all college students were 25 years or older'? Give as many reasons as possible for your answer.

3   Read the following extract (in *italics*) from Kearns and Gardiner (2007, p. 236):

> *There are hundreds of self-help books ... that argue that effectiveness can be greatly improved through practices such as writing lists, planning ahead, prioritizing the importance of tasks .... However, despite the large volume of material available, ... it appears that few studies have actually tested the empirical validity of basic time management principles.*

What suggestions do the self-help books make for ways to become more effective? Do Kearns and Gardiner believe these suggestions are correct? Give reasons for your answer.

    Finally, look at the big picture again in order to focus on the argument in the section you are reading. The argument is the position the author takes on a topic, together with the evidence provided to support it. Reread the section as a whole and ask yourself what the author is saying. Focus on the introduction and conclusion to the section. Then examine each topic sentence, especially the connecting words. These are particularly important in conveying the section argument.

    Proceed in this manner through the whole source, if required.

    Once you understand a relevant source, it is important to specifically ask yourself again how it is related to your assignment task. Glance through the source, noting what is most relevant. Mark it in the margin.

Reading to assess critically

At university you are expected to do more than understand particular sources. You are required to read critically; that is, to use critical thinking within the reading process. As was shown in Chapter 1, this involves judging the credibility of evidence and the adequacy of arguments as well as the effect of the social and power context of any claims.

For all sources assess:

- the support for claims within a source
- the support for claims across sources.

To assess the support from within a source for a claim, it is necessary to examine its relationship to the theory and research from which it was developed.

Read within a source to see how the claim is supported.

You only need to assess how a claim fits into a theory if your discipline is structured around competing theories, that is, there is a debate about how to explain what is happening. If your discipline has a fairly unified, taken-for-granted theoretical perspective, you will not need to address this issue.

In all disciplines, focus on the research that produced the claim as a means of assessing the evidence and the overall argument. In first year university, it is sufficient to notice the link between the researcher's *sample* (a sample is the particular group or event or behaviour actually studied for the research) and the claims that are made. Usually the sample is quite specific, for example, it may be students in a particular class in a particular university). A researcher should only make strong assertions about that particular group. Tentative or hesitant points may be made about larger but similar groups not directly involved in the research. Students in the final year of their degree are expected to go beyond this and examine the quality of the whole research process and the analysis of data (see Chapters 12 and 13).

It is also important to critically assess the way in which any author provides confirmation from other sources for the ideas and information that are used. Citations show the amount of support for a claim within the literature. Examine these. Assess the extent to which the literature is shown to support a claim by asking such questions as: 'Has the author used citations to show that other authors also believe the claim is correct?'; and 'What is the level of support shown for the ideas?' Very good students, particularly those in the final year of their degree or in postgraduate work, will also read some of the sources cited by an author to see if a fair and accurate account has been given.

Read across sources to examine how a claim is supported.

Critical reading also involves situating the claims of any source within the literature on the topic. This means you read across sources to assess the weight of evidence there is for any claim.

As you read any source, think of other sources that:

- discuss the same ideas
- agree on the same claim (or very similar claims)
- disagree on claims.

You will find some agreement on what is claimed, but also disagreement, gaps and inconsistencies. To read critically, notice these. If possible, see if you can discover the reasons for some of the differences. Seek out additional information to help you judge the value of the varying claims. Finally, decide on which claims are best supported, and why you might reject others. Your reasons should always be based on academic knowledge and not on your own personal preferences.

Consider also the social and power contexts in which the knowledge has been created. Critically assess the extent to which bias may be present (see Chapter 1).

Writing to create a new meaning

As you read, you should also be writing. The more you write, the deeper your learning of the source and the more you create and make coherent your own understanding of the assignment topic.

If you cannot write it, you have not yet made it your own.

Margin notes

Note key ideas in your source. Use underlining and abbreviations or symbols, anything to draw your attention to that part of the source. The aim is to emphasise those sections most related to your assignment topic. Add margin notes. These are short comments in the margin of the text. Write notes on:

Make margin notes as you read.

- the main ideas and rich detail in terms of relevance to your assignment topic
- how the ideas link to your assignment topic (support, modification, rejection)
- the amount of support for an idea
- whether an idea or piece of information is connected to one from another source.

Concept maps

Draw a **concept map** to help make the ideas in the literature yours. A concept map visually shows the connections between concepts (or categories or events or behaviours or objects), and thus helps produce sophisticated thinking about any topic (Novak & Cañas, 2006). Two techniques are traditionally used. The first makes the hierarchical relationship between concepts visible. The most comprehensive or abstract concepts (for example, 'examinations') are placed near the top of the map, and the most specific near the bottom (for example, 'examination results in Cambridge'). The second technique is employed to show the particular relationships between concepts. Those that are related are joined by lines, and the nature of the relationship is specified by a word written on the line.

Draw an academic concept map to indicate the relationship between concepts.

A further technique needs to be added when using a concept map to aid reading for an assignment. As it is always important to know the sources of any ideas or information, use different types of lines to indicate different sources. Include a legend, or list, showing the lines and the sources they represent.

In an academic concept map:

- place concepts (or categories or events or behaviours or objects) in circles
- place the most comprehensive concepts at the top of the page
- place the most specific concepts at the bottom of the page
- use lines to link concepts, and a word to show the relationship
- use a different type of line for each source
- create a legend to show which source each type of line represents.

Activity

Mapping concepts

Add the information from this claim made by Hembree (1990, p. 45):

Across all grades, female students report higher mathematics anxiety levels than males. However, the higher levels do not seem to translate into more depressed [reduced] performance.

Make sure you use a different type of line for Hembree's claim in your concept map, and that you add appropriate details to the legend.

Note taking

Write notes on any significant source.

It is a good idea to also make more formal written notes on any significant source. Structure the note taking by writing the assignment topic first to emphasise that the notes are for this purpose. Then record the publication details for the source: title, authors, year of publication and other details as required. Use two columns for note taking, one for notes from the source and the other for your additional comments (see Table 4.5).

Table 4.5 Note taking from a significant source

Assignment topic:	
Source Identification: title, authors, year and other details as required	
Note taking from source	Comments

Writing notes
• Note page numbers for each main point
• Write in your own words
• Summarise the most important points by noting:
  – a main point
  – its supporting points
  – next main point etc.
• Show the relationship between points (indicate linking words)
Select 1 or 2 quotations
• Write the quotation in full with quotation marks
• Note its page number
	Comment on the source academically
	Note:
	• how the points relate to the assignment topic
	• how well the points are supported in the source
	• how any point is related to other sources you have read
	Comment on the source in terms of your own knowledge
	Note:
	• any hesitations you might have about a point
	• any ideas you think could be relevant but that are not included
	Note follow-up tasks
	Include:
	• how you will check on or find any ideas or information
	• what further sources you need to read

In the left-hand column write your understanding of the source, in terms of its relevance to the assignment topic. Aim to provide a good summary of the main ideas and supporting points and their relationships. Notes do not need to be in full sentences; dot points are fine.

In the right-hand column, develop your critical assessment of the source and make links to your assignment. In note taking, judgments can be of two kinds: academic and personal. Both are there to help you look for further academic sources to support, modify or reject your ideas. Note any tasks that need attention following from your assessment of a source.

Reading practice: putting it all together

Below are two extracts (in *italics*). Read both of them using the techniques described in this chapter:

- Prepare to read (read title of article; read quickly through the extract; find meanings of any major words you do not know)
- Read for in-depth understanding (recognise the organisation of ideas and information, the rich details and the status of claims)

Activity

- Assess critically (assess the support for claims)
- Write to create new meaning (make margin notes).

The first extract is from Nonis and Hudson (2006, p. 152).

Along with the present trend of students spending less time on academic related activities ... today's post-secondary students are working more hours than their counterparts were years ago (Gose, 1998) ... Although working more hours per week can be one key reason for a student to be in academic trouble, available research does not seem to support this hypothesis. Strauss and Volkwein (2002) reported that working more hours per week positively related to a student's GPA. Light (2001), who interviewed undergraduate students of all majors, found no significant relationship between paid work and grades. According to Light, 'students who work a lot, a little, or not at all share a similar pattern of grades' (p. 29).

The second extract is from the first paragraph in the Conclusion section of an article by Applegate and Daly (2005).

This paper reports some results of the effects of paid employment on average grades from a survey of students at the University of Canberra ... The results do not show a large negative effect of paid employment on average grades. Doing some paid employment actually helps grades, perhaps by encouraging good time management skills but paid employment for long hours per week has a small but negative effect on average marks for a full-time student. These results are therefore in accordance with other results in the literature discussed earlier showing that paid employment does not have a substantial effect on academic grades except for particular groups including those who work long hours or who have come to university directly from school (McInnes & Hartley, 2002).

1 What ideas do both the sources agree on?
2 What idea(s) do the two sources disagree on?
3 Can you think of reasons that might explain the disagreement?
4 What would you do to help clarify this relationship between hours of working and grades? Be as precise as possible.
5 From your experience, what do you think is the relationship of hours spent in paid employment on academic grades? How would you try to find if there is academic support for your ideas?

Using reading to learn how to write

When you study, you are entering a discipline that has its own terminology and style. No matter how good you are as a general writer, you need to acquire the ability to write well within your disciplinary context.

Aim to learn the disciplinary vocabulary through reading. Start your own course dictionary. Whenever you find disciplinary terminology write it down, with its meaning. You can do the same for the 'ordinary' words that authors use, but are unfamiliar to you.

As well, use reading to develop a repertoire of useful writing skills. If you are uncertain how to write introductions or conclusions or use topic sentences, watch carefully as you read. You can also learn how to write developed paragraphs, or how to use the literature in a sophisticated manner by reading and observing these skills.

Reading can also teach you the disciplinary style of writing. Examine elements such as the sentence structures, the words, the tone or feeling, the role of the author and how the reader is addressed. It is difficult to acquire a new writing style, but constant reading and attention to style make it possible.

Activity

A reading and writing journal

Start a reading and writing journal. Write in whatever way suits you (it does not have to be neat). Date each entry. Use your journal to:

1   make notes about ideas, information, authors and sources relevant to your course
2   make lists of words and their meanings
3   make notes about any aspect of writing that you notice
4   try using words and sentence structures
5   note details about searching for sources
6   note what you find difficult, and where you might find help
7   note how you feel as you read any source
8   note if your reading skills need developing and how you will try to do this
9   note what you are good at in reading and writing
10 note ideas and information that you think are important for your assignment.

Activity

Form a reading group

One of the best ways to help yourself read is to form a reading group. Arrange to meet with friends to discuss some of the main readings for an assignment topic. However, be careful to write the assignment yourself. You cannot submit work that is the same as another student's; this is called collusion and is penalised.

Activity

Go to our website <www.oup.com.au/orc/turner2e> for more activities on the skills covered in this chapter.

SUMMARY

Reading well is quite a complex task. Before reading for an assignment, suitable sources have to be located. Skills in developing search strategies and in selecting sources are required. Then reading begins. Reading passes through three stages: an early stage with intensive examination of the most relevant sources; a middle stage in which the bulk of the reading is done, although it tends to be quite selective; and a final stage of very specific reading. It is necessary to read well in all stages by engaging in the four processes: preparation, understanding, assessing critically and writing to create a new meaning. Reading is a scholarly activity. You not only engage in understanding each individual source, but also create your own understanding by continually assessing and linking across sources, and to your assignment topic.

GLOSSARY

article an account of some research or analysis published in a journal. Sometimes an article is called a **paper**. Sometimes chapters in edited books are also referred to as articles.

authored book one in which all the authors take full responsibility for all of the material in the book.

Boolean logical operators keywords joined with AND, OR, AND NOT or sometimes just NOT and brackets, which enable a precise search statement to be made.

call number the library number used to indicate a book's content area and to make it easy to find.

catalogue an index of items held within a library.

concept map shows the key concepts and their relationships in any area of knowledge.

conference papers written documents presented (usually verbally) at a conference.

databases a term usually reserved for electronic collections of material, organised for ease of searching and retrieval.

Digital Object Identifier (DOI) uniquely names a digital object, for example, an article that is available electronically.

disciplinary terminology the specialised words within a discipline, sometimes known as technical terms, or discipline-specific terms, or even jargon.

edited book one in which different authors are responsible for different chapters.

full text a term used in databases to indicate the whole of a source.

glossary a list of the specialised terminology in a text, with meanings.

issue number of a journal designates the order of publication within a specific year.

journal a periodical devoted to some specific area of academic interest.

keyword a word (or group of words) indicating the content that needs to be addressed in an assignment topic or question.

limiting words a group of words that focus attention on a particular section of content, usually by indicating a specific time period.

paper a 'conference paper', but also is sometimes used to refer to an article in a journal.

phrase searching the use of double inverted commas around a number of words to enable a search for that exact phrase.

primary source is one which gives a direct or unmediated relationship to knowledge.

reading list a list of sources that are relevant to an assignment topic and that will probably be used in its production.

reference list a list of all the sources, and their bibliographic details, that have been used and acknowledged in a document.

search terms are keywords, alternative keywords, authors' names or titles used for finding sources.

secondary source any source that provides a secondary (or mediated) relationship to knowledge.

table of contents list of chapters and page numbers in a book; or a list of sections and page numbers in a report.

volume number indicates how many years the journal has been published at that date.

chapter FIVE

Basic Academic Writing Skills

Most of your assignments at university require that you show knowledge of the literature. As a result, you need skills both in reading and in incorporating ideas from your reading into your own work. This chapter examines the basic skills required for using the literature in your assignments. You will learn how to:

- use an objective writing style
- incorporate the literature into your own work by paraphrasing, quoting and summarising
- acknowledge sources by writing citations
- acknowledge sources by writing reference list items
- construct paragraphs around claims from the literature.

Academic writing aims to develop new ideas and to situate them in what is already known.

The most distinctive aspect of university education is the way it is linked to the literature. While assessment is structured to encourage a student to develop new ideas rather than just repeat what is already known, it also demands that these ideas are developed from and related to the literature. Not surprisingly, rules and expectations have been established to achieve this.

Writing objectively

Most academic tasks require an objective writing style.

Academic writing has particular stylistic features, as it is concerned with knowledge generated through scientific processes rather than just through personal experiences. All disciplines require that the author is **objective**. The aim is to present ideas and information undistorted by personal feelings or prejudices. Thus academic writing style is distinctly different from speaking and even from the writing in such everyday forms as newspapers. Colloquialisms are never used. As well, although academic writing uses many of the words and sentence structures found in our everyday life, it also employs a range of both general academic words and specific disciplinary terminology, and a dense style of writing (see Chapter 2). All of these are part of an objective writing style, as they emphasise that the knowledge belongs in a particular scientific community. In addition, many disciplines also avoid first and second pronouns (I, me, we, you), or pseudo third person references (such as 'In this author's opinion'). Instead, writers rely on the third person (for example, 'It is claimed' or 'Smith (2007) argued') as a means of showing the scientific basis for any **claim**. However, some styles of writing, such as reflective writing, and some disciplines, such as Education, encourage the use of personal first and second pronouns where it is appropriate. Always be guided by the style within your discipline.

Can you think of other features of an academic style of writing?

Why does this book use first ('we') and second person ('you') pronouns?

Thinking

Incorporating claims from the literature

Almost all writing and speaking at university relies on using ideas and information found in the literature. Hence, there are rules about how to bring the literature into your own work. When these rules are used well, a student clearly shows his or her intelligence and knowledge of the literature. If they are not followed, a student's work will be seen as weak, and will receive a lower mark.

The main problem in relation to bringing the literature into your own work is **plagiarism**. Plagiarism occurs when someone takes something created by an author (words, ideas, graphic, sound, image or code) and passes it off as his or her own. It is regarded as a form of cheating.

Types of plagiarism include:

Plagiarism occurs when someone takes the work of another and presents it as his or her own.

- copying words exactly from a source (without using quotation marks) with or without a citation
- copying graphics, sound or code without a **citation**
- copying words with only slight modifications from a source (keeping the same sentence structure) with or without a citation (also called patchwriting)
- copying graphics, sound or code, and making only minor alterations, with or without a citation
- patching (Wilson as cited in Biggs, 2003, p. 129): joining copied words (or graphics, sound or code) from different sources
- paraphrasing or summarising ideas but not using a citation
- buying and using work produced by another person

- using work produced by another person
- submitting work as your own that has been produced by yourself and one or more others (more often called **collusion**).

Plagiarism is penalised. A student usually receives a reduced mark, or no mark at all, for the assignment. After repeated offences, a student can be excluded from university.

Plagiarism, however, is easy to avoid, if you know how to incorporate the literature into your assignments and how to acknowledge all ideas and information.

There are three ways to bring the knowledge in the literature into your own work when words are involved: paraphrasing, quoting and summarising.

Table 5.1 Paraphrasing, quoting and summarising

	What is it?	When do you use it?
Paraphrasing	Writing an idea from the literature in your own words for your own purpose	Used very frequently in all forms of written and spoken work
Quoting	Using the 'exact' words of an author	Used occasionally in all forms of written and spoken work
Summarising	Writing a summary of an argument or idea from the literature in your own words, but keeping to the author's purpose	Used occasionally in an essay or report Used most frequently in a literature review or annotated bibliography

Paraphrasing, quoting and summarising take on particular qualities within an academic context. They are not isolated activities, as they might have been in high school or ESL classes. Rather, what is selected to paraphrase or quote, and how it is incorporated, depends on your needs as a writer. As well, an acknowledgment has to be provided to the authors whose work is being used.

Example

Academic features of paraphrasing, quoting and summarising

The essay topic is: 'Students who seek support perform better at university. Discuss.' There is information that is relevant to the essay topic in the following extract written by Krause, Hartley, James, and McInnis (2005, p. 29):

> *As one might expect, high achievers are significantly more likely to seek such advice than are low achievers. International full fee-paying students report seeking help from teaching staff more than their domestic counterparts, as do non-traditional age students. There are few significant differences in this respect across fields of education.*

The examples below show how to bring the information from the extract into your own work.

Table 5.2 Academic features of paraphrasing, quoting and summarising

Academic features	Example
PARAPHRASING: a An idea is selected. b The idea is paraphrased to show the link to your argument. c The authors of the claim are acknowledged.	The students, in any discipline, who asked for help at university were more often those who aimed for the highest marks (Krause, Hartley, James, & McInnis, 2005, p. 29). *Note:* Ideas from the first and third sentences of the extract are used as they are relevant to the topic. It would also be correct to paraphrase information from the first sentence only, although you would be making a weaker claim.
QUOTING: a A small section only is selected as a quotation. b A part sentence or an introductory sentence is used to link the quotation into your own work. c The authors of the claim are acknowledged.	Krause, Hartley, James, and McInnis (2005) commented that "high achievers are significantly more likely to seek such advice than are low achievers" (p. 29).
SUMMARISING: a This is rarely used in an essay or report. b If it is used, both the main idea and the supporting ideas are usually summarised as a means of providing depth of information. c The authors of the claim are acknowledged.	Krause, Hartley, James, and McInnis (2005, p. 29) found that some groups of students are more likely to ask for help and advice than others: those that aim to do very well, international students and mature age students. The authors claimed this pattern was mostly the same across all disciplines.

Paraphrasing

To **paraphrase** a claim for your own purpose:

To paraphrase claims, write in your own words for your own purpose.

1   Understand the claim.
2   Recognise the disciplinary terminology that may need to be kept in the rewriting.
3   Write in your own words for your own purpose.
4   Acknowledge the source.

The first step in paraphrasing is to understand the claim you wish to use. Take time to make sure you have the correct meaning and to see how it fits in with the author's overall argument (see Chapter 4).

The next step is to recognise the disciplinary terminology in the original text. All academic work is written using technical words. As they are necessary for clear and accurate communication within a discipline, keep some or all of them in any paraphrase you construct. This is not plagiarism, but essential for good academic writing.

A paraphrase often has a new sentence structure, and some of the words are changed.

Third, the claim needs to be written in your own words. A paraphrase retains the original idea or information, but restates it in a different way. This involves a transformation of the original text: the sentence structure is likely to be changed, and synonyms are used in place of many of the original words.

Paraphrases can be written mechanically.

Mechanical means can be used to transform a sentence structure. One way is to change sentences from active to passive voice (or vice versa). For example, 'John read the first chapter in the textbook last week' is written in the active voice, as the subject of the verb is 'John'; he is the one who is doing the action of reading. The sentence can be rewritten in the passive form by making the 'first chapter' the subject. The passive sentence reads, 'The first chapter of the textbook was read by John last week'.

A further means of transformation involves changing parts of a sentence. A single word, such as an adjective or adverb, can be rewritten as a phrase or clause. For example, the adjective 'first' in 'first chapter' can be rewritten as, 'the chapter which comes first'. The reverse process could also apply. As well, any complex sentence (with more than one verb) can be transformed into a simple sentence (with one verb). Equally, parts of a sentence can be reordered.

A more sophisticated way of transforming a sentence is to think of which part you want to emphasise. An easy mechanical way to do this is to begin the sentence with the part you want to emphasise. Emphasis can also be created by using 'what' or 'it'. For example, to emphasise the chapter, you can write, 'What John read last week was the first chapter of the textbook'; or 'It was the first chapter of the textbook that John read last week'. On the other hand, if you want to place emphasis on John, you could write, 'It was John who read the first chapter of the textbook last week'. The emphasis is created because 'what' or 'it' stands for, and thus points to, what is most important.

To complete a mechanical paraphrase, synonyms can be used so that the final paraphrase could read, 'Chapter 1 of *Essential Academic Skills* was read recently by John'; or 'It was John who read Chapter 1 of the book *Essential Academic Skills* last week'. These are correct paraphrases, but producing them in this manner can be clumsy, and should only be relied on if you lack confidence in using English.

Fortunately, within an academic context you are not merely performing a paraphrasing exercise but rather choosing some claim from the literature and using it as part of an argument within an assignment. In this context, paraphrasing is an easier and more natural form of rewriting.

To paraphrase well ask: why am I using this information?

When paraphrasing for an assignment, think about why you are using the idea or information. To do this, ask: 'Why am I using this?' Answer yourself by saying: 'Because I want to show that ...'. Your answer will automatically lead to a transformation of the original text and a much better writing style. For example, you may answer your question with 'I want to show John has already read Chapter 1 of the textbook'; or with 'I want to show that last week John read some of the textbook'; or with 'I want to show that Chapter 1 of the textbook has already been read by John'; or with 'I want to show that it was only a week before when John read the first chapter of the textbook'. All of these answers produce correct paraphrases of the original sentence. They are also more useful, as the purpose for using the information has been thoroughly considered.

To complete any paraphrase, always check that you have not relied too much on the language of the original and that you have only used ideas and information that can be found in the original source. You must provide a citation that shows whose idea or information it is, when it was published and where precisely it can be found. See section 'Writing citations' for more information.

Below is an example of how a particular claim from the literature can be paraphrased so that it matches different interests or purposes.

Example

Paraphrasing for your own purpose
Roig (1997, p. 121) wrote this:

> *Students lack the necessary knowledge to determine whether text has been correctly paraphrased.*

It can be paraphrased and linked into your writing in a number of different ways. See below.

Table 5.3 Writing paraphrases for your own purposes

Paraphrase	Emphasis for different purposes
Students do not have sufficient knowledge to recognise if a paraphrase has been appropriately created (Roig, 1997, p. 121).	The whole sentence is the paraphrase. It is written to emphasise students' lack of knowledge.
Recognising when a text has been appropriately paraphrased is a skill that not all students possess (Roig, 1997, p. 121).	The whole sentence is the paraphrase. It is written to emphasise the skill of recognising a correct paraphrase.
It appears that it is necessary to teach students about paraphrasing as, according to Roig (1997, p. 121), they do not have sufficient knowledge to recognise if a paraphrase has been appropriately created.	There are two parts of the sentence: the writer's claim, and Roig's claim. The language and citation show what part of the sentence is the paraphrase of Roig's claim.

Activity

Recognising plagiarism

Read the extract below (in *italics*) from page 121 of an article written by Miguel Roig, and published in 1997.

The present findings represent evidence for the position that the majority of students probably engage in inadvertent plagiarism. The overall picture that emerges from the results of both studies of students' understandings of plagiarism *is that as long as the original author is credited and/or as long as minor modifications are made to the original, the material is generally considered to be properly paraphrased. In contrast to the findings of Karlin et al. (1988) and Hale (1987), the present findings suggest that plagiarism may be a larger problem than previously thought, and that a substantial amount of this activity may stem from [a lack of knowledge of] the proper rules for correctly paraphrasing text.*

Examine each of the attempts below to use some of the ideas and information from this source in an assignment. Determine which attempts are examples of plagiarism. Explain your answers.

a   Roig (1997, p. 121) found that as long as the original author is credited and/or as long as minor modifications are made to the original, the material is generally considered to be properly paraphrased.

b   Students considered that as long as the original author is credited and only minor changes are made, the material is properly paraphrased (Roig, 1997, p. 121).

c   Roig (1997, p. 121) claimed that many students may plagiarise merely because they are unaware of what is required when paraphrasing from an original source.

d   Roig's (1997, p. 121) findings indicate that plagiarism is a larger problem than thought as students are unaware of the proper rules for paraphrasing text.

Activity

Paraphrasing

Note: In this exercise you are not expected to provide citations. You are learning the first step: how to write a paraphrase. The section 'Writing citations' teaches you how to cite.

1   Read the following extract (in *italics*). The extract is from page 24 of Peter Redman's book titled *Good essay writing. A Social Science guide*, published in 2001.

You must therefore always put arguments in your own words except when you are quoting someone directly. ... The positive side of this seemingly draconian [very harsh] rule is that you will remember better what you have put in your own words.

a   Paraphrase the extract. Begin your sentence with: 'One advantage to students of writing in their own words is that ...'

b   Paraphrase the extract again, but this time begin your sentence with: 'When writing a student must ...'

2   Read the following extract (in *italics*). It is from page 81 of an article published in 2000 by Barbara Jones and Erica Frydenberg.

> *Stress and anxiety for students is often associated with ... social factors such as, loneliness, financial problems and limited time available for their family and friends ...*

a   Paraphrase the above extract. Begin your sentence with: 'It is problems such as ...'
b   Paraphrase the extract again. This time begin with: 'Students can become anxious because of ...'

3   The extract below (in *italics*) is from page 46 of an article written by Julio G. Soto, Sulekha Anand and Elizabeth McGee, published in 2004.

> *Students committed plagiarism almost twice as frequently in the course in which no plagiarism instruction was given (Biology 21) than collectively in the two courses in which plagiarism was explicit (Biology 10 and Biology 100 ...)*

a   Paraphrase the information from the extract to show one reason students plagiarise.
b   Paraphrase the information in the extract to show what lecturers can do to minimise plagiarism.

Quoting

Occasionally we use quotations in our writing. Some ideas are written so beautifully and clearly that we honour them by keeping the exact words of the author. They enhance our work, lend further credibility to the idea we are using and reveal that we are a skilled writer.

Quotations are the exact use of an author's words.

A **quotation** may be:

- one word
- a part of a sentence
- a sentence
- a number of sentences.

To quote:

1   Select the most suitable words to use as a quotation.
2   Write the quotation using the exact words of the source.
3   For short quotations (less than 40 words), use double inverted commas as quotation marks to indicate you are quoting.
4   For long quotations, use indentation to indicate you are quoting.
5   Acknowledge the source.

Give a considerable amount of care to selecting quotations. The words should be well written and closely related to your writing needs. While a quotation must use the exact words, some very minor changes can be made to fit the quote into your writing, without any need to note the alteration. If the first word of the quotation is in upper case, it may be altered to lower case; and the final punctuation of a quote need not be used. Most quotations should be short. Also, limit the number of quotations in any assignment. As a rough guide, use no more than one short quotation per page, and one long quotation per 1000 words.

Formatting is used to show that words are being quoted.

Clearly, as quotations are using the exact words of an author, it is important to indicate that the words are consciously being used as a quotation, rather than being copied as plagiarism. Formatting is used for this purpose; double inverted commas are placed around short quotations (less than 40 words), while long quotations are indented. Citations have to be provided to show who wrote the quote, when it was published and where precisely it can be found. This is covered in the section 'Writing citations'.

Example

Using quotation marks for a short quotation
Redman on page 24 of a book published in 2001 wrote:

This ensures that you have the fullest understanding possible of the course.

You can write it as a quotation in the following manner:

Redman (2001) claimed "this ensures that you have the fullest understanding possible of the course" (p. 24).

It is also possible to make additional minor changes to a quotation as a means of creating a good fit between the quote and your writing. If this is done, the original meaning must be maintained and the alterations have to be indicated.

Table 5.4 Modifying a quotation to suit your needs as a writer

Redman (2001) claimed that "this ensures that you have the fullest understanding possible of the course" (p. 24).	
Modification	Indicating the modification
Adding a few words (that do not alter the meaning)	Use square brackets around the added words. *Example*: Redman (2001) claimed that "this [writing in your own words] ensures that you have the fullest understanding possible of the course" (p. 24).
Changing the tense of a verb	Use square brackets around the verb. *Example*: Redman (2001) claimed that "this [will ensure] that you have the fullest understanding possible of the course" (p. 24).

Table 5.4 Modifying a quotation to suit your needs as a writer (*cont.*)

Modification	Indicating the modification
Adding emphasis	Use italics for emphasis and in square brackets write: emphasis added. *Example*: Redman (2001) claimed that "this ensures that you have the *fullest understanding* [emphasis added] possible of the course" (p. 24).
Leaving out some words	Use three dots ... (called an ellipsis). *Example*: Redman (2001) claimed that "this ensures that you have the fullest understanding ... of the course" (p. 24).

Activity

Selecting and formatting quotations

Note: In this exercise you are not expected to provide citations. You are learning the first step: how to select and format quotations. The section 'Writing citations' teaches you the details of how to cite.

1   Each of the following are extracts from sources (in *italics*) about the use of quotation. *Select the part that best expresses why particular parts of a text are chosen as quotations.* Write it with quotation marks. You do not need to use a complete sentence. Try adding emphasis or leaving out some words (see Table 5.4).

a   The extract is from page 247 of a book titled *The Reader's Voice* written by Deborah Silvey and published in 2005.

You might use a quotation—the exact words used by a writer—when an idea is expressed in an especially effective way.

b   The extract is from page 84 of a book titled *Making the Grade* written by Iain Hay, Dianne Bochner and Carol Dungey and published in 2002.

Use quotations sparingly. Only use a quotation when it outlines an idea or example so well that you cannot improve on it, when it contains a major statement you must document, or when the quotation itself is the evidence or example that supports your point.

c   The extract is from page 109 of a book titled *Studying @ University* by David McIlroy, published in 2003.

Weaving suitable quotations into the tapestry of an essay is an art that can only be acquired by practice. First, quotes have to be noted at the reading stage of preparation. Some sentences or phrases are so good that they stand out and are best used in their original form.

2 Select a quotation from the extract below (in *italics*) to show the type of teaching in Chinese education. The extract is from page 159 of an article written by Joseph Kee-Kwok Wong and was published in 2004. Write the quotation.

> *... the mode of teaching might not be through simple transmission of knowledge. It actually occurs in a complex and interactive environment.*

Summarising

Summarising is used as a means of briefly conveying the main points of a piece of work.

Summarising a source, or part of a source, involves writing the main points in your own words and possibly also the supporting points. Summarising is useful as a learning tool. It is also an important skill in some types of assessment. Both an **annotated bibliography** and a literature review (see Chapter 13) involve summarising the claims of authors. Summarising is less often used in general writing tasks, such as essays and reports. However, if you are asked to compare the position of various authors, or to evaluate a particular author, then it is essential to summarise their positions.

To summarise:

1 Understand the section.
2 Summarise the main points (and possibly the supporting points).
3 Write in your own words.
4 Use disciplinary terminology.
5 Acknowledge the source.

It is important to understand the section or source you wish to summarise. Read the source many times if necessary. Look carefully for the main points and their connections. Also underline any disciplinary terminology that you are likely to need. Write the **summary** in your own words, using appropriate terminology. Your aim is to produce a coherent outline of all the main points, their supporting points, if necessary, and their connections, exactly as the source has presented them. How much of the original text is included in a summary depends on your purpose in using it. Sometimes you will only use the main points. At other times, a summary is best written covering both the main points and their supporting points. Illustrative points such as examples are not incorporated into a summary.

In your writing you must acknowledge the source of the ideas you have summarised.

Activity

Summarising

Note: In this exercise you are not expected to provide citations. You are learning the first step: how to summarise. The section 'Writing citations' teaches you how to cite.

1   Summarise the main points of this section: 'Writing claims from the literature'.
2   Summarise the main points of the section: 'Paraphrasing for your own purpose'.

Paraphrasing, quoting and summarising: relationship to the source

Paraphrasing, quoting and summarising transport ideas from the literature in a fair and accurate manner into your work. Each of these writing tools has a different relation to the source, as outlined in Table 5.5.

Table 5.5 Differences between paraphrasing, quoting and summarising

	Degree of modification of the source	Amount of the source usually involved
Paraphrasing	• Own words • Written for your own purpose	From a sentence to a paragraph
Quoting	• 'Exact' words of source	From part of a sentence to a number of sentences
Summarising	• Own words • Written with the same purpose as the source	From a paragraph to an entire source

Writing citations

At university we need to acknowledge the authors of any claim or quotation or any other material we use by providing basic publishing information for the author's work. In acknowledging sources we:

Acknowledge the source of all claims and quotations and any other material used within your work.

- give our writing credibility
- show the extent of the reading on which we are basing our ideas
- enable readers to follow up on any idea that interests them.

Both Australian and international students can find acknowledging sources a problem. Domestic students may well need to develop their abilities to meet the greater demands placed on them by university assessment requirements. Students from other educational cultures, such as Eastern Asia, the Indian subcontinent and the Middle East, may have no familiarity at all with the process of acknowledging sources.

It is extremely important to learn the skill of acknowledging sources (or referencing). Failure to do so leads to a loss of marks, whereas the ability to

It is essential to learn how to acknowledge sources.

acknowledge sources is rewarded. Often in first year courses, marks are given just for the technical skills involved in referencing. More importantly, a student is likely to gain a much higher mark for content in any assignment that is well referenced, as skilful acknowledgment of sources reveals the depth and breadth of a student's reading and thinking.

Although only a few major systems of acknowledging sources exist, there are many variations. The most commonly used style is the author–date referencing system, which is generically known as a Harvard style. It contains:

- in-text citations
- a **reference list**.

The APA 6th is an example of such a style. The American Psychological Association (APA) developed it as an authoritative guide to referencing, and the APA 6th is the most recent update. It is quite widely used across many different disciplines, as it covers referencing for all source types, and is particularly good at producing guidelines for new types of electronic sources. Some courses at university also use what is termed a Harvard style. The Australian Government Publishing Service (Snooks, 2002) produced a comprehensive guide to this style, but it does not cover all the types of sources published in an electronic environment. Universities, lecturers and publishing houses may create their own versions of the Harvard style. For example, this book uses an Oxford University Press version. The examples being shown to you are, however, APA 6th.

Use one referencing style consistently throughout any piece of written work.

Other types of referencing system are:

- the note style (for example, the Chicago note style, which uses footnotes and endnotes to provide referencing information)
- the notational style (for example, the Institute of Electrical and Electronic Engineers (IEEE) Style, which numbers the citations and provides a numbered list of references at the end of the document).

It is usually best to use the system recommended by your lecturer. Whatever style you choose, use it consistently throughout a document.

Thinking Activity

- Why do you think most lecturers will accept any referencing style as long as it is consistently used?
- Different disciplines have different preferences for styles. Can you think of reasons why this might occur?
- Why do you think Oxford University Press does not use the APA 6th style?

To acknowledge sources using the APA 6th style, provide:

- short acknowledgments of each of the sources *within* the text (called an in-text citation, or citation, or reference)
- a list at *the end* of the text containing the full bibliographic details of each cited source (called a reference list or references)

Provide a citation for each:

- paraphrase
- summary
- quotation
- other forms of information or material produced by an author and used in your own work (statistic, graphic, image, sound, code or film).

No acknowledgment is needed if the idea or information is general knowledge.

A citation normally gives three pieces of information about the original claim:

Citations identify the source by indicating: who, when, where.

- *who*: the family name(s) of the author(s)
- *when*: date of publication
- *where*: page number.

In the examples on the following pages, the basic citation patterns are shown. The examples indicate how to include page numbers as well as author names and dates of publication. The APA *Publication Manual* (2010) does not give advice on where to place page numbers for paraphrases and summaries, although it does encourage their use. An APA style expert (S. Lazer, personal communication, 11 January 2011) suggested that page numbers for paraphrases and summaries always follow the date of publication. That advice is used in examples throughout this book.

Table 5.6 illustrates the most common ways of incorporating citations for paraphrases, short quotations and summaries into sentences.

Techniques for citing ideas or information found not in their original source but cited in another are also shown on the following pages.

An example showing how to cite long quotations is provided. These are cited differently from short quotations. As discussed earlier in this chapter, if the quotation is long (more than 40 words) indentation is used, rather than inverted commas, to indicate quoted material. A period is placed at the end of the indented quote. When the citation is inserted, the page numbers are written in parentheses as usual, but placed after the period.

There are, however, many other possible variations. For example, sources will have different numbers and types of authors; different types of date for different sources, including no date; and may or may not have page numbers. Table 3 of Appendix A shows how to write citations containing any of these variations.

Table 5.6 *Typical ways of incorporating citations for paraphrases, short quotations and summaries (APA 6th style)*

Structure	Example
Author's family name (date, p. X); a verb in the past tense; the paraphrased claim	Greetham (2001, p. 240) advised students to be aware that different lecturers will have different preferences for how referencing is to be done.
The paraphrased claim written as a sentence (Author's family name, date, p. X)	Students need to be aware that different lecturers will have different preferences for how referencing is to be done (Greetham, 2001, p. 240).
'According to' author's family name (date, p. X); paraphrased claim	According to Greetham (2001, p. 240), students need to be aware that different lecturers will have different preferences for how referencing is to be done.
Author's family name (date); verb in the past tense; and additional words as needed to create a sentence "quotation" (p. X)	Barrass (2002) claimed that one way to learn referencing skills is to "look at appropriate books and journals to ... see how sources are cited" (p. 113).
'According to', Author's family name (date); additional words to create a sentence "quotation" (p. X)	According to Barrass (2002), one way to learn referencing skills is to "look at appropriate books and journals to ... see how sources are cited" (p. 113).
Author's family name (date, p. X); verb in the past tense; summary	Krause, Hartley, James, and McInnis (2005, p. 29) found that some groups of students are more likely to ask for help and advice than others: those that aim to do very well, international students and mature age students. The authors claimed this pattern was mostly the same across all disciplines.

Example

Writing a citation for a claim cited in another source (APA 6th style)
Cite the source of the claim as well as the source it was found in. For example, on page 191 of an article published in 2009, Michael Sheard wrote:

In higher education generally, mature-age students have outperformed young students in first-year academic performance (McKenzie & Gow, 2004) ...

This idea would be cited as:

... (McKenzie & Gow as cited in Sheard, 2009, p. 191).

OR

McKenzie and Gow (as cited in Sheard, 2009, p. 191) claimed that ...

Writing a citation for a claim cited in another source when more than one source is cited

Cite the first source of the claim only, as well as the source it was found in. For example, on page 479 of an article published in 1997, Maryanne Martin wrote:

> *In recent years there has been increasing concern (e.g., Tanner and Tanner, 1983; Goodhart, 1988; McCrum, 1991, 1994, 1996) that female students at Oxford and Cambridge have tended to achieve lower degree classifications than male students.*

This idea would be cited as:

… (Tanner & Tanner as cited in Martin, 1997, p. 479).

or

Tanner and Tanner (as cited in Martin, 1997, p. 479) argued that …

Example

Writing a citation for a long quotation (APA 6th style)

Use: Author's family name (date); verb colon; quotation indented; with no quotation marks. (p. XX)

As Redman (2001) has pointed out:

> You must therefore always put arguments in your own words except when you are quoting someone directly … The positive side of this seemingly draconian rule is that you will remember better what you have put in your own words. This ensures that you have the fullest understanding possible of the course. (p. 24)

Continue writing from here.

Example

Writing citations

See Appendix A for how to write citations for different types of sources and different types and numbers of authors.

1   Return to Activity: 'Paraphrasing' on pages 102–103. Write the paraphrase and provide a suitable citation for 1a, 2a and 3.
2   Return to Activity: 'Selecting and formatting quotations' on pages 105–106. Write the quotation for 1a, 1b, 1c and 2, and give a correct citation.
3   Return to Activity: 'Summarising' on pages 106–107. Write a citation for Question 1.
4   Read the following extract (in *italics*). It is from page 198 of an article written by Pamela A. Jackson and published in 2005.

Activity

Koehler and Swanson (1988) show that ESL (English as a Second Language) students, even those from within the US, have difficulty conducting library research.

Paraphrase the relevant part of the above extract to show one of the difficulties faced by second language speakers, and provide a citation. Notice this is a citation to an idea that is itself cited in the source. See the example in this chapter.

5   The following extract (in *italics*) was written by Nicole J. Auer and Ellen M. Krupar and was published in 2001. It is on page 417.

There is a lack of consistency among citation style guides, particularly regarding online information (Malone & Videon, 1997; Fletcher & Greenhill, 1995).

Paraphrase the relevant part of the above extract to show the problem of citing material from the internet. Notice this is a citation to an idea that is itself attributed to a number of different sources. See the example in this chapter.

6   The extract below (in *italics*) was published in 2006 and written by Ruth Barrett and James Malcolm. It is part of a web document, and is from paragraph 2 in the 'Discussion' section.

A high percentage of students had submitted work that was unacceptably plagiarised, but most of these students were new to UK higher education, and most were from overseas. We believe that for the majority of these students this was due to difficulties in writing in their own words or in quoting sources correctly.

Paraphrase the relevant part of the above extract to show why, according to these authors, some overseas students may experience difficulty with plagiarism. Notice this is a web document and has no page numbers. See Appendix A.

Writing reference lists

A reference list provides all the relevant bibliographic information for each cited source.

When you use citations, you must also include a reference list. A reference list provides comprehensive bibliographic details for each of the cited sources in your work. It helps your reader judge the quality of your work, and also makes it possible for your reader to find and check up on any of your sources.

Some courses may ask you for a **bibliography**, rather than a reference list. A bibliography includes all items cited in your work plus any other items you consider relevant. Usually, however, you are not asked to write a bibliography as, particularly at undergraduate level, you do not have the depth of knowledge to sensibly add extra readings. Unless told otherwise, use a reference list.

To create a reference list:

- select the referencing style
- recognise the type of source to be referenced

- use the rules for writing the reference list item for the particular source
- format a reference list
- (possibly) use technology to create a reference list.

Referencing styles

You may find that different lecturers and different disciplines have their own preferred referencing style. The first step is therefore to be aware of the recommended style and to use that.

Source types and referencing

There are numerous source types (see Chapter 4). It is essential, when constructing a reference list, to note the type of source, as publishing details depend on that.

Rules for writing reference list items

Although there are many rules about how to reference any source, there are two general principles governing these rules. The first is about differences in how a source exists: whether the item is a stand-alone piece of work, or whether the source is embedded within a larger unit. A **stand-alone source** exists in its own right (for example, a book or a website). In this case, the reference list item is simple; it merely needs to supply details about that source. However, an **embedded source** is one that has its own author or authors but does not exist independently. It is contained within a larger unit (such as a chapter in an edited book, an article in a journal or a page within a website). The reference list entry is therefore more complex, as it has to supply a double set of details—some for the source, some for the item in which it is published.

The second principle is about the differences between **non-periodical** (published once) and **periodical** (published periodically) sources. For a non-periodical, specific details have to be supplied (for example, the publisher; the author or editor). For a periodical, as it is published many times, often over a long period, specific information about editors and publishers is irrelevant. Instead, details are required to specify which issue of the periodical is being referred to.

All of the kinds of publishing information are **fields** within, or components of, a reference list item. When constructing a reference list item manually it is thus necessary to know:

- which fields need to be completed
- what order the fields need to be presented in

The details needed for any reference list item depend on what type of source is being referenced.

- how to format the information within a field
- how to punctuate within and between fields.

When a reference list is being constructed manually, consult a guide to see what is required for each field. If you are using an electronic means of creating the reference list item, the formatting within and between fields is mostly done for you. You may need to check a guide to see which fields need to be completed, and to ensure that the generated reference is accurate.

See Appendix A for more information on writing reference list items.

Below are a number of examples of reference list items for the most commonly used source types. See Appendix A, Table 1 for information on formatting each field; Table 2 for creating reference list items for other source types; and Table 3 for how to deal with variations in each field.

Example

A reference list item for a printed book (APA 6th style)
Fields: Author's family name, Initial. Initial. (Date of publication). *Title of book*. Place of publication: Publisher.

Example:
Greetham, B. (2001). *How to write better essays*. Basingstoke, UK: Palgrave.

Example

A reference list item for a chapter or section in a printed edited book (APA 6th style)
Fields: Author's family name, Initial. Initial. (Date of publication). Title of chapter or section. In Initial. Initial. Editor's family name (Ed.), *Title of book* (chapter or section page numbers written as pp. XX-XXX). Place of publication: Publisher.

Example:
Volet, S., & Renshaw, P. (1996). Chinese students at an Australian university: Adaptability and continuity. In D. A. Watkins & J. B. Biggs (Eds.), *The Chinese learner: Cultural, psychological and contextual influences* (pp. 205–220). Hong Kong: Comparative Education Research Centre.

When a journal article is accessed electronically this location needs to be included in the reference list item. A Digital Object Identifier (DOI) system has been established to provide a reliable digital location that can be used for referencing. As yet, however, not all articles have been allocated a DOI. The first task is to note if a DOI is present. If it is, it should be available on the first page of the article or on the web page containing the full bibliographic details for the article. If you are unsure, copy and paste the bibliographic details for the source into the CrossRef DOI finder (www.crossref.org). It will return the DOI for the source if it has one. The reference list item for an article will vary depending on whether it has a DOI, or not.

A reference list item for an article in a journal (APA 6th style)

When a DOI (digital object identifier) is available.

Fields: Author's family name, Initial. Initial. (Date of publication). Title of article. *Title of Journal, volume*(issue), page numbers written as XXX–XXX. doi: XXXXXXXXXXXX

Example:
Biber, D., & Gray, B. (2010). Challenging stereotypes about academic writing: Complexity, elaboration, explicitness. *Journal of English for Academic Purposes, 9*(1), 2–20. doi: 10.1016/j.jeap.2010.01.001

Example

When there is no DOI, and the article was accessed electronically, according to the APA (2010) rules, you are required to reference the home page URL for the journal in which the article is published. However, as this requirement leads to additional work, with little or no benefit to readers, many universities suggest a different approach. It is recommended that as students are writing within a community that has access to the same databases, the URL for the database site from which the item was downloaded be used instead. This choice is supported by the APA Style Blog (Jackson, 2009, 25 September). If you use the database URL shorten the article URL to just the host or domain name (the part of the URL that ends with 'org', or 'edu' or 'com', or with a country code; for example, 'au').

If a printed article does not have a DOI, omit that part of the reference.

A reference list item for an article in a journal (APA 6th style)

When no DOI (digital object identifier) is available.

Electronic article: Using journal home URL
Fields: Author's family name, Initial. Initial. (Date of publication). Title of article. *Title of Journal, volume*(issue), page numbers written as XXX–XXX. Retrieved from journal homepage URL

Nield, K. (2004). Questioning the myth of the Chinese learner. *International Journal of Contemporary Hospitality Management, 16*(3), 189–195. Retrieved from www.emeraldinsight.com

Example

Electronic article: Using the URL for the site from which the item was downloaded

Fields: Author's family name, Initial. Initial. (Date of publication). Title of article. _Title of journal, volume_(issue), page numbers written as XXX–XXX. Retrieved from URL of download site

Nield, K. (2004). Questioning the myth of the Chinese learner. _International Journal of Contemporary Hospitality Management, 16_(3), 189–195. Retrieved from www.proquest.com

Paper copy of an article

Fields: Author's family name, Initial. Initial. (Date of publication). Title of article. _Title of Journal, volume_(issue), page numbers written as XXX–XXX.

Nield, K. (2004). Questioning the myth of the Chinese learner. _International Journal of Contemporary Hospitality Management, 16_(3), 189–195.

Activity

Writing reference list items
Go to Appendix B for practice in writing reference list items for a variety of source types.

Constructing a reference list

Reference lists are organised alphabetically by the first significant word in each item.

Reference lists are organised alphabetically. Use the first significant word in the reference list item. If there are authors, use the first author's family name to determine alphabetical order. If the reference list item begins with the name of a company or an organisation, or is a title of a work, then use the first significant word, ignoring articles, such as 'the' and 'a'. If there are two sources, both of which are written by authors with the same family name, use the first initial as a way of determining the alphabetical order. If there are two or more sources from the same author, organise these by date of publication where the earliest publication date is first.

The full reference list appears on a separate page at the end of the main writing task.

The reference list is formatted for ease of reading:

- place immediately after the main writing task
- start on a new page
- provide a heading: 'Reference List' or 'References'
- use a 'hanging indent' paragraph format for each item.

Using technology for referencing

Use technology to make referencing easier.

Referencing is very difficult to do correctly manually. Fortunately, there are a number of electronic means of creating reference list items. In order to use these well, you need to know all the principles involved in referencing, as outlined above.

The electronic referencing possibilities are:

- 'cite' (or similar name) function in databases and some library searches
- Word 2007/2010 referencing tool
- referencing management software, such as EndNote and RefWorks.

Many databases now have a 'cite' function that automatically generates a reference list item for a number of different styles. Once you open the Abstract or the full text of an article, the function is available. Be careful to check the accuracy and completeness of the generated reference. To use 'cite':

- click on 'cite' (or other similar word)
- select the referencing style
- copy and paste the reference list item into your document
- check for accuracy and completeness.

Searches of the entire library collection, or of most of it, also have a 'cite' function. Open a document's details by clicking on the title, then select 'cite'. Always check that the citation is complete and correct.

Word 2007 and Word 2010 have a very useful referencing tool that will automatically generate reference list items in a number of styles. It also enables you to 'cite while you write' as a means of both generating in-text citations and an automatic reference list. The 'references' tab on the toolbar leads to the commands. To find out how to use these, use the help menu and search for 'bibliography'.

The most sophisticated and most useful technology is referencing management software, such as EndNote and RefWorks. Among other things, such software enables you to 'cite while you write' and to create reference lists. It also has a very comprehensive range of styles, and covers all source types. Your university may give you free access to referencing management software. If so, you can access it on your university website for downloads or you may be able to borrow it for download from the library. Your library will offer training and/or guides on how it can be used. One of the best features of this software is that some databases can directly link to it. If they do, you can export all bibliographic details from any source directly. To do so:

- open the Abstract or full text of a source in a database
- click on 'Export' (or similar name) and follow instructions.

Checking technological means of referencing

Activity

1   Use a general database, such as ProQuest or Academic Search Premier. Use the search term "academic integrity" to generate a list of sources on that topic.

2　Open the first article and use the 'cite' function to create a reference list item for the source in the APA style.

3　Compare the reference with the APA 6th style (see Appendix A). What changes would you need to make to ensure the reference list item was fully written in the APA 6th style?

4　Create a reference list item for the same source using the Word 2007/Word 2010 referencing tool. How accurate is this?

5　Find out if your university offers free access to referencing management software. If it does, download it, and learn how to use it.

Constructing a paragraph around claims from the literature

All content paragraphs in any academic writing task are built around a claim from the literature.

Writing good paragraphs is not easy. Many students, both domestic and international, find that they cannot write paragraphs. Often their essays are returned with comments such as 'This is not a paragraph', 'This paragraph does not have a topic sentence' or 'Your writing is not structured. It is all over the place'.

Your ability to shape how ideas are read depends on skill in controlling paragraphs. After all, the paragraph is the basic unit of meaning in any academic writing. The most common form of paragraph, and the one that has to be mastered, is the content paragraph: it carries a claim from the literature.

The basic content paragraph has:

- a topic sentence
- a background or introductory sentence (or sentences)
- the claim (with a citation)
- the claim explained and/or elaborated
- a final linking sentence (if suitable).

Topic sentences

A topic sentence:

- (usually) is the first sentence of the paragraph
- (always) indicates the main idea in the paragraph
- indicates how its paragraph relates to the paragraph before it (if appropriate).

Table 5.7 How to write a topic sentence

Ask:	Write:
What is the general topic of this paragraph? What comment do I want to make about this general topic? or Why am I writing this paragraph?	Write your response to your question in your own words.
How does this idea link to the idea in the paragraph before?	Add a linking word (if appropriate).

The **topic sentence** is the key to controlling the paragraph internally. It is a statement about the main idea in the paragraph. A topic sentence consists of two parts: the name for the general topic area and a comment on it. It is the comment that the whole paragraph will explore. That is the main idea in the paragraph, and so is often referred to as the **controlling idea**. As a paragraph is built around a claim from the literature, that claim must be referred to in the topic sentence. Indeed, the topic sentence is a summary of why you are using the claim. Without a topic sentence, you do not have a paragraph and your writing appears disjointed.

A paragraph explores the comment contained in the topic sentence. It becomes the controlling idea for the paragraph.

The topic sentence is 'your' sentence. Use it to control how your ideas are read. It is usually placed first in a paragraph, and generally does not include a citation.

Topic sentence

NOTE: The topic sentence names the general topic 'many university students' and makes the comment 'studying less than expected'. The paragraph explores this comment. It is the controlling idea for the paragraph.

Example

It appears that many university students are studying less than expected. Students in Australia are often instructed to spend 3 hours per week for each of the contact hours in their courses (Applegate & Daly, 2005, p. 160). Yet evidence exists from both Australia and the US that students are much less diligent. Applegate and Daly (2005, p. 160) reported that Australian students spend 8.2 hours in total for each of their courses which is equivalent to only 1.7 hours of study per hour of teaching time. Nonis, Philhours, and Hudson (2006) found an almost identical pattern for business students in the US. Their research showed that Marketing students were the least involved in outside of class study, spending less than 1 hour on academic work for each of their credit hours. Nonis et al. (2006) commented, "this is much less than the [USA] proverbial standard of two to three hours of study per credit hour" (p. 124).

Activity

Recognising the general topic and the comment (or controlling idea)
In each of the sentences below, underline the general topic, and circle the comment made on it.

1 Test anxiety lowers the performance of university students.
2 One of the main causes of test anxiety is a course with a large study load.
3 Females experience greater test anxiety than males.

Activity

Writing topic sentences
Below is a badly written paragraph, as it does not have a topic sentence. Read it, then answer the questions.

While there is a vast quantity of literature available on any topic, students are not expected to read it all. However, they are required to read many of the most relevant sources (Clanchy & Ballard, 1997, p. 6). Extensive reading allows students to find suitable ideas and to show a good knowledge of the available literature.

1 Examine the sentences and phrases below. Each is *unsuitable as a topic sentence* for the above paragraph. Explain why.
   a Students need skills in reading.
   b All students have to read widely for their assignments (Clanchy & Ballard, 1997).
   c Reading is an enjoyable activity.
   d Reading widely.
   e Students can find ideas by reading.
   f How much of the literature does a student have to read?

2 Write a suitable topic sentence for the paragraph.

A topic sentence is also the most important means of linking paragraphs externally, that is, linking one paragraph to another. Connection between paragraphs is made by, first, ensuring all topic sentences are written from the same point of view (see Chapter 2). To test if they fit together, read the topic sentences one after the other, and see if they make sense. Second, connection between topic sentences is created by using connectives (see Chapter 2). Both of these techniques link the topic sentences, and hence also the paragraphs.

Examining topic sentences

Take any section of a piece of academic writing and examine the topic sentences. Look for:

a   the way a topic sentence announces the main idea of a paragraph

b   how the topic sentences use words to link to each other

c   how the topic sentences have the same focus (how they fit together).

Activity

It can seem illogical to start a paragraph with a topic sentence. Certainly, the paragraph story line (the linear logic of the paragraph) usually begins with the second sentence. A topic sentence works against this 'natural' flow, as it indicates the topic before it has been introduced. However, with practice your ability to write good topic sentences increases, and then they will appear 'natural' and logical to you.

Background and introductory sentences

Typically, the 'paragraph story' begins with the second sentence. It often either offers some background or an introduction to the main point within the paragraph. A background sentence provides some context for the claim within the paragraph. It helps the reader understand its significance. An introductory sentence begins the description of the main idea, but does so in a general way. Citations will be needed if the background or introductory sentence contains information from the literature.

The background or introductory sentence helps the reader understand the claim by leading into it.

Background sentence

The extract is from page 21 of a book written by Rudolph and Kathleen Verderber and published in 2003.

Background sentence

Example

A third cause of public speaking apprehension comes from having underdeveloped speaking skills. This 'skill deficit' was the earliest explanation for apprehension and continues to receive attention by researchers. It suggests that many of us become apprehensive because we don't understand or cannot do the basic tasks associated with effective speech making. These tasks include ...

Topic sentence

Description of the main point begins

Example

Introductory sentence

The extract is from pages 40–41 in a book written by Joseph DeVito and published in 2004.

Because culture permeates all forms of communication, it's necessary to understand its influences ... to understand how communication works and master its skills.
As illustrated throughout this text, culture influences communication of all types (Moon, 1996). It influences ...

Description of the main point begins

Introductory sentence

Topic sentence

Sentence(s) carrying the claim

The central ideas in a paragraph must come from the literature.

If you are using a paraphrased claim from the literature, it is typically written following the background or introductory sentence. Paraphrase the claim so that it fits in with the flow of the paragraph, which means that it is written in terms of the comment provided in the topic sentence. It may be written in one or more sentences. Include a citation.

Elaboration and/or explanation of the claim or quotation

After presenting the claim it needs to be further incorporated into your writing. This involves elaborating on it or explaining it. You can use:

- further ideas or information from the literature (with citations) as a means of elaboration
- a quotation (with correct formatting and citation) used to support the claim
- your explanation of the claim (keeping to the meaning of the claim; that is, not adding any of your own ideas or information)
- your ideas about how the claim links to your argument.

It is always impressive when a writer ties together ideas and information from various sources as a means of elaborating an idea. It shows depth of reading and good organising and writing skills. Paraphrased claims are most often used to elaborate or explain. Ensure that all additional ideas are connected to the main claim and that they fit under the topic sentence. A quotation is also an excellent means of elaboration. It cannot just appear in your work, however, but must be introduced. Use a sentence written in your own words providing a very brief summary of it, or use a partial sentence to lead into it. In addition to elaborations from the literature, all paragraphs usually include some sentences, or partial sentences, which clearly indicate how the claims fit into the argument.

Paragraph with claim elaborated

This is an extract from pages 46–47 of a book by Gary Buck, published in 2001.

Example

It is important to note that in many spoken interactions, the relevant linguistic information is conveyed not only by the sound. Kellerman (1990) has argued that looking at the speaker's mouth—the lips, jaw and tip of the tongue—provides   Claim

information about what the speaker is saying, and listeners use that to help them understand. <u>And not all the relevant information is conveyed by the language.</u>   Quotation introduced

<u>As Abercrombie suggests, 'we speak with our vocal organs, but we converse with our bodies' (1967:55).</u> Visual information is important in communication, and of particular interest given the increased availability of video and multimedia.   Claim further elaborated by writer

Topic sentence   Claim elaborated with additional information in a quotation

---

Final sentence

Many of you have learned that a final sentence should summarise the paragraph. While this may be true for isolated paragraphs, it is almost never true in academic assignments. If a paragraph marks the end of a section, then no summarising final sentence is required as the whole paragraph performs that task. Within a section, final summarising sentences for paragraphs are not required, as paragraphs need to flow together rather than exist as unrelated units.

A final sentence is not required in an extended piece of writing.

Use the final sentence of paragraphs to create a flow in writing by either:

- finishing a paragraph without a summarising sentence, or
- using a final linking sentence that leads subtly into the following paragraph.

If a final linking sentence is used, it should have a double reference: first, to the paragraph in which it is embedded, and second, to the paragraph which follows. Usually a subtle link is provided to extend the paragraph idea towards the new idea in the following paragraph. Think of it as a hint, preparing the reader to shift thinking. Do not give the whole idea for the next paragraph. If you are uncomfortable with hinting, leave out the final sentence.

Ways to hint at the following paragraph in the final sentence:

- link into a key word for the next paragraph
- indicate there are more issues or examples.

Example

Final sentence of a paragraph used to link to the next paragraph
These sentences are from page 111 of an article by T. Dean Thomlinson, published in 1996.

Paragraph:

Ethnocentrism results in the belief that we and our culture are the center [sic] of the universe. All incoming data is evaluated accordingly. Tourists the world over are notorious for comments such as 'but why do they drive on the WRONG side of the road?' ... These evaluative structures apply to everything from table manners to mourning a death. As Kim and Gudykunst observe: 'Those who believe that their culture is the only one—or the only "real" one—treat communication patterns appropriate in other cultures, but not their own, as "mistakes" rather than "differences"' (1988, p. 22).

Hint about the content of the next paragraph

Topic sentence for the following paragraph:

One of the basic barriers to effective listening is judgmental thinking during the listening process.

Content of the next paragraph indicated more specifically

Coherence

For a paragraph to read coherently:

- the topic sentence needs to indicate the main idea in the paragraph
- each sentence from the background sentence to the final one needs to address the comment contained within the topic sentence
- each sentence is linked by using repetition of exact words or variations on the words, or pronouns, by the use of labelling techniques to refer backwards (or forwards) to a section of text within the paragraph, by

maintaining the same point of view or focus for each sentence, and by the use of connecting words (see Chapter 2).

Paragraph writing

Activity

1   Recognising the functions of sentences within a paragraph.

Examine the two paragraphs below. Each sentence has been numbered. Indicate the role each sentence plays in the paragraph. You may choose from the following (a number of sentences may have the same role):

- topic sentence
- introductory sentence
- background sentence
- main claim for the paragraph
- claim elaborated (by a paraphrase from another source)
- claim elaborated (by a quotation)
- claim elaborated (by the writer)
- claim explained with information from the literature
- claim explained with information from the writer
- claim linked into the writer's argument.

a   [1] Many of the aspects of time management are effective in producing a good work outcome. [2] Kearns and Gardiner (2007) studied the perceptions of staff and students at a university in relation to time management. [3] They found that three features led to favourable results. [4] When staff and students were directed in their activities by having a clear aim, and when they planned and also avoided distractions they perceived themselves to be effective in their work and experienced higher morale and less stress (Kearns & Gardiner, 2007, pp. 241–242). [5] The results are not surprising as they conform to the general beliefs about the usefulness of time management.

b   [1] It appears that many university students are studying less than expected. [2] Students are often instructed to study an average of 3 hours per week for each hour of contact time in lectures or tutorials (Applegate & Daly, 2005, p. 160). [3] Yet evidence exists from both Australia and the US that students are much less diligent. [4] Applegate and Daly (2005, p. 160) reported that Australian students spend 8.2 hours in total for each of their courses which is equivalent to only 1.7 hours of study per hour of teaching time. [5] Nonis, Philhours, and Hudson (2006) found an almost identical study pattern for business students in the US. Their research showed that Marketing students were the least involved in outside of class study, spending less than 1 hour on academic work for each of their credit hours. [6] Nonis et al. (2006) commented, "this is much less than the proverbial standard of two to three hours of study per credit hour" (p. 124). It is likely that similar patterns of study occur in other Western countries.

2   Writing a developed paragraph

Write a paragraph using information from the two sources below (in *italics*) and with the following topic sentence:

> *Second language students find it difficult to fully understand lectures due to their lack of skills with discourse markers.*

Vocabulary note: 'discourse markers' are words that indicate how the ideas in a text are organised and connected.

EXTRACT A

The article is titled 'The role of discourse signalling cues in second language listening comprehension' and was written by Euen Hyuk (Sarah) Jung and published in *The Modern Language Journal*, Vol. 87, No. 4 (Winter, 2003), pp. 562–577. The extract is from p. 562.

> *Pertinent research indicates that many L2 [second language] learners, even those with adequate English language proficiency, have difficulty comprehending academic lectures and fail to grasp the main points of the lectures (Allison & Tauroza, 1995; Hyon, 1997; Thompson, 1994; Young, 1994). A large body of research demonstrates that L2 learners' difficulties in understanding lectures lie at the discourse level i.e. at the level of the organisation of all ideas within the lecture as a whole as well as at the sentence level (Clerehan, 1995; Olsen & Huckin, 1990). Olsen and Huckin, for example, reported that most L2 learners with proper comprehension of English at the sentence level had difficulty identifying the main ideas in a lecture, mainly as a consequence of their inability to utilise discourse level cues [e.g. words that indicated previews, summaries, emphasis, and connectives or linking words] that signalled the organisation of the lecture.*

EXTRACT B

The title of the article is 'Voices from Chinese students: Professors' use of English affects academic listening'. It was written by Jinyan Huang and published in the *College Student Journal* in 2004. It is in Volume 38, Number 2, and on p. 215.

> *Studies have shown that non-native English-speaking learners have difficulties in recognizing these discourse markers. Yuan (1982) conducted a study on Chinese scientists' difficulties in comprehending English science lectures at UCLA ... The results of this study showed that the subjects, generally, 'were rather weak at paying attention to the sequence of the lecture because of their neglect of the logical connectors of sequence and their lack of recognition of transition from one main idea to another. Additionally, they paid more attention to decoding the speech sentence by sentence than to extracting the science information from the lecture through understanding' (p. 48).*

Go to our website <www.oup.com.au/orc/turner2e> for more activities on the skills covered in this chapter.

Activity

SUMMARY

This chapter has examined the basic skills required for doing any assignment that involves using the literature. You have learned the three ways in which the literature can be brought into your work: paraphrasing for your own purpose, quoting and summarising. You have also learned how to write citations and create reference lists. Finally the chapter has shown you how to write a well-constructed paragraph built around claims from the literature.

GLOSSARY

annotated bibliography a list of sources with, for each source, a summary of its main points and a critical assessment of it.

bibliography an alphabetical list of sources with full bibliographic details, attached to the end of a text. The sources may or may not be cited in the text.

citation the short in-text acknowledgment of the source of some idea or information (sometimes called 'a reference' or an 'in-text citation').

claims ideas or information found in the literature.

collusion occurs when a student works too closely with one or more other students on an assignment, and so submits individual work that is very similar to, or the same as, that of the other student(s).

controlling idea is the comment made about the general topic contained within the topic sentence of a paragraph. It becomes the controlling idea of the paragraph as the whole paragraph is organised to explore it.

embedded source a type of publication that does not exist on its own, but exists within some other larger unit (for example, a chapter in a book, an article in a journal or a part of a website).

field a particular space in which the same type of publishing information is recorded (for example, an author field or a date-of-publication field).

non-periodical a publication that is published once only. It may be reprinted (but the material stays the same) and it may pass through a number of editions (where the content undergoes some changes but remains basically the same).

objective the presentation of information undistorted by personal feelings and interpretations.

paraphrase a technique for using the literature which retains the original idea or information but restates it in a different way.

periodical a publication that is published periodically (regularly), each time under the same title, but with different content.

plagiarism occurs when someone takes the work of an author (words, ideas, images, graphic, code, sounds or film) and presents it as his or her own.

quotation a technique for using the literature, which keeps the exact words of an author, but formats them to show they are being quoted.

reference list an alphabetical list providing full bibliographic details for each cited source in any piece of writing.

stand-alone source a type of publication that exists in its own right. It is a single unit, in that a person or group of people or an organisation is responsible for the whole of the work (for example, a book or a whole website).

summary a technique for using the literature that gives a brief account of the content but does so by restating it in a different way while retaining the purpose of the original author.

topic sentence usually the first sentence of a paragraph. It consists of two parts: the name for the general topic area and a comment on it. It is the comment that the whole paragraph will explore.

chapter SIX

Further Academic Skills: Working on an Assignment

Every assignment should be a well-organised response to its set topic or question. As university assignments are typically quite long and cover complex ideas and issues, their organisation takes considerable effort and ability. This chapter is devoted to examining the skills needed in:

- responding to the assignment task
- understanding how to organise ideas and information through the use of:
  - lists
  - comparison
  - evaluation
  - argument
- planning
- drafting (editing and proofreading).

The general processes involved in the production of any assignment are the same. Reading and writing are always engaged in together over a number of weeks. As well, the production of any assignment passes through the same stages, as outlined in Figure 6.1.

Responding to the assignment task

Although the assignment task or question is carefully examined during the reading process, it needs to be reexamined prior to writing. To maximise understanding of an assignment task, focus on its:

- content
- structure
- instruction words.

Figure 6.1 Reading and writing work together

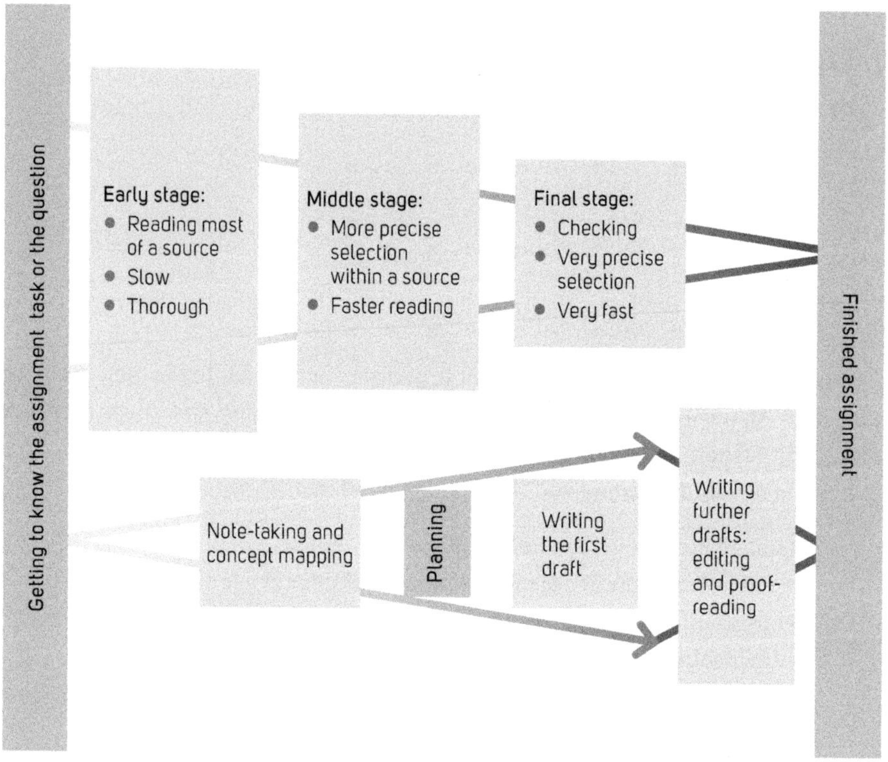

Getting to know the assignment task or the question

Early stage:
- Reading most of a source
- Slow
- Thorough

Middle stage:
- More precise selection within a source
- Faster reading

Final stage:
- Checking
- Very precise selection
- Very fast

Note-taking and concept mapping

Planning

Writing the first draft

Writing further drafts: editing and proof-reading

Finished assignment

Content

Focus on the limiting and content words in a question to become aware of what the assignment must address.

The purpose of an assignment is to test your ability in moving around a body of literature. Focusing on the limiting words and content keywords in the assignment task makes this possible, as it enables you to recognise the rich information and complexities in the literature relevant to the assignment topic.

Limiting words indicate the specific focus required (for example, 'during the last decade'). Notice if your assignment topic contains such words. Next, use the content keywords as a guide to examining the literature within this focus. Examine the literature for:

- the distinctions made within the keywords
- the relationships and connections made between the keywords
- the explanations offered.

Some keywords in a topic are quite general. Your task is to note all the distinctions the literature makes within each of these. Consider the topic:

Test anxiety causes university students to underperform in their examinations. Discuss. The content keywords, as shown in Chapter 4, are: "test anxiety", "university students", performance, examinations. All these are general terms. The literature, however, discusses quite specific aspects of each of these: for example, different kinds of test anxiety, different kinds of university students (in terms of level of study, discipline, gender and age), different ways of measuring performance (such as results in a test, final results in a course and Grade Point Average), different types of examinations (such as different types of questions and examinations in different subjects). It is these distinctions that you need to notice, as they lead to rich information and so make it possible for you to show that you know all the complexities in the literature.

Table 6.1 Focusing systematically on the literature addressed in an assignment task

Step 1: Look for: meaningful clusters of content keywords	Ask: What are the content keywords in this task?
Step 2: Look for: distinctions (in the keywords) addressed in the literature	Ask (thinking of the keywords): Who or what is discussed in the literature?
Step 3: Look for: claims and/or connections made (in terms of the interests given by the task)	Ask: What is said about these in the literature? Ask: How are these connected in the literature?
Step 4: Look for: explanations for the claims and connections in the literature	Ask: Why does the literature say these patterns exist?

As well, a topic often asks for some discussion of a relationship between keywords. Even though a topic indicates a specific relationship (for example, 'underperformance' as the relation between test anxiety and examination results), your task is to examine all the literature says about that relationship. Hence, for the topic on examinations above, you would need to note if there is underperformance, and also if performance is not affected, only affected slightly, or even enhanced. The ability to do this shows you understand the complexities in the literature and so leads to a very good assignment.

Finally, as the literature offers some explanations for the patterns you are examining, they must also be noted. Four steps can be taken (see Table 6.1) to produce a systematic questioning of the task and the literature.

Is there a relationship between the questions you ask yourself about the content keywords in an assignment task and the way you structure a concept map (see Chapter 4)?

Thinking

Different assignment tasks require slightly different approaches. The techniques offered above may have to be modified. Try whatever is necessary to help focus on the complexities in content and level of understanding that the question addresses.

Structure

Focus on the structure of an assignment task to understand what has to be addressed.

To focus on the structural aspects of an assignment task, look for the number of parts to the question, indicated by punctuation or logical operators or **connecting words**. As each part of a task or question must be addressed in an assignment, it is necessary to determine how many parts there are. Punctuation and the use of words indicating a logical connection (such as 'or', 'and' and 'not'), and some connecting words (such as 'although', 'however', 'yet', 'despite' and 'but'), separate the assignment into discrete sections. Emphasise these aspects of a task by circling them, then underlining and numbering each part.

Instruction words

Focus on instruction words to find the form of organisation of ideas and information required in your assignment.

Almost all assignment tasks at university are set up, at least in part, to test your ability to organise ideas and information. **Instruction words** within the task indicate the dominant type of organisation of ideas you are to employ (see Figure 6.2). Words such as 'describe' and 'outline' ask for a basic organisation of ideas. Instruction words such as 'compare and contrast' and 'evaluate' focus on specific types of connections and a particular type of criticism. Words such as 'analyse', 'critically analyse', 'explain' and 'discuss' are directly asking for an argument form and for a critical focus.

You are almost always expected to produce an argument.

Be careful with instruction words. Despite the focus on a particular organisation of ideas as given by the instruction words, it is almost always implied that some level of argument is to be included. Thus, for example, although you are asked for a specific organisation with the instruction words 'compare and contrast' or 'evaluate', it is implied that you also come to some conclusion (your position), and that you organise the comparison or evaluation to support that conclusion.

By working on the assignment task, in terms of content, structure and instruction words, you find the main ideas that need to be spoken about in your assignment and how they are to be organised. However, this is not the end of your preparation. In the next stage of the process you need to think about how you write this content.

Figure 6.2 Instruction words and their focus on ways of connecting and organising ideas

1 Organising basic connections	2 Organising to illustrate a point	3 Organising groups of ideas	4 Organising to advance an argument

Instruction words	Levels of connection			
Describe, define, outline, state	1	2	3	4
Compare and contrast, evaluate	1	2	3	4
Analyse, assess, critically analyse, critically evaluate, discuss, explain, justify, 'to what extent'	1	2	3	4

Activity

Focusing on content keywords, limiting words, structure and instruction words in an assignment task

Mark the following in each of the assignment tasks or questions below:

a   content keywords (underline in colour)

b   limiting words (circle and star)

c   logical operators, punctuation and connecting words (circle)

d   number of parts (underline and number)

e   instruction words (box)

TASKS

1   Outline why reading is generally considered important at university. Assess to what extent students are required to read critically during their course work.

2   Discuss the claim that test anxiety can lead to lower results in examinations.

3   The internet has given students easy access to a wide variety of knowledge. However, the ease of copying and the lack of clear guidelines for citing internet sources have led to a large increase in plagiarism in the last decade. Discuss.

4   Compare and contrast concept maps and brainstorming as aids for working on an assignment task.

5   Describe the equity policies at your university in relation to students from rural and isolated areas. Evaluate how successful they have been in the period from 2000 to the present.

Organising ideas and information

All assignments call for the ability to organise ideas and information. It is assumed you have mastered the basic skills of creating continuity between ideas, and using definition, examples, clarification and emphasis to illustrate a point. This section focuses on the more sophisticated forms of connection: lists, comparison and contrast, evaluation and argument.

Lists

A list presents related ideas in an ordered way, using an additive logic. All assignments call on your ability to describe well. Usually, you will need to describe a number of aspects of some event, behaviour or experience, and so will employ a list form of organisation. You may also have a list of points included in explanations or theories.

A list is organised through the use of:

- **categorisation**
- ordering.

Place similar items together in a list.

The basic requirement for a **list** is that the items belong to the same category. In practice, you are likely to have one list of abstract (or comprehensive) features, which allows you to organise all the aspects you are interested in. Then, under each of these abstract categories, you will build other more concrete (specific) lists. For example, if you were describing the film *The Lord of the Rings*, you could create a list of three very abstract categories: 'story', 'characterisation' and 'setting'. Then, within each of these, you could create more concrete lists of, for example, specific stories, characters or settings).

Thinking

Why does a list need to contain items at the same level of abstraction?

Recognising different levels of abstraction

1   Each of the following is a jumble of points. Produce organisation by arranging them from the most abstract (or comprehensive) to the most concrete (or specific).
    a   Sydney Opera House; Sydney; tourist destinations in Australia
    b   *Avatar*; science fiction; movies
    c   Girl bands; Spice Girls; pop music.
2   For each of the above, create another list, at the *second* level of abstraction, containing two more items.
3   For each of the above, create another list of two more items at *the most concrete* level.

List making is simple, but it can be made much more interesting and informative. The primitive form of a list implies an equality of importance between all items. It merely gives information in terms of 'first', 'second', etc. Although it can be useful sometimes, it is much better, wherever possible, to create a sophisticated list that indicates an order of importance. In such a list, the items of most significance are placed first, and those of least significance placed last (though sometimes the reverse order is used), and words are used to reveal the basis for the judgment of significance.

Organise the order within a list.

Figure 6.3 A sophisticated list structure (note: it can be reversed)

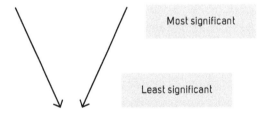

Most significant

Least significant

Table 6.2 Different types of list

Words indicating an equal relation	Words providing additional information in a list structure
first, second ... finally, additionally, in addition, another, a further **Example** *One way to search for sources is to use a suitable database.* *Another way to search is to use a single search such as Summon or LibrarySearch.*	the most ... the least One ... a more ... a much more ... Oldest ... newest ... As well Moreover **Example** *A good way to search is to use a suitable database.* *A more useful way to search is to use a single search such as Summon or LibrarySearch.*

Thinking

Which is the stronger list in Table 6.2?
Why is it stronger?

Activity

Organising lists

1 Describe your experience of learning at university, using a list structure.
   a Create a list of at least two comprehensive categories that would allow you to offer a good description.
   b Create a list of two specific items for each of the comprehensive categories.
   c Order the items in all your lists.
   d Write your description.
2 Describe different types of students at university using a list structure.

Comparison (compare and contrast)

Comparison organises ideas into similarities and differences.

Another common way of organising ideas is to use **comparison** and contrast to portray similarities and differences between items.

Comparison requires:

- the items being compared belong to a common category (for example, high schools and universities can be compared as both are institutions for education)
- bases for comparison that are recognised as significant in the literature (for example, teaching, discipline)
- justification for the choice of the bases of comparison
- a comparison for each basis (look for complexities).

Comparison can be presented in one of two ways. The weaker form of organisation is to state all similarities first, then all differences. A more sophisticated comparison first justifies the choice of the bases of comparison, drawing attention to the fact that they are the most significant issues in the literature, then organises the information in terms of the bases for comparison. Thus the similarities and differences for one basis are given, then the same for the next.

Usually, aspects will not be perfectly the same or different. The point is to display the complexities.

Using a table as a means of organising comparison and contrast

What is being compared: *high school and university*			
First basis of comparison: *teaching*		Second basis of comparison: *discipline*	
High school	University	High school	University
Small classes	Some large classes (lectures); some small (tutorials)	Imposed by teacher, but with increasing emphasis on self-discipline	Self-discipline mainly; some reminders of how to behave
Interactive	Not interactive in large lecture classes; Interactive in tutorials		

Compare and contrast

Compare and contrast the processes of finding relevant journal articles and websites:

1 Develop two bases for comparison.
2 List what is similar and dissimilar for each of the bases of comparison (look for and note complexities).
3 Write out the results, organising the information in a suitable manner.

Evaluation

Some assignments (or parts of assignments) ask for an **evaluation** of an idea, a practice, a theory or a policy. How the evaluation is done depends on what you are required to evaluate.

There are two types of evaluation.

If you are asked to evaluate a claim, your evaluation takes a particular form. For example, if you were given the topic *Evaluate the claim that test anxiety can lead to lower results in examinations*, you are being asked 'to what extent can this claim be seen to be *true*?' Your evaluation will be based on your assessment of all the evidence available, much as a judge assesses evidence in a court. In this case, give the evidence and clearly assess it in terms of its ability to support, reject or modify the claim.

However, if you are asked to evaluate a policy, or a company's profitability, or even a theory, then the evaluation is different. You are not being asked a question about truth, but rather 'to what extent does this policy or theory etc. meet certain *criteria of usefulness*, or *adequacy*, or *good performance*?' In this case, a set of criteria have to be developed as a basis for an evaluation.

Criteria should be:

- relevant to the item that is being evaluated
- recognised as significant in the literature
- comprehensive.

You may find the item you are evaluating meets some of the criteria, but not others. It is also likely that the item may meet the criteria to some extent, but not totally.

Activity

Evaluating

Evaluate the quality of the meal you ate last night.

1 Develop two criteria for evaluation of the meal.
2 Assess to what extent the meal met the criteria (totally, somewhat, not at all).
3 Write an evaluation by:
   a describing why the criteria are significant
   b describing (with examples) your evaluation.

Argument

'Argument' has a specific meaning within a university context.

You are required to produce an **argument** in almost every form of assessment that you do at university. Indeed, assignment topics are written to encourage an argument. For example, the inclusion of instruction words such as 'discuss', 'analyse', 'evaluate the claim that ...', 'critically evaluate the theory ...', and 'to what extent ...' alert you to the need for an argument.

As well, assignment tasks are often deliberately written to provoke an argument. One technique is that either the whole question, or at least part of it, is stated in a general form (such as 'Democracy is *always* good'). Another method of writing questions is to overly limit some claim. For example, 'Test anxiety *always* leads to lower results in examinations. Discuss.' Yet a further way of forcing an argument is to use a concept that is itself debatable. For example, a question might be: 'Stress is an *unfortunate outcome* of the higher level demands placed on students at university. Discuss.' All of these tasks, by being extreme in some manner, are deliberately provoking you into creating an argument in which you may agree with the statement, disagree or partially agree.

The argument is such a taken-for-granted aspect of assignment writing that even if the question does not explicitly indicate the need for one, it is always implied that an argument has to be presented. For example, though some assignment tasks call for a comparison and contrast approach and others require an evaluation, it is expected that both will also offer an argument based on these organisations of ideas.

However, students often find it difficult to write an argument. One reason is that students may confuse the meaning of the word 'argument', as used in ordinary life, with the meaning it has in university work. Some mistakenly believe that an argument means to 'take sides' or 'to disagree with'. This is not the case. Another reason is that some students, particularly second language speakers, are misled because of the particular meaning given to 'argument' within English language courses. They believe that having an argument is the same as stating what 'should' be the case. Again, this is not its meaning within an academic context. Further, many students, both from some Australian high schools and from overseas, have not learned to write an academic argument, and in some cultures, arguments are not even presented in the form used in a Western university. Perhaps, for most students it is difficult to create an argument because the ideas and information are unfamiliar.

In fact, it is easy to learn how to write an argument. Start by recognising that the meaning of 'argument' in an academic context is closer to 'discussion' than it is to the meaning of 'argument' in everyday life.

An academic argument consists of three aspects:

1   The position
2   The evidence to support the position
3   The organisation that shows the argument is a response to a particular question or topic.

> An academic argument consists of a position supported by evidence and organised so that it is a response to an assignment topic.

Position

A **position**, within an academic context, is the opinion formed about the topic given all the information available. It is, strictly speaking, not a personal opinion, as it is developed from wide reading of the literature, rather than being derived from merely an individual's own ideas and knowledge. A position may be either basic or comprehensive. The basic position contains one idea (for example, 'The Lord of the Rings is a great movie'). You are probably familiar with this type of position from high school or ESL classes. At university, however, positions are more comprehensive, because both the information and the analysis of it are more complex.

> Develop comprehensive position statements at university.

A position can consist of:

- basic idea (essential)
- additional details named (for example, reasons or causes or aspects)
- additional details indicated (by the use of words such as 'mainly', 'main', 'usually', 'sometimes')
- an indication of contradictory ideas
- an indication that one point of view will be shown to be incorrect.

A position can also be a combination of the above possibilities. See examples below.

Example

Positions

Basic: Test anxiety reduces the academic performance of university students in examinations.

Comprehensive (addition of ideas): Test anxiety reduces the academic performance of university students in examinations mainly because it leads to the development of interfering thoughts that prevent a proper focus on examination tasks.

Comprehensive (contradictory ideas): In general, test anxiety lowers performance, although this is not evident in all situations, nor with all types of students.

Comprehensive (showing one point as incorrect): Test anxiety is usually measured in terms of levels of debilitative anxiety; however, such a measurement does not capture all forms of test anxiety.

Comprehensive (combination): In general, test anxiety lowers performance slightly, although this is not evident in all situations, nor with all types of students. The main mechanism for this result appears to be that test anxiety leads to the development of interfering thoughts that prevent a proper focus on examination tasks. It is caused by awareness of an inadequate level of course knowledge, and also by difficulties within the testing situation.

Evidence

Evidence is derived from the literature, and consists of rich descriptions, explanations and examples.

All arguments must provide evidence to support their position. As Chanock (2007) claimed, 'arguments are meant to be demonstrations of how these opinions [positions] are inferred from evidence' (p. 275). At university, evidence is derived from the literature, and consists of rich descriptions, explanations and examples for each point. The whole of any assignment is constructed to provide evidence to support a position (see Chapter 7).

Organisation

Organisation turns a list of separate points into an argument.

Finally, the ideas must be organised as an argument. This starts with organising how the position is written (see example below). The position must always:

- focus on the main topic
- address each part of a topic if there is more than one part
- link ideas to show how they are connected both to the topic and to each other.

As all positions are developed in response to an assignment topic, they must be organised in terms of that topic. The techniques for maintaining a single point of view or focus are used (see Chapter 2). Also if a topic is presented as a number of parts, each of these must be addressed.

Connection is the essential feature of an argument. Students find this aspect very difficult, and sometimes resort to either presenting a series of unconnected points or providing incorrect connections (for example, by merely listing the points as 'first', 'second' etc.). Both of these techniques lead to poor results. In order to create connection, first recognise how ideas can be related by having a very good knowledge of the literature. Second, use language to show the way ideas are linked. Typical connecting devices, as discussed in Chapter 2, are:

- connectives that join ideas (such as 'which', 'although', 'because'; 'when'; 'however' and 'therefore')
- repetition of names (either exact repetition or repetition with variation)
- pronouns that refer to names (such as 'this', these' and 'it').

Activities for developing skills in creating connection are on pp. 142–143. The entire assignment also has to be organised to display and support the argument.

Features of a comprehensive position indicating an argument structure
Topic: *Test anxiety causes university students to underperform in their examinations. Discuss.*

| Main topic stated (underlined) | Topic fully addresses all relevant aspects | Ideas linked using suitable connectives (in bold) |

Example

In general, <u>test anxiety lowers performance</u> *slightly*, **although** this is not evident in all situations, **nor** with all types of student. The *main* mechanism for <u>this result</u> appears to be that test anxiety leads to the development of interfering thoughts **which** prevent a proper focus on examination tasks. <u>It</u> is caused by awareness of an inadequate level of course knowledge, and also by difficulties within the testing situation.

Focus maintained on the topic (underlined words)

Techniques for writing an argument

Claims in an argument need to be fully supported with evidence. At a minimum, one paragraph is devoted to the description, elaboration and explanation of each point. Some points will take many paragraphs. Topic sentences are used to indicate the content of each paragraph, and also the **argument line**. See if you can read topic sentences only, and understand what your argument is.

Provide a rich description and explanation for each point in the argument.

The literature is used to provide legitimate support for each claim. The descriptions, explanations and examples provided must be appropriately cited. See Chapter 7 for more details on how to write an argument in full.

Activity

Recognising how connection is created

Topic: Test anxiety causes university students to underperform in their examinations. Discuss.

Examine each of the positions in the example on page 140.

1 What techniques have been used to ensure there is a continual focus on the topic (that is, how has the same point of view been maintained)?
2 What language techniques have been employed to create connection between ideas?

Activity

Examining positions

For each of the questions below:

1 Circle the author's basic position statement.
2 Underline the evidence offered to support the author's basic position (if provided).
3 Place a box around any additions to the basic position and note if the addition is named or merely indicated.
4 Shade any contradictory position that is presented.
5 Underline and star any information that the author indicates is incorrect.

   a *Rabbit-Proof Fence* is a very successful Australian movie because it tells an incredible story of resilience and has an excellent director, Phillip Noyce.

   b The Indian Bollywood movies are exhilarating as they have enchanting music, vibrant colour and exaggerated love stories.

   c *The Lord of the Rings* is a great movie partly because of the use of a range of computer enhancement techniques. Although some critics believe that the actors were of such a high calibre that no enhancement was necessary, the ability to change size and shape of the characters was essential because of their mythical qualities.

   d Political movies do not always engage the audience fully. However, the Japanese animation, *Grave of the Fireflies*, is an exception. It is an extremely powerful antiwar movie because of the simplicity of its story and the way in which the plight of its two main characters touches the audience.

Using connecting words to create arguments

Each of the items below is a series of disconnected points, not in argument form, although they are in the correct order for an argument. Write each one as an argument by using connecting words to show how the ideas are linked (see Chapter 2). You may need to alter the sentences slightly once you have inserted connecting words.

1   Students need to learn how to use claims from the literature in an essay. An essay has to be built around ideas from the literature.
2   Some students think listening is easy. Listening well is a skill. Focus is required to listen well. Students need to use intelligence in listening.

Using contradictory ideas

Much of the literature you read will have contradictory evidence. It is your task when writing an argument to show that you know this. To present the information:

- describe each idea fully, then provide, if possible, some reasons for the different conclusions; or
- organise the information in terms of the factors that create the difference; for example, 'In X context, it has been found that … However, in Y context, the findings are different …'

Showing disagreement

An argument that rejects or modifies an opposing idea is achieved through two very simple devices: order, and use of words.

The argument carrying two different points of view is structured in the following order:

- the ideas of those you disagree with are written first
- your point of view is written second.

In presenting an opposing point of view, attention needs to be paid to order and use of words.

Table 6.3 Using words to structure an argument with opposing views

First point of view: use words that imply you disagree	*Second (your) point of view:* start with words that indicate a change in direction of the argument
Some authors believe … It is generally agreed that … One view is … An earlier (etc.) view is …	However, … There is evidence to the contrary … A more fruitful (or comprehensive, or better, or sound etc.) view is …

As there are two views being stated, language has to be used carefully so the reader is aware of what is happening. Indicate that the first section contains ideas that will later be rejected by using words to imply the rejection. As well, use words to create a change in direction of the argument before giving the ideas you agree with (see Chapter 2).

Strengthening an argument by building ideas using a number of sources

Within any paragraph an argument can be strengthened by showing the amount of support there is for it within the literature. One way to indicate support is to show that a number of sources contribute to the idea. This indicates that the idea is generally accepted, allows a rich description to be developed and enhances the status of the idea. To build an idea using a number of sources:

- start with the simplest statement of the idea
- add information from other sources to fully describe it
- provide an in-text citation after each source as it is used.

Example

Strengthening an argument by building an idea using different sources

It is important to allow time between the first and second drafts of an essay. While the original attempt is often in need of improvement, rewriting should not be done immediately. Ideally, the first draft is set aside for a day or two before the second is commenced (Lashley & Best, 2001, p. 143). This creates the possibility of the writer becoming critical of his or her work. It gives time for a shift from the initial writer perspective to the audience perspective that is required in the final work (Clanchy & Ballard, 1997, p. 65). The change in viewpoint is necessary in producing a good second draft.

Using different sources to build an idea

Strengthening an argument by showing sources agree

Another technique for indicating the level of support for an idea is to show the amount of agreement on any point within the literature. To do this:

- use words to indicate that a number of sources agree
- provide a citation for each source.

Words such as: 'A few authors ...', 'A few sources ...' or 'Many authors ...' flag the agreement of a number of sources. Citations for all relevant sources are inserted within parentheses after the claim. The citations are organised alphabetically, using the first family name of each source, and a semicolon is placed between sources.

Strengthening an argument by showing the agreement on a point
A number of authors (Clanchy & Ballard, 1997; Cooper, 2003; Lashley & Best, 2001) have agreed that it is best to leave some time between the first and second drafts of an essay.

Three sources agree

Example

Planning

The aim in planning is to produce an overall structure of ideas to help writing. It involves indicating the main points, their relationship to each other and any supporting points.

The level of detail in the plan depends on your own preference. Some students like to begin with a detailed plan, while others like to start with a broad outline and use writing to help with further planning.

To produce a plan:

- recognise the planning already provided in the assignment task
- find your argument
- create a structured plan.

Recognising the planning in your assignment task

Not all the planning needs to be done by you. Many assignment tasks, particularly in first year courses, are designed to provide a basic structure. Some assignments contain a series of instruction words (such as 'describe', then 'evaluate', then 'recommend'), or have a series of parts presented in an ordered manner. These provide a clear outline plan for your assignment. You need to follow it.

On the other hand, tasks that consist of a statement and a general instruction word, such as 'discuss' or 'analyse', give little indication of the plan that has to be followed. However, they do indicate the focus for the content, and that has to be maintained.

Before beginning planning, pay careful attention to instruction words in your assignment, as they indicate the type of organisation required in the response.

Creating a structured plan

Many students need to create a structured plan before writing. The structure is already prepared for you in your position. Typically, the plan will begin with a description of the main topic concept. This is not just a definition, but rather an exploration of the various ways in which the concept has been understood.

The position provides the outline of the plan.

The remainder of the plan will follow the position. You can add in bullet points or arrows at each step to indicate the evidence that will be provided as support for each point (see example below).

Example

A plan

Position

In general, test anxiety lowers performance slightly, although this is not evident in all situations, or with all types of students. The main mechanism for this result appears to be that test anxiety leads to the development of interfering thoughts that prevent a proper focus on examination tasks. It is caused by awareness of an inadequate level of course knowledge, and also by difficulties within the testing situation.

Plan

Test anxiety

Discussion of concept (if required).

Test anxiety and performance

In most situations, test anxiety reduces the academic performance of university students slightly: *evidence.*
Situations in which test anxiety does not appear to reduce academic performance: *evidence.*
Types of students who have a reduced academic performance because of test anxiety: *evidence.*
Types of students whose academic performance is not affected by test anxiety: *evidence.*

Reasons

Interfering thoughts: *evidence.*

Causes

Inadequate level of course knowledge: *evidence.*
Difficulties within the testing situation: *evidence.*

Writing drafts

All assignments need to pass through a number of drafts. The first **draft** enables you to organise all ideas in a reasonable manner and provide all supporting details. However, this is not a final assignment. It always needs some editing.

Edit for good overall structure and content.

After the first draft has been written, put it aside for a day, then return to edit it. At this stage **editing** should focus on checking the large features of the assignment.

A good second draft will take quite a bit of rewriting. Once it is complete, **proofread** for accuracy in: citations, reference list, grammar, spelling and flow of ideas. Make any changes that are necessary to produce a polished final assignment.

Proofread for accuracy in the details.

Table 6.4 Checklist for editing at second draft stage

Check the assignment to see if it:
• Addresses each part of the task
• Covers all the content required by the task
• Is written with the organisational pattern(s) required by the instruction words

• Has a clear overall argument evident in:
   – the topic sentences
   – the introduction
   – the conclusion

• Has coherent paragraphs

• Has ideas well supported by the literature:
   – good use of ideas with citations
   – good selection of quotations with citations
   – evidence of working across the literature (to build ideas, show agreement, to reject opposing ideas)

• Is appropriately formatted.
• Has the correct word length.
• Has a reference list.

Go to our website <www.oup.com.au/orc/turner2e> for more activities on the skills covered in this chapter.

Activity

SUMMARY

In this chapter you have developed your assessment skills by learning how to work on an assignment. You have learned the skills needed to create an assignment that responds in a complete manner to the set topic and that is well organised and well written. Creating assignments takes time, but the long gestation allows you to develop a high level of knowledge, and a good ability to express what you know coherently and competently.

GLOSSARY

argument in an academic context means a position the author takes in relation to the information in the literature and the evidence provided to support each point within that position. It is organised as a response to a question or topic.

argument line the direction of the argument.

categorisation the organisation of the ideas and information by placing similar items together.

comparison (compare and contrast) the organisation of ideas into similarities and differences.

connecting words indicate a relationship between points or groups of points (also known as transitional words or linking words).

draft a version of a piece of work that is subject to being changed.

editing checking and correcting a draft.

evaluation assessment of the value of ideas or information.

instruction words in an assignment, the instruction that indicates what form of organisation of ideas and information should dominate.

list provision of evidence in an additive manner that can imply an order of importance.

position an opinion about a topic, based on the evidence in the academic literature, or based on primary research.

proofread reading and marking corrections that need to be made.

chapter SEVEN

Essays and Reflective Writing

All assessment tasks at university test your understanding of the knowledge within the discipline you are studying. The formal academic essay is one of the traditional means of assessing your knowledge. It is built around a thorough knowledge of the relevant literature, and the use of that, to construct an argument in response to a question.

A somewhat less traditional form of assessment uses reflection. The ability to think about what you do, and alter your actions or ideas to produce a better outcome, is an essential skill in learning. In some disciplinary areas (such as education and interpersonal development) assessment can be structured around your reflections about your own actions and outcomes.

This chapter builds on the skills already acquired in Chapters 4, 5 and 6, and addresses the particular requirements of essay writing and of assessment tasks involving reflection. You will learn:

- the specific structure of a formal academic essay:
  - introduction
  - body
  - conclusion
- the specific requirements for reflection:
  - how to reflect upon experiences
  - how to link experience to course concepts and theories
  - how to write a reflective journal
  - how to write a reflective essay.

Essays

Some students wonder why they have to write **essays**, as they cannot see a link between essays and their future work. However, there are many skills you acquire by writing essays, all of which are extremely useful and easily able to be applied in other contexts. Essays develop skills in assessing and finding information, thinking clearly, making judgments and putting ideas together in a coherent and powerful manner. An analogy may help. Top football players train at a gym. They do not use gym work when they are engaged in their sport; but the gym prepares them so they can play well. Essay writing is just like that: it is mind gym (M. Browne, personal communication, 15 February 2007).

Most students need to acquire skills in essay writing. Some students, despite exposure to essay writing in high school, are likely to feel that their skills are not adequate. Others, particularly many international students, have only practised writing the types of essays found in English language courses. As an academic essay is quite different from these, a significant range of new writing skills has to be developed. However, by this time, you have already learned many of the skills that are required for essay writing, so the task is not so daunting.

When writing an essay, use all the processes required for the production of a good assignment:

1 Read thoroughly in the topic area.
2 Create a concept map.
3 Take notes.
4 Work on the topic to find how to respond to it.
5 Plan your response.
6 Write using ideas and information from the literature.
7 Acknowledge all ideas and information (using citations and a list of references).
8 Write a number of drafts and edit your work.

An essay is like any other assignment in many respects. However, what is specific to it is the emphasis on argument, and the fact that the argument needs to be carried in writing.

Using the essay format to reveal the argument

An essay format presents an argument as a continuous piece of prose.

An academic essay is almost always written in an **essay format**. This means you use words to indicate the structure and to lead the reader from point to point in the argument. An essay is structured in the following manner:

- introduction (including background)
- body
- conclusion
- reference list

Introduction

An **introduction**:

- states the topic addressed in the essay
- provides some background information
- gives a summary of the essay argument (the argument statement or thesis statement).

Typically an essay begins with a statement indicating the topic to be addressed. A short sentence, in the present tense, is used. It operates like a heading or title but in sentence form. The most common way to write it is to begin with words such as 'This essay examines/explores/analyses' followed by a statement of the topic. It does not refer to the essay argument.

The first sentence of an essay announces the topic.

Essay topic: Test anxiety causes university students to underperform in their examinations. Discuss.

Possible topic statement: This essay examines the relationship between test anxiety in university students and their performance in examinations.

Example

Often the statement of topic is immediately followed, within the same paragraph, with some background information. **Background** provides context as a means of helping the reader understand the importance of the topic being addressed. The essay topic itself is not discussed in this section. Rather, the background focuses on the broad topic contained within the essay question.

The background provides a context for the essay argument.

Table 7.1 Background

Essay topic	Broad topic to address in the background section
Test anxiety causes university students to underperform in their examinations. Discuss.	Significance of examinations at university level or The significance of examination results for students
Evaluate the impact of the internet on the occurrence of plagiarism in university assignments.	The growth of internet resources for academic work or The importance of university assignments in assessing student knowledge

Example

In the background section you might:

- provide some history relevant to the broad topic
- give statistics to show the significance of the broad topic
- provide examples of the significance of the broad topic.

Ideas and information used as background should come from the literature, and so need to be cited. A good background makes an impressive beginning. It may be just a few sentences in a very short essay (of 1200 words, for example) but will be a paragraph or more in longer essays. If you are unsure what a background is, omit it or seek advice.

The introduction includes a clear statement of the essay argument.

The final and most important part of the introduction is the statement of the essay argument (or 'thesis statement' or 'argument statement'). An **argument statement** can be:

- a basic position and the evidence used to support it, or
- a comprehensive position.

While an argument always consists of a position and evidence, this is not the case for the statement of an argument at the beginning of an essay. If a position is comprehensive, a summary of evidence for each point cannot be provided, as it would be too clumsy. Hence, the comprehensive position itself becomes the argument statement. As you are expected to produce comprehensive positions (see Chapter 6) at university, you will find that in almost all cases your argument statement will be the same as your position.

The statement of argument is so important that it needs to be highlighted by the following writing techniques:

- if the argument statement is two or more sentences in length, use a separate paragraph without a topic sentence
- begin the sentences outlining the argument with words such as 'This essay argues that' to alert the reader to the presence of the argument statement (use the present tense)
- write each sentence so that it is clearly part of the argument by repeating words such as 'argue', 'argument', 'further argues', 'points out' and 'shows'
- do not use citations, as these are your sentences describing the main points of your essay.

A concise summary of the argument creates a strong introduction. Many students merely list a range of issues that will be addressed in their essay. This is an extremely weak introduction. An argument statement is much stronger, as it not only indicates what will be addressed, and in what order, but also how the ideas are linked together. A powerful beginning is made when you clearly and confidently state the essay argument.

Topic: Test anxiety causes university students to underperform in their examinations. Discuss.

Comprehensive position as an argument statement: <u>This essay argues</u> that in general, test anxiety lowers performance slightly, although this is not evident in all situations, nor with all types of students. <u>Further, it is argued that</u> the main mechanism for this result appears to be that test anxiety leads to the development of interfering thoughts, which prevent a proper focus on examination tasks. <u>The essay also points out</u> that test anxiety is caused both by an awareness of an inadequate level of course knowledge, and by difficulties within the testing situation itself.

Example

Some essay guides suggest that an outline of the sections of an essay (or essay map) be supplied in the introduction. However, when you have a well-written argument statement, there is no need to do this, as the range of topics and the order of presentation are contained within the argument statement itself.

Not all sources follow the above format for an introduction. For example, you will find that many articles do not present their argument in the introduction. Where is it stated?

Thinking

Why are you expected to present your argument at the beginning?
Many students find presenting an argument first difficult. Why? Consider all possible reasons.

Thinking

Revision: examining arguments
Below are two essay questions and brief summaries of arguments that could be made in response to them. For each:

1 Circle the author's basic position statement.
2 Underline the evidence offered to support the author's basic position (if provided).
3 Place a box around any additions to the basic position and note if the addition is named or just indicated.

Activity

4   Shade any contradictory position that is presented.

5   Underline and star any information that the author indicates is incorrect.

Question 1: *International students find it difficult to write an academic essay. Discuss.*

Argument: Some international students initially experience difficulty in writing an academic essay, for both cultural and language reasons.

Question 2: *The ability to read critically is an essential skill in university assignments. Discuss.*

Argument: The ability to read critically is certainly a highly valued skill at university, but it is not essential in all areas of study. While some students, particularly in humanities and the social sciences, are expected to possess this ability, not all students are. It appears that critical reading is rarely used in some disciplines, and in others it is not encouraged until third year.

If you need to provide a definition, use one from an academic source.

Many sources suggest that students include definitions in their introduction. While this practice may be appropriate for essays in high school and English courses, it is not usually suitable for a university essay. Most knowledge at university is complex, and hence a definition of a concept is often not capable of being presented in a sentence or two. Moreover, some essay questions are written to force a discussion of a concept. Here the whole essay is devoted to arriving at some suitable position on what the meaning of the concept is (Clanchy & Ballard, 1997), so an initial definition would be useless. Of course, there will be some exceptions. If a definition is required, find one from an academic source rather than from a dictionary.

Thinking

Why would a definition from an academic source be preferred over one from a dictionary?

Body (short essay)

The **body** is the essay proper. It is here that your argument is presented in full detail, correctly cited. As the logic of the essay is carried in words, very careful thought has to be given to the order of paragraphs and especially to the topic sentences (see Chapters 5 and 6).

The body of the essay is structured to display the argument.

If an essay is addressing a concept that is variously understood in the literature, then it could begin with a paragraph discussing these meanings. Be careful, as it requires a sophisticated approach. You should neither just list a series of definitions, nor argue for the use of a particular one. Rather, the aim is to display the range of understandings of the concept in such a way that you can return to this information later in the essay as a means of better understanding some of the claims in the literature. This is likely to be too difficult initially. However, as you advance in your studies keep in mind that this approach will be required for some topics.

The body of an essay follows the order given in the argument statement (see 'Creating a structured plan' in Chapter 6). Each point in the argument statement is:

- addressed in the order indicated
- elaborated in one or more paragraphs
- fully supported with examples and evidence from the literature.

Topic sentences are used to hold the paragraphs together as one argument. Thus careful attention has to be given to ensuring that each topic sentence:

- states the point contained in its paragraph
- reveals the connection between paragraphs.

A short essay is constructed as a number of paragraphs, each of which is linked to create the essay argument.

Create links between topic sentences with the devices discussed in Chapter 2:

- repeat key words either by using the word again or using variations on the word
- use a labelling word to refer to the content in a previous paragraph or paragraphs
- Use the same point of view for all topic sentences
- Use connectives, where needed.

If topic sentences have been well constructed, you will be able to read just the topic sentences and see a coherent essay argument. Check that this is the case.

Example

Topic sentences revealing coherent content

Essay topic: Test anxiety causes university students to underperform in their examinations. Discuss.

1st paragraph: Test anxiety is normally understood as a form of debilitating anxiety, although how it is measured varies.

2nd paragraph: Evidence points to the fact that, in general, test anxiety lowers performance slightly.

3rd paragraph: However, in some situations, and for some students, examination results are not negatively impacted by test anxiety.

4th paragraph: It appears that when there is a reduction in performance it occurs mainly because of the presence of interfering thoughts.

5th paragraph: There is little agreement in the literature as to the causes of this phenomenon. Some argue it arises because of an awareness of being inadequately prepared.

6th paragraph: There is also evidence that a number of features, both surrounding and within the test situation itself, lead to the development of test anxiety.

Figure 7.1 Structure of a short essay with linked topic sentences

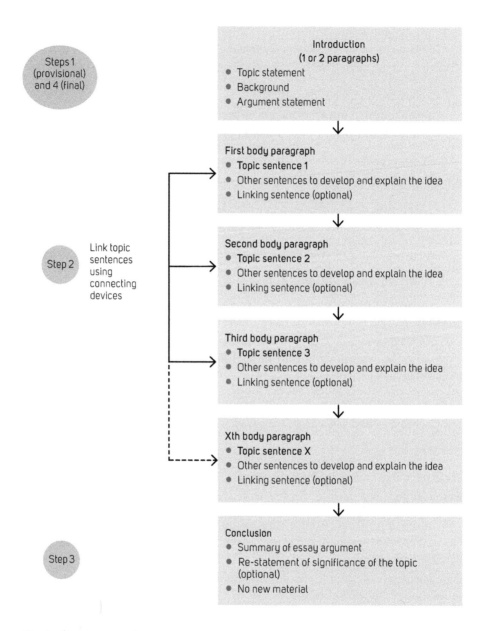

Body (long essay)

The body of a long essay (2000 or more words) has a more complex structure. It is often constructed as a series of connected sections. Each section holds a major point within the overall argument. These will be quite comprehensive (or abstract). Within each section, there is likely to be a series of minor points (at a more specific level) used to provide a rich description and explanation (see Figure 7.2).

A long essay is constructed as a number of sections, each of which is linked into the essay argument.

Figure 7.2 Structure of an essay with long sections

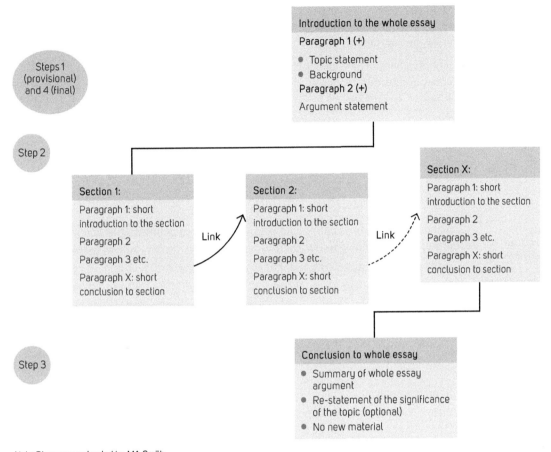

Note: Diagram constructed by MA Smith.

In a long essay each section has:

- an external logic
- an internal logic.

A section is structured like a short essay. It has a very brief introduction that sets up an external logic (linking the section to the overall essay argument) and an internal logic (outlining the argument within that section). The body of a section is fully developed, with each paragraph describing and explaining a point in the section argument. A section concludes with a short paragraph (perhaps even just two sentences) that finalises the section by summarising it, and then addresses the external logic by leading into the following section.

Conclusion

An essay always includes a **conclusion** to the essay as a whole. This paragraph summarises the argument of the essay without any citations. A conclusion

The conclusion summarises the essay argument.

cannot contain new ideas, and so it is difficult to make it different from the introduction. One way to conclude, is to restate the essay argument with greater confidence than in the introduction (but without overclaiming). A better way is to make some link between your argument and the background as a means of highlighting the importance of the topic. Again, it is a good idea to watch closely how authors of academic work conclude in order to develop a repertoire of concluding skills.

Reference list

An academic essay always includes a list of references (Chapter 5).

Writing order

In an essay, remember to use course terminology, use citations, write in a formal style and write in the third person (usually).

Although an essay is constructed to be read from beginning to end, it is usually not written in this order. A position or argument statement has to be developed first, although it will be provisional as you can expect to modify it as a result of the writing process. The body of the essay is written next, and then the conclusion. After this, return to the introduction to refine the argument statement. The reason for this approach is that writing the body helps clarify the essay argument.

Activity

Short essay
Go to our website <www.oup.com.au/orc/turner2e> to see an example of a short essay.

Being critical

Most essays assume you will take a critical perspective on the literature. Indeed, the ability to be critical is highly prized in Western universities. It is also, unfortunately, often an ambiguous demand. However, in practice, the basic ability of being critical is shown in a number of normal aspects of essay writing:

- selecting some ideas rather than others
- linking ideas from the literature together to show how they relate
- creating an argument.

All of these processes involve your making judgments about what is important and what is not. This is having a critical approach to the literature.

In second and third year courses, and especially in any postgraduate work, the ability to be critical has to be further developed, with a more conscious selection and assessment of ideas. This will involve your judging the basis for making any claim and the implications of that by assessing:

- the quality of the research on which the claim has been based (see Chapter 12)
- the implications for the claim of being embedded in a particular theory.

Being creative

Students often feel that they cannot express themselves in an essay. As an essay is built so tightly around the literature, there appears little room for the writer's own intelligence and thinking to show. Certainly, students cannot add their own ideas directly. However, there is still a large amount of room for creativity. Something new is created when we choose what to read, think about the links between sources, construct an argument and support that from the literature. A well-written, well-researched essay is an original piece of work that very clearly shows a student's own creative thinking and understanding.

Reflective writing

In some courses at university you are asked to reflect upon and write about your own experiences. The aim is to help you understand the particular course at a much deeper level, to embed the skills taught in the course more thoroughly and to help you to use learning to improve (transform) yourself and/or situations.

The process of reflection

Being able to reflect requires four skills:

- awareness
- thinking
- planning
- trying.

Awareness

Awareness can lead to change. Often we act more or less automatically. This is particularly so in situations or relationships that are habitual. Even when our behaviour patterns create problems for us (and/or others), we tend not to be aware of the pathways that have led to the problems. However, we can learn to become aware and use that awareness to change a situation. Awareness is an essential element in most learning.

To be aware is to have the skill of acting in the world, while at the same time being conscious of what is occurring. This can seem daunting, but with practice we can become good at it. To begin, we can develop a curiosity about how events and behaviours occur.

Our first aim is to focus awareness on the processes involved. One way of examining a situation is to view it in terms of its content (for example, what happened; what was said). Another point of focus is to look at the processes involved (for example, how something was said; how it caused a reaction). Clearly content and process are not able to be totally separated. However, we can focus on one, rather than the other.

We can develop awareness of both external and internal processes.

The second aim is to focus, in particular, on our own processes. As the aim of using reflection is to develop understanding and skills, then the focus needs to be on ourselves: both on our 'external' actions and reactions (for example, how I say something; how others react to what I do or say; how I react to what is done or not done); and on our 'internal' ones (what I think; what I feel).

1   My external processes include:
    - how I do something
    - how others relate to this
    - how others act
    - how I act in reaction to this
    - what helps achieve an outcome
    - what hinders an outcome.
2   My internal processes include:
    - what I am thinking and/or feeling as I act
    - what I am thinking and/or feeling as I react.

Activity

Recognising awareness of content and process

1   Examine the following statements: Decide which ones *mainly* describe:
    a   the content
    b   the process.
2   Give a reason for your answer, and if it is a process, indicate whether it is mainly external or internal.
    a   A tutor is marking an essay.
    b   When the tutor said, 'I don't understand what is being said here', I felt confused.
    c   When the tutor looked annoyed and said, 'I don't understand what is being said here', the tutorial became quiet.

d   A tutor asked me, 'Please explain what you mean here.'

e   I think, 'I'm going to get a low mark', so I say nothing.

f   I felt pleased with our meeting and so happily offered to help Patricia with her work.

Becoming aware

Activity

1   In this activity try to become aware of all the aspects of what occurs. The more detailed your awareness is, the better.

a   Find a partner. One student will be 'A'; the other 'B'. Student A will argue that the death penalty should be used as a punishment for murder. Student B will argue that it is wrong to use it. Fully imagine that you hold the beliefs assigned to you.

b   Take a few minutes to produce some notes about points you could use. Do not worry if your statements seem extreme. Remember these are only to help in the discussion. Do *not* read them to your partner.

c   Now argue the topic with your partner. Maintain your position throughout. While you are doing this become aware of how you say things; how your partner reacts; how that makes you react. Try to notice any thoughts and feelings you have. Try to be as specific as possible.

d   After a few minutes, write down what you have noticed about the processes involved in the argument. Make sure you describe both external and internal processes (for example, how it was said, how it affected you, what it made you do, how your partner reacted to what you said).

e   Share this with your partner, and/or with the tutorial as a whole.

2   Repeat the above process but this time Student A will try to teach Student B how to add up (for example, how to add 29 + 2; or 13 + 7). Student B is not interested. Student A is to keep trying.

Thinking

What are the consequences of not being aware of what you do?

What kind of impact do you think your feelings have on the actions you are engaged in?

Sometimes, while we are speaking to someone, we have thoughts that are not related to the topic (for example, thoughts of what I might do next, thoughts that I am bored, that I really like this person, that I think this person is talking too much). In what way can you imagine such 'irrelevant' thoughts affecting what you do?

Thinking

Reflection also involves thinking. There are two interrelated aspects to consider:

- the assessment of the outcome and processes
- the link to course concepts and theories.

Think about what occurred, and how it may be related to your course.

There is a close relationship between the two aspects, as recognition of successes and problems cannot be fully achieved without knowledge of the course concepts and theories.

As part of the activity of thinking, assess your experience. First examine the outcome. Develop some criteria for success. Ask yourself to what extent the outcome was successful. Next, think carefully about the external and internal processes involved. Try to select those steps that worked well, and those steps that could have been better.

As a natural response, you will draw on any of your prior knowledge or experience in helping to assess your experience. This is important. However, as you are doing the exercise as part of a course, it is essential to place a large emphasis on course content.

Knowledge of the relevant course material is an essential part of reflection used as an assessment item. Even before you begin the process of reflection, some knowledge of the relevant concepts and ideas helps you focus on the most important aspects. Once you move to the thinking stage, consciously and actively relate your course concepts and theories to what occurred. In order to help, reread any relevant course material. Examine the course material for any:

- concepts that can be used to name aspects of the situation you have experienced
- theories about why the problems you experienced may have occurred
- theories about what can be done to make such situations better.

Remember: most theory is contested at university, so make sure you also note any disagreement among the theories and ideas you are thinking about.

Planning

The third stage of reflection is planning how to improve a situation. Again think in terms of your course for ideas that can help. You may also think of ideas from other courses, or even from your experience. Develop a plan of action with the aim of using it to improve the outcome and/or process. Your plan needs to be:

- about what you can change in yourself
- specific.

Planning is about creating specific actions you can take to improve a situation.

If your plan involves changing others (for example, I will make X do his share of work), alter this to produce steps that you can do to try to achieve this aim (for example, I will meet X and offer to help if he has difficulty; I will remind X of his group commitments). If your initial plan is too general (for example, I'll be more supportive in group work), change this into something specific (for example, I will message X and ask him how he is going). Planning is about creating specific actions you can take to improve a situation.

Why would you plan for actions that *you* can do, rather than actions that *others* can do?

Thinking

Trying

Once you have made a plan, try it out. Select a suitable time, remembering that the primary focus in the particular situation is not your plan, but the activity itself. Be aware of both how you implement your plan (internally and externally) and what the outcomes are.

Try out your plan at a suitable time and with awareness.

Activity

Thinking, planning and trying

Continue with Activity: 'Becoming aware', Question 2, on page 161.

a   Student A and Student B (individually): think about the outcomes of the activity (What worked? What did not? Why?)

b   Student A and Student B (individually): make a specific plan to change something about how you acted or reacted, or thought, or felt. The plan must be about what *you* can do.

c   Try the exercise again (with awareness).

d   Think about the outcomes the second time. Share your experience with your partner.

Reflecting over time

Normally, you are asked to be reflective about some ongoing activity. In this case the cycle of awareness, thinking, planning and trying is used over and over. In this situation:

- Evaluate your process of reflection. Look back over the whole activity and consider if different actions could have been taken at any point.
- Evaluate the effectiveness of course concepts and theories for the whole situation.
- Evaluate your own learning over the time.

Figure 7.3 Reflection over time

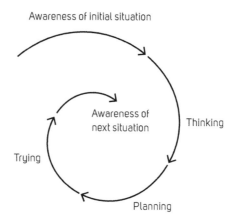

When you engage in reflection over a long period you can evaluate, not just individual actions and behaviours, but also the process as a whole. Look back and consider whether the steps you took at any stage were the most useful. Do not worry about imperfections, as they are to be expected.

To evaluate the course concepts and theories, consider how useful they are in categorising and explaining the activity you are engaged in. Expect that neither will fit your experience exactly. They are abstract and useful for applying generally, and so are not a perfect match for any particular situation. Make an assessment of which aspects of your course material:

- are useful
- need modification
- need to be omitted
- need to be developed in new ways or new areas.

The aim of reflection is to aid learning. Thus, when looking back on what happened it is important to assess what you have learned. Again, don't expect to be perfect. When assessing your learning be realistic about what you have achieved and indicate what further areas can be improved.

Can learning how to act in the world ever be perfect? Why or why not?

Thinking

Reflective journals

You may be asked to write a **reflective journal** for either a whole learning module or for some specific aspect of it. A journal is a record of your continual process of awareness, thinking, planning and trying in a particular area.

Finding a way of beginning a journal may be difficult. The content of a journal is very open, so you will not receive explicit directions. Start by reminding yourself that the basic aim is to learn the concepts, theories and skills within a course, so this has to be a focus. Then ask yourself questions like those in the Critical Incident Questionnaire (Brookfield, 1998):

1   At what moment in the class [or team or task] this week [was I] most engaged ...?
2   At what moment in the class [or team or task] this week [was I least involved] ...?
3   What action that anyone ... took this week did [I] find most affirming or helpful?
4   What action that anyone ... took this week did [I] find most puzzling or confusing?
5   What surprised [me] most about the class [or team or task] this week? (Critical incident questionnaire: Critically reflective practice in action section, para. 2)

Answer each of these, giving as much detail as possible about the processes. The answers lead to the issues that are most important for you. From that point you can begin your practice of reflection.

Usually you can include what you like in a reflective journal. Hence you can have rough notes; incomplete sentences; sketchy diagrams; pertinent images from magazines or the net; links to relevant books or movies or music; quotations from course material; notes of class discussion. The general rule is that the more links you make as you reflect upon the task, the deeper (and better) your learning will be.

Despite the openness of presentation there are some features to attend to when writing a journal:

- write frequently and date entries
- focus on processes
- continually reflect on the situation and the course content
- evaluate continually.

Sometimes a journal is used as a private learning tool. Some lecturers and tutors use it to engage a student in dialogue (the student writes a journal entry and the tutor provides feedback, and so on). Sometimes journals are assessed. If

A reflective journal is a freely written record of your continual process of awareness, thinking, planning and trying.

this is the case, you will need to trust your tutor or lecturer to treat your work with respect. If you do not feel confident in this, seek an alternative form of assessment (if that is possible) or be circumspect (careful) with what you write.

Reflective essays

A reflective essay presents a coherent account of a process of reflection.

A **reflective essay** is a means of assessing your learning. It is a coherently presented account of a process of reflection. Normally you will be asked to keep a journal, and will be expected to use it in the production of the essay.

The reflective essay reveals and explains the details of the reflective process. To write it well:

- organise the material
- provide details from your experience
- create links from your experience to course concepts and theories
- evaluate.

The most important task in a reflective essay is to organise your material. A good way to start is to organise in terms of a sequence. Draw a timeline indicating what happened, when, concentrating on problems, transformations in the problem areas, and successes or difficulties. Then categorise your information. This is best done with the use of course concepts. Finally, consider if there is any overall theory that can explain much of your experience (there usually is).

Once you have created some order in the material, attend to how you will present it. The overall aim in a reflective essay is to weave together seamlessly details from your experience and course concepts and theories. It is quite a difficult task. At the basic level an essay will be organised chronologically (according to a time sequence) with the emphasis on separate items of experience, each linked to some aspect of the course. More sophisticated essays aim to produce an overall coherence based usually on a particular theory that proved useful. The theory rather than the experiences then becomes the basis of organisation.

Provide detailed descriptions of your experiences.

Whatever your mode of presentation it is necessary to provide details from your experience. The richer you make your details, the more interesting and informative your essay will be. General statements lead markers to assume you have not engaged in any reflection.

Your experiences will be linked to the course concepts and theory in two ways at least. First, the course concepts will be used as a means of talking about the details of your experience. Second, theories will be introduced to explain the experiences.

Finally, your reflective essay should also contain some evaluation of both your learning process and of the usefulness of course concepts and theories.

It is not expected that either will be perfect. In fact, limitations in both areas are usual. You are assessed not on whether you reached your goals, but on your ability to understand the processes involved in learning, including your ability to judge the usefulness of course theories.

Presentation of a reflective essay

A reflective essay must meet many of the requirements of a formal academic essay: a good introduction, some background, a clear argument carried in well-organised paragraphs with good topic sentences and a conclusion. You probably will have to use citations and a reference list.

A reflective essay must also be able to present both personal information and course information. This means that in the writing of the essay you will move from personal pronouns (describing your own experiences) and emotive (if necessary) prose, to more formal accounts of course theories (using third person and in-text citations). The weaving together of these two forms of writing is a considerable skill.

Go to our website <www.oup.com.au/orc/turner2e> for more activities on the skills covered in this chapter.

Activity

SUMMARY

This chapter has examined two forms of assessment: the formal academic essay and the reflective essay. While both are built around a good knowledge of the course and the relevant literature, they differ significantly in how this knowledge is used. The formal academic essay requires the development of an argument based on the literature. The reflective essay, like the formal essay, needs to follow an essay structure, have an argument and show knowledge of the literature. However, it is significantly different in that its main focus is on your reflections about your experience.

GLOSSARY

argument statement a statement of a basic position, with the evidence used to support it, or a statement of a comprehensive position.

background context provided so the reader can more easily understand the significance of an argument made in an essay.

body (of an essay) the part of an essay that fully develops the argument.

conclusion the last paragraph(s) of an essay, or other piece of work, that summarises the argument.

essay a piece of continuous prose that carries an argument, often made in response to a question.

essay format the presentation of an argument as a continuous piece of prose.

introduction the first paragraph(s) of an essay, or other piece of work. It indicates the topic addressed, and provides background and a clear statement of the argument.

reflective essay a coherent account of a process of reflection, so involves both personal experiences and academic comment.

reflective journal a freely written record of your continual process of awareness, thinking, planning and trying during a particular task.

chapter EIGHT

Doing Case Studies and Writing Reports

In this chapter we examine two other forms of assessment you are very likely to use at university: case studies and reports. Case studies are used as a means of teaching the link between what you learn and what happens in the 'real' world. They are invaluable in courses with a large practical element. Reports are not strictly speaking a form of assessment, but a way of presenting information. They use formatting and other graphical devices to present information in a very clear, easy-to-read manner.

In this chapter you will learn how to:

- do case studies:
    - understand the case
    - link the case to course concepts and theories
    - create a range of solutions and recommendations
    - write up the case study
- write reports:
    - structure a report
    - write each section in a report.

Case studies

The knowledge in your courses at university is well organised, often abstract and offers ideal solutions to problems. The 'real' world of actual events and behaviours and situations, on the other hand, has very specific problems with messy and chaotic features. As a result, many students often wonder what the relation of university knowledge is to their lives.

A **case study** is a story of some actual situation designed to allow students to learn skills in applying their course knowledge to the 'real world'. It is either based on research, or is a fictional account, of particular events or behaviours or institutions.

The simplest case studies are 'real life' accounts with specific questions aimed at assessing your ability to:

- recognise course concepts and ideas in a 'real life' situation (for example, a case may contain an account of a particular manager and her way of working with staff; you may be asked to name her management style using a course concept)
- perform some calculation using 'real life' data (for example, you may be given a story of some real company's transactions, with questions that require you to use the data in the case to perform some accounting calculations)
- show your course knowledge in a case study context (for example, you may be asked to examine two different computers and recommend which one would be suitable for a company described in a case study). See *Case study report* (n.d.) <www.monash.edu.au/lls/llonline/writing/general/report/1.xml> for an example of such a case study).

Case studies help students learn how to link their knowledge to a particular 'real life' situation.

These types of case studies are relatively simple. The key skill is to link what you know in the course with what is presented in the case.

A more demanding case study requires problem-recognition and problem-solving skills as well. This gives students the chance to learn how to use the knowledge in their course in order to:

- make sense of the complexities in any particular situation
- find the problems that need addressing
- present viable solutions.

The four steps in doing a problem-solving case study are:

1 Get to know the case.
2 Identify the problems.
3 Create recommendations.
4 Write up the case study.

Getting to know the case

Very focused work has to be done to reveal the nature of a long and complex case. The key tasks in this process are:

- reading the case
- linking to the course material
- reordering the case details into suitable categories.

Reading the case

Start by reading the case a number of times to get to know all the details. Focus on:

When reading the case, aim to find its details.

- the details in the case by looking for answers to questions such as: What has happened? When has it happened? Who are the main actors in the case? Who did what?
- the claims made by the actors or by the case. Don't take any description as necessarily correct. Always check to see if the claims are backed up by some evidence from the case details.

Reading a case study

Read the following case study and answer the questions below.

Activity

As Bao Mei was a very good student at her high school in northern China, her parents carefully saved money to send her to Australia to study. They have great expectations that she will become an accountant and help them run their business. Bao Mei is halfway through her first semester in Australia.

The money her parents send her is not enough to cover the cost of living, so Bao Mei has found a job at a Chinese restaurant, where she works for 20 hours each week.

Bao Mei knows it is best to study as much as she can. She usually gets up at 4 a.m. and studies for three hours before going to university. When she doesn't have lectures, she keeps studying, only stopping to eat noodles at lunchtime, and to go to work in the evening.

Her greatest difficulty, at the moment, is writing an essay on the topic: 'A leader is important for successful team work. Discuss.' The essay is worth 30 per cent of the course marks, and Bao Mei is not sure what she has to do. She tries to ask the librarian, but the librarian is not at her desk, so Bao Mei decides it is better to start searching, rather than wait. She carefully copies her essay topic into a database and retrieves so many articles it is impossible to select what to read. She then types the essay topic into the library catalogue and finds nothing.

Bao Mei is becoming quite desperate and disheartened. She has passed in the mid-semester examination, receiving 25/40 marks, but that is not a good mark and now she doesn't know what to do for her essay. She thinks of what it would be like to fail her course and what her parents would think. Bao Mei is beginning to panic because she also has to study for tests in other courses. She feels stupid not knowing what to do.

Finally, Bao Mei asks a friend, Chamika, for advice: 'How do I find sources for the essay?' 'That's easy,' Chamika replies, 'it says "teamwork". That's what you look for.'

Bao Mei and Chamika find numerous articles on teamwork. Then it seems easy to write the essay.

Bao Mei is very careful to write well-developed paragraphs. She checks all her topic sentences. She writes everything she knows about 'teamwork' and cites all her ideas.

She submits her essay, very pleased because she feels she has done well.

When Bao Mei receives her essay back, the tutor has written on it 'Bao Mei, I can see you have read a lot of articles and books. You have also written good topic sentences and paragraphs. However, your essay is not on the topic. Unfortunately, you must fail. Your mark is 12/30.'

Bao Mei is distraught. Her final exam in this course is an essay worth 30 per cent of the course marks. She feels sure she will fail.

Questions

1   Who are the main 'actors' in the case?
2   What are the main events in the case?
3   The case says: 'Her (Bao Mei's) greatest difficulty at the moment is writing an essay.' Do you think this is a true assessment? Give reasons for your answer.

Linking to the course material

Once you know the case fairly well, you should be in a position to judge the general course content area the case is addressing. If this is not obvious (perhaps you have not yet had a lecture on the area and so it is unfamiliar to you), then ask your tutor. You cannot proceed without this knowledge.

When the general content area is established, leave the case and return to your course material. Read any relevant lecture notes, chapters in text books, or search for and read other relevant sources. Deepen your knowledge of the concepts and theories in your course so that all the relevant ideas will be in the forefront of your mind as you do further work on the case.

To find the links between case details and the course, ask questions of the case using course concepts and theories.

Return to reading the case with your course knowledge. A case rarely uses course concepts and terminology; rather, it describes actions and events. Look at these details to find the relevant concepts, terminology and theories that could be used to describe and explain them. In order to do this, ask questions of the case, for example, 'Is there any evidence of X concept in this case?' Write down all the course concepts that are related. These are extremely important for your analysis of the case. Expect to reread the case with this viewpoint a number of times.

Linking the case to the course

1   What content area in this book do you think Bao Mei's story is linked with (try to be as specific as possible)?
2   Reread the section in this book that is most relevant to Bao Mei's case.
3   Find two course concepts that would be helpful in naming and describing parts of Bao Mei's case.

Reordering the case details into suitable categories

All your reading is preparation for the next step, which is to reorganise the information in the case for your own purpose. The case will not be neatly categorised into information directly related to your course. Nor will it be organised in a manner that is helpful for immediate analysis. To create a useful form of the information, the case details need to be reorganised.

Reorganise the information in the case into a useful form.

Each discipline has its own models or tools that enable a student to reorder case information (see, for example, *Problem-solving techniques*, n.d.). We will examine just two that are able to be used in any context:

- a timeline
- a SWOT analysis.

A **timeline** allows us to regroup the case information in an ordered manner with a focus on what happened, when, to the company or person (etc.) involved in the case.

A timeline shows what happened, when.

A **SWOT analysis** is a conceptual tool or model that creates a focus on qualities in the case that are relevant to its problems and solutions. It breaks up the chaotic information in the case and regroups it into Strengths and Weaknesses *internal* to the organisation or individual, and Opportunities and Threats that are *external*.

A SWOT analysis reveals qualities related to problems and solutions.

- The Strengths are those features within the organisation or individual that help (ask: 'Who/What makes it easy or successful?')
- The Weaknesses are the qualities that hinder (ask: 'Who/What makes it more difficult? Who/What creates a problem?').
- The Opportunities are aspects of the external world that could help if used (ask: 'Who/What could help?')
- The Threats are possible external problems (ask: 'Who/What is a possible problem?').

Activity

Reordering the information in a case

1   Draw a timeline for Bao Mei's case.

2   Do a SWOT analysis on Bao Mei's case. Use the question guide below. Provide specific details from the case to support your answers.

Note: the questions asked about Bao Mei's case are relevant to this learning situation *only*. When you are doing a case study in another discipline, choose questions that reflect the interests in that discipline. For some useful questions in a business context see *SWOT Analysis: Discover new opportunities. Manage and eliminate threats* (n.d.).

Strengths	Weaknesses
What helps Bao Mei in her current situation? Consider: • personal characteristics • skills • resources (people and things that help her)	What hinders Bao Mei in her current situation? Consider: • personal characteristics • lack of skills • lack of or inadequate resources (people and things)
Opportunities	**Threats**
What is available to Bao Mei which she could use to help herself? Consider: • resources (people and things) • future events	What is in Bao Mei's context that could cause a future problem? Consider: • future lack of resources (people and things) • future events

Identifying the problems

Begin your identification of the problems by highlighting all the difficulties in the case study. The SWOT analysis helps.

Most often the problems will not be described using course concepts. Rather, you are presented with signs or symptoms of the problem. Your task is to examine these and recognise the concept within your course that would be used to name them.

For example, a case may describe an angry manager. Think of this as a symptom of a course-related problem. Ask: 'What course concept does this symptom relate to?' You may find that the symptom of an angry manager relates to a failure in interpersonal skills in one course or to the use of a particular management style in another, and perhaps is entirely irrelevant in other courses.

Look for relationships between all aspects of the problem(s).

A case often presents a complex problem or problems. It is helpful to draw a concept map to highlight some of the aspects of the problem(s):

- the causes of any problem
- the effects and/or symptoms of any problem
- the connection of one problem to another
- the connections of any problem across the past, present, future.

Making recommendations

The most important task in a case study is the creation of **recommendations** to solve the problems identified in the case. Recommendations offer clear and specific advice on what needs to be done. They are developed from a good knowledge of both the case, and of the relevant literature.

A recommendation is a clear and specific statement of what needs to be done to solve a problem.

Generating solutions

Your task is to find to what extent the ideal solutions provided in the literature can be used in the case. First, reread the literature, giving particular emphasis to the kinds of solutions relevant to the problem(s) identified in the case. Also consider solutions you have used in your workplace or elsewhere. Think very carefully of the case details, as the solution has to fit the case.

Next, use techniques to help generate a range of possible solutions for the particular case you are dealing with. Brainstorming can be used as a way of producing innovative ideas. To brainstorm ask yourself what would be useful. Record all ideas without judging their value. Then assess the ideas. This approach would be particularly useful in a case study in, for example, marketing, where creative solutions are required. It also works well in a group discussion of solutions.

Create both innovative and systematic solutions.

Systematic solutions are also needed. To do this, it is best to use criteria around which solutions can be built. Select the criteria from the ones relevant to the particular case, for example:

- low cost; medium cost; high cost
- short term; long term
- high profit/high risk; medium profit/medium risk; low profit/low risk.

Then for each criterion, develop solutions that can fit the details of the case and the knowledge in the literature.

Activity

Generating solutions

Brainstorming

1   Do this activity in groups of three or four. Select one member who will record all ideas. Remind yourself you are not to judge ideas and that any idea is useful at this stage. Brainstorm solutions to the problem in the Bao Mei case study—what could Bao Mei do to maximise her opportunities and minimise her threats?

Thinking systematically

2   Systematically generate solutions for Bao Mei using two different criteria:

   a   receiving a mark above 60 per cent in her course

   b   receiving a passing mark for her course.

Make sure specific details are provided for each solution and that these are suitable for the case.

Evaluating solutions

Select the solution(s) that is most likely to be successful given the nature of the case.

Evaluate the range of solutions generated. Ideally, a solution that solves all the problems identified in the case is the one that should be used. However, the whole point of a case study is that the 'real world' is not ideal, but rather chaotic and messy. So a more realistic approach needs to be taken. The solution that is likely to be most successful, given the nature of the case, is to be preferred. In selecting be aware of:

- any assumptions that need to be made (not all details are supplied in a case; you may have to assume some)
- the changes in the case situation that would be required to create the solution
- the Strengths that could be used to help in the transformation
- the way Weaknesses could be minimised
- the Opportunities that could be utilised
- the Threats that need to be avoided
- the costs
- the expected outcomes if the solution were adopted
- any problems likely to remain.

Once a solution has been selected it becomes a recommendation.

Once a solution(s) has been selected, it becomes a recommendation. Provide the details of:

- who is to do what, when, and how
- the expected outcome
- the limitations—any problems likely to remain or any assumptions used.

There is no one right answer. Your task is to show you know how to apply the concepts and theory in your course to the case.

Evaluating solutions

In your groups:

1   Examine the solutions you have generated for Bao Mei. Select the one that is the best fit for the case, or create a new solution that is a combination of aspects of those you have generated.
2   Decide why you see it as the best option.
3   Give details about how it is to be implemented within the case context.
4   Decide which problems are likely to remain, even if the recommendation is followed.

Writing up the case study

A case study is normally written using the following structure:

- Introduction
- Background
- Method
- Analysis and discussion
- Recommendations (alternatively, recommendations may be written after the conclusion)
- Conclusion.

In writing up a case study, aim to show your thinking on the case and your knowledge of the literature.

An introduction needs to be given in which the following elements are briefly presented: a statement of the topic area; and summaries of the method employed, the main problems found in the case, and the major recommendations.

As well, some background should be included. A brief summary of the case story can be made. Material from the literature (with citations) indicating the significance of the type of problem in the case, or general information about the company or situation dealt with in the case, can be presented.

The method section briefly provides a description, with citations, of the conceptual tools (such as SWOT) used to help explore case details.

The analysis and discussion section is a comprehensive description of, and comment upon, the problems identified in the case. Each problem is fully described using case information. A discussion is then included in which comments are made about the problem. The relevant literature is addressed as a means of highlighting the significance of the problem or explaining it further. Citations need to be used when referring to the literature. To create links between the case and the literature, tentative statements are used to indicate that possible connections are being made. For example, you might write: 'This situation is similar to that described by ...', or 'It appears that the problem has many features in common with ...'.

Recommendations are fully described and justified.

The final section in the body presents the recommendations with full justification. It includes:

- a brief restatement of the problem
- a statement of the recommendation with full justification for it using both the literature and the case
- comprehensive details about how the recommendation should be carried out within the case context
- an assessment of the extent to which the recommendation will solve the problem in the case
- (optional) a numbered summary restatement of the recommendation.

When justifying a recommendation, explain fully why it is the best recommendation for the particular problem in the case. Give details so that it is clear exactly what needs to be done in the case situation. Also show that the recommendation has some support in the literature, by noting, with citations, why it is valued or when it has been used in a similar situation.

If a recommendation summary is included, title and number it (for example, Recommendation 1) and provide a clear summary, usually beginning with: 'It is recommended that ...' Subpoints are used (if necessary) to indicate steps in the process needed to achieve the outcome.

Example

Recommendation summary

Recommendation 1.0

It is recommended that Student X learn how to do her case study by:

- reading Chapter 8 of the textbook
- doing some initial analysis of the case using a SWOT analysis
- highlighting where she is experiencing difficulty
- asking her tutor for help with the specific difficulties.

A conclusion is essential. It provides a clear summary of all stages. It can be stronger and fuller than the summary contained in the introduction.

Different disciplines will have their own preferred way of presenting a case study. The sections outlined above are the most common. However, the order may vary. Some disciplines, for example, prefer the recommendations to follow rather than precede the conclusion. Sometimes a case study is presented in an essay format. If this is the case, it is usual to use headings. More often the case study is written in a report format. The next section outlines the general features of a report.

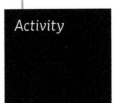

Activity

Writing up the analysis and discussion section for a case study

1   Use the case study presented in this chapter (see Activity: Reading a case study).
    Write one or two paragraphs to present an analysis and discussion of Bao Mei's
    problem of not knowing how to select and use keywords:

    a   Fully describe Bao Mei's specific problem as presented in the case study.

    b   Provide a tentative statement linking the case problem to the literature.

    c   Outline, with citations, what the literature says about this problem. Use the extract
        (in italics) published in 2004 and written by Jenny Ellis and Fiona Salisbury. It is a
        web document, and the relevant section is titled 'Keywords'. It presents results
        from a study of first year students at the University of Melbourne.

EXTRACT

*Students were asked to underline the keywords in the following essay topic: Examine
the use of suspense in Alfred Hitchcock's films* Psycho *and* Rear Window.

*Of the total group, 32 per cent were able to identify a suitable number of
appropriate keywords that would have given a sensible starting point for constructing
a search strategy. However, 31 per cent underlined too few keywords. For example,
underlining of only the words 'Examine' and 'suspense' was not considered sufficient
coverage of the topic. Twenty-eight per cent displayed a tendency to underline too
many keywords in the topic, sometimes underlining almost every word in the
sentence. Others underlined instructional words such as 'examine' and 'use of' as well
as the key concepts required for searching. Eight per cent of students did not attempt
this question.*

2   See Appendix D for a further exercise on writing the analysis and discussion of a
    case problem.

Reports

A report is a style of presentation of ideas that uses formatting and other
graphic modes of presentation to simplify reading and understanding.

You will almost certainly be asked to present some of your work at university
in a report format. A report is constructed so that reading is simplified. Instead
of using words to carry an argument, as an essay does, a report uses formatting
and other graphic devices.

All reports have three main sections, each with their own formatting features:

- preliminary matter
- report text
- endmatter.

Order of report content

The order of presentation of each of these sections in a report varies depending on the nature of the report, the practices within a discipline and even the preferences of individual lecturers. Always be guided by your lecturer. See Table 8.1 for some possible structures, but expect to find variations on these. Also, Chapter 13 provides one possible outline of the structure for a report on primary research.

Table 8.1 Some different report structures

Basic report of secondary research	Basic problem-solving case study report
Title page Table of contents Executive summary (or Abstract) 1.0 Introduction 2.0 First body section 2.1 subheading 2.2 subheading 3.0 Second body section 4.0 etc. 5.0 Conclusion Reference list	Title page Table of contents Executive summary (or Abstract) 1.0 Introduction 2.0 Background 3.0 Method 4.0 Analysis and discussion 4.1 First problem 4.2 Second problem 4.3 etc. 5.0 Recommendations (Recommendations may also be placed after the Conclusion) 6.0 Conclusion Reference list Appendices
Basic report for engineering students	**Full report**

Title page
Abstract
Disclaimer
Acknowledgments
Contents
Figures
Tables
Symbols
1.0 Introduction
2.0 First body section
    2.1 subheading
    2.2 subheading etc.
3.0 Second body section with subheadings
4.0 etc.
5.0 Conclusion
6.0 Recommendations
References
Appendices
	Title page
	Letter of transmittal
	Table of contents
	List of Illustrations and Tables
	Acknowledgments
	Executive summary
	1.0 Introduction
	2.0 First body section with recommendations if appropriate
	3.0 Second body section with recommendations if appropriate
	4.0 etc.
	5.0 Conclusion
	List of recommendations (if appropriate)
	Appendices
	Abbreviations
	Glossary
	Reference list

Note: From Report Writing. Style Guide for Engineering Students by A. Winckel, & B. Hart, 2002. University of South Australia Learning and Teaching Unit webpage.	*Note: From Style Manual. For authors, editors and printers* (pp. 236–237), 2002, Milton, Queensland: John Wiley & Sons.

The order of working on a report is different from the order of the final presentation. A report is presented with the **preliminary matter** first, but, in fact, that has to be written after the text section is completed. Thus we will begin an examination of the features of a report with those to be found in the text section.

The report text

Overall structure

The **report text** carries the content. It contains:

The report text has the same basic overall structure as an essay.

- an introduction (including background),
- body
- conclusion.

The introduction begins the report. It usually contains:

- the name and position of the person who commissioned the report (if appropriate)
- a statement of the general topic of the report
- a statement of the main purpose of the report (for example, to give recommendations)
- a description of the scope of the report (for example, what exactly the report investigated)
- background to establish a context for, and the significance of, the information in the report
- an indication of which sections are included in the report or a summary of report content.

An introduction to a report is likely to be written over a number of paragraphs. It is even possible for each part of the introduction to be given a subheading. For example, it may be written as:

1.0   Introduction (with a short paragraph saying who commissioned the report, if appropriate and indicating the general topic area)
1.1   Purpose
1.2   Scope
1.3   Background
1.4   Report outline (or Report summary).

An introduction to a report of primary research may be significantly different. See Chapter 13.

The body of the report is the largest part of the report text. It is logically organised as a number of linked sections, each of which may have subsections.

The body of the report consists of linked sections.

Each section and subsection is placed in a carefully selected and meaningful order. Its style of presentation is distinctive, and will be discussed more fully below.

The conclusion summarises the report. It can also remind the reader of the importance of the report by linking to the background. The conclusion is normally presented as one or more paragraphs, and does not have subheadings.

The presentation of recommendations is different in different reports.

Recommendations, if used, can immediately precede the conclusion section, or occur throughout the text, or follow the conclusion. The placement is determined mostly by how comprehensive the justification for the recommendations is.

If the report is lengthy (such as over 5000 words) and includes recommendations that require a full justification and explanation, this section can be placed before the conclusion and only the summary of each recommendation be placed after the conclusion. If the report is very comprehensive, recommendations are included within each relevant body section, so are not given a separate section in the report. In this case, a list of recommendations must be included after the conclusion.

On the other hand, if the report is short and the recommendations require little justification as they follow obviously from the conclusions of the report, then they may be placed after that section. Even in this situation, however, one or more paragraphs should be written to persuade the reader of the suitability of any recommendation before it is presented.

Formatting and graphic presentation of ideas and information in the report text

The report text consists of many paragraphs, all of which require the same abilities as needed in essay writing: coherence within each paragraph, a logical order indicating an argument between paragraphs, use of topic sentences and use of citations (where appropriate).

The report text uses headings, bullet points and graphic representation of information to make reading easier.

The report text also includes very distinctive features. In order to create a document that is easy to read, it uses devices that make the content highly visible, such as:

- headings and numbering
- bullet points
- graphic representation of information.

Headings are short titles for sections indicating content and order.

Headings and numbering

Each section of the report text is given a **heading** to indicate its content. To create a heading:

- name the content of the section
- use only a few words
- do not use verbs.

Headings are numbered in the report text so that the order of sections is obvious. The first level indicates the major sections within the report (such as 1.0; 2.0; 3.0). Separate subsections *within* these larger units are also numbered (such as 3.1; 3.2). It is possible to also break the text into smaller sections with a third (and even a fourth) level of heading, but this should not be attempted unless the report is quite long and complex.

Headings are formatted to produce maximum visibility. Usually a heading is on a line by itself, often in a larger font from the text and in bold. Typically the heading is aligned to the left page margin. The following should be used:

- different sized fonts for different levels of heading
- numbering to indicate the relationship between headings
- (sometimes) indentation of the text under the lowest level headings.

Creating headings

Turn each of the following sentences into a major heading or a subheading and number it, starting at 3.0.

a   This report examines internet marketing.
b   Email is sometimes used as a tool for marketing.
c   Advertisements on popular webpages are a good way to market products.

Activity

Bullet points

Bullet points allow information to be presented in a very visible manner. They use an abbreviated form of a list with each item clearly displayed. They appear simple but, in fact, require considerable skill. A bullet point list needs to be:

- well categorised and ordered (see Chapter 5)
- linked into the argument, so there is a continuity of ideas
- introduced, using part of a sentence with a colon
- written so that each point fits in grammatically with the introductory sentence (each point has a parallel structure)
- fully described in the text following the listing of points.

Typically, bullet points are linked into the argument by an introductory sentence that summarises why the list of points is being presented. As well, a partial sentence always precedes the bullet points, and provides the grammatical structure for the list. Once the bullet points have been presented,

Bullet points are used when a number of items of information can be briefly presented in a list form.

each point needs to be fully explained in the text with appropriate explanations, descriptions and examples. Good bullet points show that you are a skilful writer; however, they should be sparingly employed, for maximum impact, and not used if the content is complex.

Activity

Creating bullet points

Write bullet points with an introductory sentence for each of the following. Make sure the points are well ordered and that they grammatically fit with the introductory sentence (have a parallel structure).

1   List three ways of organising ideas.
2   List two entry paths into university.
3   List three good reasons for using bullet points.

Graphic representation of information

Graphic information presents data or ideas in a highly visible form.

Reports can and should use a range of graphic presentation of information. In reports dealing with statistical information, **tables** and **figures** are used. Tables present the information in columns and rows. Figures give a visual depiction of the information (figures include: bar charts; pie charts; graphs). **Diagrams** can also be included to give a simple graphical view of a set of relationships being discussed. All of these are normally included within the report text, though some disciplines expect them to be placed in appendices.

All forms of graphic presentation of information need to be presented professionally. Each requires:

- an identifier (such as Figure 1 or Table 1)
- a title.

Usually tables, figures and diagrams have a separate numbering system. Hence, there may be Table 1; Table 2; Figure 1; and Diagram 1. The identifier and title can be written in bold above the graphic.

Graphic information needs to be discussed within the text. Before or after presenting any illustration, explain fully what it means. Repeat, in words, the information contained in a table or figure. Refer to the graphic being discussed (for example, write: 'See Figure 2').

If you have used a graphic from a source (rather than generated it yourself), acknowledge the source below the graphic (use smaller font):

- for a journal article write: *Note.* From 'Title of article', by A. A. Author, date, *Journal Title, volume number,* p. X
- for a book write: *Note.* From *Title of book* (p. X), by A. Author, date, Place of Publication: Publisher.

Page numbering

The report text is often presented as one continuous item. Although it is divided into a number of different sections and subsections, these may not be divided by page breaks. However, some disciplines prefer that each major section begins on a new page. Be guided by your lecturer.

The report text is numbered using arabic numerals (1, 2, 3 etc.), starting with the introduction on page 1.

Preliminary matter

Overall structure

All reports contain some preliminary matter. It is material that is not part of the content and is included before the report proper (the text). Possible preliminary matter includes (the order can vary):

Preliminary matter is included before the report text.

- title page
- disclaimer
- letter of transmittal
- terms of reference
- table of contents
- list of illustrations
- acknowledgments
- abbreviations
- symbols
- executive summary (or abstract).

Content of preliminary pages

The **title page** of a report is like a title page of a book. Give your report a title, rather than just copying the question asked; provide your name(s) and student ID(s); indicate who the report is for by naming your lecturer and providing the course title, or naming the authorising person and company; and insert the date of submission of the report, which is technically called: 'date of release'. Use formatting to make the page attractive.

A **disclaimer** is occasionally added to large reports. It is a short sentence stating that the report is the work of the author(s) and is hand signed by the author(s). Typically, if a student is required to present such a disclaimer, the wording will be provided.

The **letter of transmittal** is a short business letter attached to some reports as an accompaniment. The letter is formatted using the usual layout for a business letter. As it is personal, use first and second person as appropriate. See the example below.

Example

Letter of transmittal

35 Whitlam Avenue
Canberra
ACT 2610
Telephone 6225 5907
E-mail wendysmith@anu.edu.au

← *Your address and contact details*

24 October 2024

← *Date*

Professor Iain M Banks
Department of Science Fiction
Australian National University
Canberra

← *Name and address of person to whom the report is addressed*

Dear Professor

I am pleased to present you (*provide the title of the report*).

This report (*provide a brief summary of the report's content*).

I look forward to (*indicate willingness to discuss the report or gratitude for being asked to do the report*).

Yours sincerely

Signature

Wendy Smith
Consultant

← *Your signature, name and position*

Some reports require you to address **terms of reference**. These are the areas a company or agency wishes to be covered in a report. If you are given these, copy and paste them onto a page and use a heading: Terms of reference.

Example

Terms of reference
To make recommendations on how the purposes, shape, structure, size and funding of higher education, including support for students, should develop to meet the needs of the United Kingdom over the next 20 years, recognising that higher education embraces teaching, learning, scholarship and research.

Note: Section of Terms of Reference. From *Report of the National Committee*, by The National Committee of Inquiry into Higher Education, 1997, retrieved from <www.leeds.ac.uk/educol/ncihe>.

All reports include a **table of contents**. Use a heading: either Contents or Table of contents. List the main divisions within the report, and provide their initial page numbers. The following are listed:

- all items in the front matter except the title page and the table of contents
- all major sections and subsections (with numbering and indentation)
- all endmatter.

It is usual for the titles of major sections, including their numbers if appropriate, to be lined up on the left margin. Subsection numbers and titles are often indented one tab space. Page numbers are listed on the right margin.

Examining a table of contents

Look at how the table of contents has been constructed for this book.

Activity

The list of illustrations provides a list of all graphic material in the report and the page number where each can be found. A heading is used. The term 'List of illustrations' is used when a range of different types of illustrative material is contained in the report (such as figures, diagrams, tables and photographs). If only tables and figures are used, the list can be called a List of tables and figures. If there is a range of different types of illustrations, the order of presentation is: figures; diagrams; tables. Each of these is given a separate subheading.

For each illustration include:

- identifier (for example, Figure 1)
- title
- page reference.

Format as for the table of contents.

List of Illustrations

Figure 1	Portfolio structure	9
Figure 2	Organisational chart at 30 June 2005	12
Figure 3	Portfolio outcome and Optus structure and prices	15
Table 1	Consultancy contracts for the past three financial years	71
Table 2	Summary of all consultancies by division	72

Example

Note: From *Annual Report 2004–2005* (List of Illustrations), by Australian Government. Department of Industry, Tourism and Resources, 2005, retrieved from <www.industry.gov.au/annualreport/04_05/index.html>.

In some reports the author wishes to acknowledge specific help in the production of the report. If you wish to do this use a heading (**Acknowledgments**) and write a description of the help received and acknowledge those who provided it. Clearly this is a personal note and needs to use first and second person pronouns.

Example

Acknowledgments

Acknowledgments	Comment
My thanks are due to a range of people and organisations who helped in the research.	*General introduction*
Thanks also go to my colleagues at PSI, in particular to Karen Mackinnon who undertook computer analysis.	*Particular acknowledgment of anyone helping in the project*
And finally I thank the students who took part in the survey and gave up their time to complete the questionnaires.	*Acknowledgment of those who were the subjects of the research*

Note: The National Committee of Inquiry into Higher Education. Report 2. Full and part-time students in higher education: Their experiences and expectations (Acknowledgments), by C. Callender, 1997, Retrieved from <www.leeds.ac.uk/educol/ncihe>.

A list of **abbreviations** can be included if a report uses abbreviations for significant institutions or features. For example, if the report used 'DITR' to refer to the Department of Industry, Tourism and Resources, or 'ACT' for the Australian Capital Territory, then these need to be noted in the list of abbreviations. Abbreviations for words (for example, 'e.g.') are not included. In some reports, the list of abbreviations is placed in the endmatter. In a scientific report that uses a significant number of **symbols**, a separate page should be used to list each symbol with 'definition, quantity to which the symbol refers, and the unit of measurement' (Winckel & Hart, 2002, section 3.1.8 Symbols).

All reports contain an **executive summary** (also called an abstract). The executive summary gives a succinct summary of all the sections in the report. It is mostly written in the present tense, except where it discusses actions in the past. The executive summary gives a good indication of the quality of the report. Use it to:

- state the topic area
- outline the purpose (for example, to create recommendations)
- describe the scope (the specific investigation undertaken)
- summarise the main results (or findings)
- mention the main recommendations (if included).

Page numbering

The preliminary matter is presented in a different manner from the report text. Each item is on a separate page. As well, the page numbering system is different. The preliminary matter is numbered using roman numerals (i, ii, iii, iv etc.). The title page is regarded as the first page, but is not numbered. The page following the title page is thus page ii.

Each item of preliminary matter is on a separate page.

Endmatter

Overall structure

The **endmatter** includes (the order can vary):

The endmatter is inserted after the report text.

- list of recommendations (if included)
- appendices
- glossary
- reference list.

Content of endmatter pages

If there are recommendations that are fully justified within the report text, then a list of recommendations is included on a separate page after the conclusion. If the list is very short it may be placed immediately after the conclusion. All recommendations are presented in summary form and are numbered. The most comprehensive and important recommendations are placed first.

List of recommendations

A Wholistic Approach: Gender Mainstreaming

1   That the WA government take a gender mainstreaming approach to policy and practices in its commitment to closing the gender pay gap by applying a systematic process of 'gender analysis' to existing policies and policy proposals to identify any differential impact the policy would have on each gender.

Voluntary Strategies

2   That a combination of voluntary and regulatory strategies be adopted to address the gender pay gap.

3   That employers conduct gender pay equity audits ...

4   That these audits become part of the annual reporting process.

Note: From Report on the Review of the Gender Pay Gap in Western Australia, *by T. Todd and J. Eveline, 2004, retrieved from <www.commerce.wa.gov.au/labourrelations/PDF/Publications/Gender_Pay_Final_Rep.pdf>.*

Example

Appendices are additions to the report that may be useful but would make the report too cumbersome if they were included in the text. Typically, appendices are:

- numbered using alphabetical numbering (such as Appendix A, Appendix B)
- given a title indicating the content.

If a report contains technical words, a **glossary of terms** is included. The heading Glossary is used, and the term and its full explanation listed alphabetically.

Reports must contain a correctly formatted reference list (see Chapter 4).

Example

Glossary

Term	Meaning
Accrual Accounting	The accounting basis that brings items to account as they are earned or incurred (and not as cash received or paid) and recognises them in financial statements for the related accounting period.
Administered items	Revenues, expenses, assets and liabilities that the Government controls, but which an agency or authority manages on the Government's behalf.

Note: From *Annual Report 2002–2003 (Glossary)*, by Australian Government. Department of Finance and Administration, n.d., retrieved from <www.finance.gov.au/publications/annual-reports/annualreport02-03/glossary.html>.

Page numbering

Separate pages are used for the list of recommendations, unless they are included immediately after the conclusion; each appendix; the glossary; and the reference list. Page numbering, using arabic numbers, continues from the report text section.

Activity

Examining different types of reports

1 Use an internet search engine and a search statement to find examples of different reports (search for: marketing AND report; or accounting AND report).
2 You can even search for specific features in a report (such as marketing AND report AND "executive summary").
3 Examine the reports you find to notice different report features.

Table 8.2 Summary of headings and page numbering in reports

	Format for headings	Page numbering
Preliminary matter	• larger font than text • bold	• roman numerals (i, ii, iii, iv etc.) • numbering begins at the title page
Report text	• Use a range of font sizes to indicate levels of heading • bold • numbered	• arabic numerals (1, 2, 3 etc.) • numbering begins at the Introduction
Endmatter	• larger font than text • bold • alphabetical numbering for appendices (Appendix A etc.)	• Arabic numerals • numbering continues from the report text section.

Go to our website <www.oup.com.au/orc/turner2e> for more activities on the skills covered in this chapter.

Activity

SUMMARY

In this chapter we have examined how case studies are used to test your ability to apply course information to a chaotic 'real life' situation. Skills in problem recognition and the generation of solutions have also been presented. Finally, we have described how information can be presented as a report. In particular, we noted the way reports use formatting and graphic presentation of information to make reading easy.

GLOSSARY

abbreviations shortened versions of terms, either in the form of initial capital letters ('UNESCO') or contracted versions of the words themselves ('Dip. Ed.').

acknowledgments a description of the help received by the author of a book or report, including a list of those individuals and institutions who provided it.

appendices additions to the report that may be useful, but would make the book or report too cumbersome if they were included in the text.

bullet points a brief ordered list with a parallel grammatical structure.

case study an account of a 'real life' situation used to help students learn to apply abstract theory and concepts to a particular problem.

diagrams a simple graphical view of a set of relationships.

disclaimer a statement occasionally added to large reports, stating that the report is the work of the author(s) and hand signed by the author(s).

endmatter the material placed after the conclusion of a report.

executive summary (abstract) a succinct summary of all the sections in the report.

figure a visual depiction of statistical information, such as bar charts, pie charts and graphs.

glossary an alphabetical list of all the main technical terms used in the report, plus a full explanation of each term.

headings short titles for sections indicating content and order.

letter of transmittal a short business letter attached to some reports as an accompaniment.

preliminary matter material included before the report proper (before the report text).

recommendations clear and specific statements of what needs to be done to solve some problem.

report text the content of the report from the introduction to the conclusion.

SWOT analysis reveals strengths, weaknesses, opportunities and threats of a situation (or person).

symbol non-letter or non-number used to represent words or ideas (such as '¶' for 'paragraph').

table presents statistical information in columns and rows.

table of contents a list of the main divisions within a report and the pages on which each of these starts.

terms of reference a list of the areas a company or agency wishes to be covered in a report.

timeline shows what happened, when.

title page the first page of a report, including information such as the title, name of the author(s), destination of report, and date of submission.

chapter NINE

Collaborative Learning: Working in Groups

A significant part of your learning at university involves collaboration with other students. This chapter focuses on the kinds of collaboration that you are required to participate in as part of your formal, or prescribed, learning experience. In most cases this kind of collaboration is called assessable group work.

Educational benefits of students working collaboratively are well recognised. Researchers have found that the most effective learning happens when students learn together; that is, when they help each other to learn. By working in a collaborative way students not only improve their understanding of the material they are studying, they also develop skills in working in teams or groups.

However, undertaking group work for assessment can be very challenging. By reading this chapter and putting into practice some of the suggested strategies you should be able to avoid some of the pitfalls of group work, and in the process reap the many potential benefits.

In this chapter you will find some basic information about group work to assist you to work effectively as a group member, and to help your group work towards achieving its goals. The chapter includes:

- a definition of group work, and a description of collaboration and cooperation
- an outline of the importance and benefits of studying and working in groups
- a description of the important roles that members implicitly and explicitly play when working in groups
- a description of how groups develop
- a description of some of the challenges of group work, and ways to overcome those challenges (includes conflict, social loafing and leadership)
- an overview of some of the micro processes of group work, including some tips for making the processes work.

Collaborative group work

Group work is generally defined as work (for example, activities, exercises, tasks, discussions, problem solving, presentations and projects) undertaken by a number of people all striving towards one primary goal or purpose. Group work is commonly used in courses that require judgment; for example, where there is a requirement to apply theory to real-world problems, make decisions and problem-solve. The reason group work is used in these types of tasks is because superior decisions generally result from collaborative decision-making.

Group members collaborate to help each other to learn and to succeed.

In the majority of cases, when you undertake group work you are jointly rewarded for the work completed by your group; that is, each person in the group is awarded the same mark for the one piece of work submitted. With this approach to group work, the expectation is that all group members will be dependent on one another and collaborate fully in the completion of the assessment task. Johnson, Johnson and Holubec (1998) call this 'positive interdependence'. In a relationship that is positively interdependent, you are linked to others in a group in such a way that for one person to succeed, the whole group has to succeed.

Collaboration used this way, early in your study career, can be quite challenging. In spite of this, the benefits of collaboration are expected to outweigh the difficulties, as all group members are assumed to gain from the broader learning experience.

Cooperative group work

In some cases, a group assignment may be able to be broken into distinguishable parts that can then be divided among the group members. Each member has a specific part to complete; for example, different subtopics of a research project. The final product might then be a combination of what each member has produced. In this case, one group member is usually given the responsibility of pulling the parts together into, for example, a final report. With this kind of group work all members are still generally awarded the same mark. However, their activities are more akin to cooperation rather than collaboration, and as such each student may or may not experience as broad a learning experience as if each had collaborated across the entire assignment.

In other situations, individual marks can be awarded to assessment that in the beginning starts out as group work but culminates in the submission of individual pieces of work. This can be the case, for example, with written assessment or presentations. You might be required to work with others on the research, analysis, decision-making and/or problem-solving stages of an assignment, then go your separate ways to write your individual response to the assignment. You can also each play individual parts in a presentation that has been collaboratively or cooperatively developed. In these cases you may be assigned an individual mark for your work. These latter uses of group work can reduce some of the challenges that group work poses, but can also increase the likelihood of other problems arising. Some of the challenges or problems students face when doing group work are discussed later in the chapter.

Formal and informal group work

Whether it is collaborative or cooperative group work, if it has been prescribed by your lecturer and it attracts a mark, it is considered to be **formal group work**.

Group work can also be informal. As an individual you may engage in collaboration or cooperation with class members or with friends outside of class. Groups working together this way are usually referred to as informal study groups. Students usually develop study groups so they can:

- pool resources needed for an assessment item
- clarify and discuss ideas
- share the task of collecting and recording lecture notes
- share in the development of revision material for exam preparation.

Informal group work can also be initiated by your lecturers. For example, while you are in class, your lecturer may ask you to work in a group to complete short activities, solve problems or engage in discussions. These activities may be assessed; however, in most cases they are not. In-class group activities are usually used by your lecturers to enhance the classroom learning experience for all involved. They are generally used to increase interest and creativity, and also to improve the generation of more effective ideas, information and solutions.

Benefits of group work

Group work at university is undertaken to satisfy many different teaching and learning goals. It is used to help you learn, understand and retain as much as possible of what you are taught, and to help make your learning an enjoyable and fulfilling activity.

The development of effective group work skills not only ensures greater success and satisfaction in your university study, but it also ensures greater success in obtaining and retaining satisfactory employment when you graduate. Among the many generic skills that graduates are expected to have on entering the workforce are good teamwork skills. In industry, teamwork skills are

Developing group work skills can help you educationally and professionally.

increasingly being seen as the answer to many challenges that face organisations, especially where managers are looking for maximisation of output, creativity, accuracy, efficiency, productivity and profits.

Advantages of group work:

- feelings of connectedness, engagement and inclusiveness or shared purpose, leading to higher levels of satisfaction (Davis, 1993)
- performance at higher intellectual levels (Vygotsky, 1978)
- development of effective functioning as a member of a group; that is, of good teamwork skills
- deeper and more sustained learning and understanding
- increased creativity
- access to greater amounts of information
- greater confidence in involvement and participation
- accomplishment of more (quantitatively and qualitatively) as a result of synergy
- exposure to new and different perceptions
- minimisation of errors or mistakes
- greater support from peers
- preparation for professional life (provides more of a 'real-world' experience)
- development of skills that include time management, coordination, communication, conflict resolution, organisation, negotiation, problem-solving, delegation, leadership and following.

While many of the benefits occur in any type of group work, deeper and more sustained benefits to learning and understanding, and the development of creativity and higher-level reasoning strategies, are more likely to come from formal collaborative group work.

Activity

Share your group-work experiences

Take a moment to think about your experience of working in groups. Join with your group members to share your experiences.

1   Has your past group work been more like collaboration or cooperation? Give examples.
2   In what ways has your group work been successful or enjoyable?
3   What were the challenges you faced in previous group work?

Roles people play in groups

While working in a group, each individual member usually plays one or more **roles**. A role refers to the particular behaviours or functions that a group member undertakes as he or she participates within the group. There are many roles that group members play that help the group to function effectively, and there are some roles that can prevent the group from achieving its goals.

Roles are socially recognised patterns of behaviour.

Even though there are many different roles that people can take within a group, they fall within two main types. The first includes roles that are largely implicit or informal; that is, they emerge within the group as part of the natural process of group development. These roles include *task*, *maintenance* and *dysfunctional* roles.

The second type of role is one that the group consciously or explicitly allocates to members of the group. These are *procedural* roles.

Task, maintenance and procedural roles keep the group on track and working well as a team.

Task roles

Task roles are those that are focused on achieving specific aspects of the group's goals and tend to give the group a sense of purpose and accomplishment.

Table 9.1 Characteristics of task roles

Task roles	Characteristics
Initiator	• Generates new ideas and actions
Information/opinion giver	• Gives information • States opinions
Information/opinion seeker	• Asks the group for information • Asks the group for their opinions
Elaborator/clarifier/coordinator	• Listens carefully to help to explain ideas • Asks questions to clarify ideas • Offers examples and makes links between ideas
Evaluator/critic	• Judges ideas or work produced by the group
Orienteer	• Redirects the group's thinking or work
Energiser	• Gives the group energy • Makes the group feel it can achieve
Summariser	• Restates the main ideas, decisions and plans, to keep the group on track

Note: Adapted from Benne, K., & Sheats, P. cited in *Small Group Communication*, by T. Borchers, 1999, Allyn & Bacon, Communication Studies website: <www.abacon.com/commstudies/groups/roles.html>.

Activity

Task roles

In your group, discuss:

1   What task role or roles do you recall playing within a group you have previously worked within?
2   What did you do in your task roles?
3   Were there any task role or roles you felt a group needed but were not done? How did this have an impact on the group?
4   Give positive feedback to your group members (that is, provide information that can help team members recognise their contribution to the group) on the task roles you see they are performing within your current group. See if you can:
    • name the role a team member performed
    • describe what was done that helped you recognise it as part of that role
    • comment on how that role helped the group perform their task.

Maintenance roles

Maintenance roles are those that are focused on the social aspects of the group. They help to build a cooperative and safe environment for all group members. **Maintenance roles** ensure that relationships in the group are conducive to the effective functioning of the group.

Table 9.2 Characteristics of maintenance roles

Maintenance roles	Characteristics
Encourager/supporter	• Supports the ideas and work of others • Builds group member confidence • Invites quiet members to speak
Harmoniser/mediator	• Works to resolve differences between group members
Compromiser/reconciler	• Solves disagreements and maintains harmony by making concessions (giving up some of his or her favoured ideas)
Gatekeeper	• Keeps ideas flowing (e.g. asks for clarification and advises others when the discussion drifts off track or is being dominated by a few)
Group observer	• Monitors group processes and offers feedback to the group on how the group is progressing
Follower	• Agrees with *all* group decisions

Note: Adapted from Benne, K., & Sheats, P. cited in *Small Group Communication*, by T. Borchers, 1999, Allyn and Bacon, Communication Studies website: <www.abacon.com/commstudies/groups/roles.html>.

Maintenance roles

Take a moment to think about the following questions. Then discuss your responses with your group.

1   Who do you know that would be good at being a harmoniser? Think of an example of how you have seen that person perform this kind of role. What kinds of things did that person do or say to make you think of him or her as a harmoniser? Do you think how the person behaved was effective? Perhaps that person was you!

2   What is the value of naming particular task and maintenance roles? Prepare a summary of your group position and report back to the class.

Dysfunctional roles

Not all roles within groups are functional. Some roles reduce the likelihood of the group achieving its goals, or make it very difficult for the group to function effectively. Some people refer to **dysfunctional roles** within groups as individualistic; that is, they are roles motivated by self-interest.

Table 9.3 Characteristics of dysfunctional roles

Dysfunctional roles	Characteristics
Aggressor	• Acts aggressively towards group members by criticising or blaming • Makes other group members feel inadequate or wrong or inferior
Blocker	• Interferes with the group's progress
Rebel	• Breaks group norms (expected ways of behaving) and refuses to cooperate
Self-seeker (includes: recognition seeker/show-off/lobbyist/help seeker)	• Tries to make him- or herself the centre of the group's focus. Attempts to achieve personal goals ahead of the group's goals • Tries to grab the group focus by taking no responsibility and *always* asking for help
Dominator	• Tries to control the group through any means, for example, by using flattery, or fear, or bullying/aggression • May give directions abruptly, or interrupt when others are speaking
Social loafer/free loader/hitchhiker	• Lacks commitment to the group, makes few or no contributions (see explanation outlined later in the chapter)

Note: Adapted from Benne, K., & Sheats, P. cited in *Small Group Communication*, by T. Borchers, 1999, Allyn and Bacon, Communication Studies website: <www.abacon.com/commstudies/groups/roles.html>.

Activity

Dysfunctional roles

In your group discuss dysfunctional roles. Consider:

1 What happened in any group you have been a member of, if someone played a dysfunctional role? (Give examples from your own experience.)
2 What would you do if any member showed dysfunctional behaviours in a group?
3 Each of the dysfunctional roles has a useful aspect. What could be useful in each of the dysfunctional roles above?
4 What could you do to encourage a person playing a dysfunctional role to use his or her insights and energy in a productive manner?

Procedural roles

Procedural roles are explicitly adopted by group members.

Whether roles develop explicitly or implicitly, everyone in a group plays a role. A well-organised group usually formally or explicitly allocates some roles for group members; in particular those that are procedural in nature. **Procedural roles** are important pragmatic roles that help the group to achieve its goals. They need to be decided early in the life of the group. Group members who are allocated procedural roles rely heavily on the assistance of those that undertake implicit task and maintenance roles.

Table 9.4 Characteristics of procedural roles

Procedural roles	Characteristics
Leader/coordinator/chairperson	• Takes responsibility for overseeing, managing and guiding structure, purpose, roles and responsibilities within the group • Sets the agenda of meetings and ensures the group keeps to the agenda • Establishes and maintains a positive group environment
Recorder/secretary	• Takes notes and keeps a record of group actions, decisions and plans • Reminds group members of meeting times
Technical support	• Provides resources and access to resources needed by the group (e.g. obtains any electronic equipment that the group might need, such as tape recorders, computer equipment) • Completes practical tasks for the group (e.g. copies resources for the whole group, navigates computer software when others are not familiar with it)
Diplomat	• Reminds group members of work that is due • Follows up on members who have not completed their work • Encourages and supports any member who is having trouble with his or her work • Involves the whole team in deciding what to do when work cannot be completed

Finding what roles suit you best
Go to our website <www.oup.com.au/orc/turner2e> and use the Group Roles Inventory to identify the role that best suits you when working in a group.

Activity

How groups develop

Groups that come together formally to achieve a particular goal usually go through a number of stages in their development. The four stages are: forming, storming, norming and performing (Tuckman, 1965).

Groups pass through four stages of development: forming, storming, norming and performing.

Forming

During the **forming** stage, members are getting to know one another. They are usually polite and reserved, and there is often quite a bit of uncertainty about the goals of the group and the roles that people will play. In spite of the uncertainty, there is little overt conflict or disagreement over what is discussed. Criticism is avoided or kept to a minimum, and any decisions that are made about the goals of the group and how it is to function are for the most part tentative.

Figure 9.1 Group development

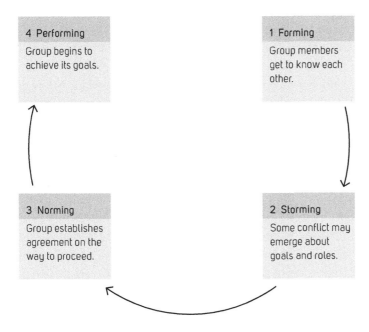

At this stage in the development of the group it is very important to focus on developing effective social relationships within the group. The group's social relationships are just as important as the task. When your group first comes together, as you are getting to know each other, it might be useful to remind everyone of the importance of keeping an eye on how the group is working together as well as keeping an eye on the task. In your first meeting, talk about the stages of group development and acknowledge the difficulties that the group might experience. Share your experiences of group work and talk about ways to avoid the pitfalls of group work.

At this stage, group members can help the group move forward by:

- getting to know group members
- getting to know the group task
- looking for procedures the group can use to help group functioning (see 'Meetings: setting up the group', on pages 212–213)
- setting out expectations for group behaviour (see 'Creating a safe-ideas climate', on pages 214–215);
- suggesting ways to organise the work.

Storming

Conflict sometimes arises once a group begins decision-making. This is the **storming** stage. At this point in the group's development the uncertainty of the forming stage is still present, but individuals are more willing to express their disagreement about how the group should function and what the aims of the group should be.

Group members need to work together to resolve the conflicts experienced in the storming stage. Conflict that is managed well in this stage usually results in decisions that serve the group well as a foundation for effective group processes. The section on 'Managing group work challenges' below describes a number of skills that are useful in dealing with conflict within a group.

Norming

After passing through the storming stage, groups usually move into the **norming** stage. This is when the group unites and rallies with a spirit of collaboration, cooperation and coordination, and consolidates the commonly understood procedures and guidelines that either endured or emerged as new during the storming stage. Communication at this point tends to be more positive, with members feeling more secure with their place and role within the group. Effective groups begin to express viewpoints openly and respectfully, and ideas and opinions are listened to in an active and productive way.

Performing

With a common view of the goals of the group and the ways in which the group is to achieve them, the group automatically moves into the **performing** stage. Members productively and supportively engage in tasks that more effectively achieve the group's goals. It is at this stage that the benefits of collaboration, or working as a group, really become clear.

The single iteration of the cycle, which incorporates the four stages of group development as has just been described, of course is the ideal. There is no guarantee that if your group reaches the performing stage, group interaction will be straightforward and trouble free. Once at the performing stage, problems can emerge, and where they do your group may find itself back in the storming stage. If problems do arise in the performing stage it is likely that they are by-products of problems not fully resolved in the storming and norming stages.

Managing group work challenges

Because of the well-known benefits of group work, you will no doubt find yourself undertaking at least one or two formal group work assignments each semester. However, while there are obvious benefits to be gained from group work, it is not always easy. The skills needed to make teams work can take a long time to develop. As well, no matter how skilled you may be, all groups are likely to experience difficulties as a natural part of group development. Moreover, other members may not have either the skill or interest to support good group working.

There are three main reasons that groups fail or are not as successful as they could be: conflict, social loafing and a lack of leadership. In this section we examine these challenges and consider ways they may be overcome.

Conflict

Conflict within groups can be caused by many things. For example, it can come about as a consequence of misunderstandings about roles and responsibilities, personality clashes, cultural misunderstandings and uncooperative behaviour, or simply as a symptom of the stress and frustration that can come from trying to balance the demands of study, work and life.

Conflict is a very natural part of all groups. It can occur at any time. However, as outlined earlier, it typically occurs in the storming stage of group development, and sometimes in the performing stage. During this stage, disagreements and criticisms emerge over such things as values, perspectives, goals, power and roles.

If conflict does occur in your group it can be very dysfunctional. If it is allowed to escalate (for example, by gossip, isolation of group members or antagonism) it is likely to result in reduced output from the group, a lack of creativity and a hostile and unpleasant group environment. Ignoring or avoiding conflict can also result in similar outcomes.

Conflict, however, can also be a healthy and creative aspect of group work. Conflict can result in a greater understanding of the issues being contested and the problems being investigated. Drucker (1977), for example, believes that when there is a clash of opinions competing alternatives can be seriously considered, which results in better outcomes and those involved gain a greater appreciation of the issues.

When conflict does arise in your group, you should aim to involve all group members in any attempt to overcome the negative impacts and to maximise the possibility of a positive outcome. Managing conflict so that it does not impact too negatively on the group is difficult. It takes a conscious effort and good communication skills.

Activity

Handling conflict

Before moving on, take a moment to discuss the following points with your group, and then share a summary of your conclusions with the class.

1   Each group member should think of an experience he or she has had where engaging in conflict rather than avoiding it has resulted in positive outcomes.
2   Discuss how the conflict was handled so that those involved benefited.

Preventing and dealing with conflict: key communication skills

Effective collaboration that turns conflict into positive outcomes requires communication skills that include active listening and respectful open communication. It also requires attitudes and attributes that include mutual trust, tolerance and sensitivity to different values, especially when you are working in mixed cultural groups.

Preventing and dealing with conflict: effective listening

Conflict can lead to positive outcomes when you use good communication skills.

Good listening skills are very important in dealing with conflict and ensuring an effective collaborative relationship. Most people consider themselves good listeners; however, in truth, listening is not easy. Many of us hear, but do not listen.

Listening involves two main aspects:

- receiving a message without distraction
- understanding the message that has been sent.

The second aspect identified above is what really distinguishes listening from hearing. When we listen for understanding, we are said to be actively listening. This form of listening is particularly useful when there is conflict. **Active listening** is partly about giving the speaker feedback about what we have understood him or her to say, and partly about seeking more information to check our understanding of what the person has said.

Active listening leads to better understanding.

Active listening involves three main behaviours:

- attending: focusing on the person who is speaking;
- encouraging: inviting the speaker to provide more detail about what he or she thinks and feels
- reflecting: checking your understanding of what the speaker has said by restating what he or she has said and/or asking for more information.

Effective active listening can be used to improve interpersonal communication and reduce conflict, and is particularly effective in groups.

Practise your listening skills

In your group, prepare a short report on Australian culture.

1   Discuss the topic, making sure that all opinions are listened to well.
2   Make sure all ideas are fully explored.
3   Use the listening skills of attending, encouraging and reflecting.
4   Report your findings to the class.

Activity

Preventing and dealing with conflict: assertiveness

All group members, in spite of their role in the group, need to be *assertive* (have respectful open communication) in their interactions with other members of their group. Being assertive can overcome two communication barriers: passivity and aggression.

When group members behave passively, they may not be respecting their own right to express an opinion. In addition, they may not be showing respect for the rights of others to hear all possible opinions. By being passive the whole group may be disadvantaged. If you have an idea or an opinion, express it openly, as it may lead to more effective outcomes for the group.

Aggressive behaviours can also be equally as disadvantageous for the group. When individuals speak or behave aggressively they demonstrate a lack of respect for those they are communicating with. Aggressive behaviour can cause other group members to feel frustrated and alienated, which may lead to reduced collaboration and second-rate problem-solving.

Use the principles of assertiveness to help avoid conflict.

For some people **assertiveness** comes naturally. They speak their ideas confidently and respectfully. Others are shy or they speak and act aggressively. For those in the latter group it is useful to keep the following key aspects of assertiveness in mind when working in groups.

Assertive group behaviours include:

- open expression (sharing your ideas confidently)
- respectful disagreement
- respect for your own rights
- respect for the rights of others
- respect for the interests of the group as a whole.

Assertiveness is not an easy skill, but it is one of the key behaviours of effective collaboration. If at all times you are guided by the five basic principles of assertiveness in groups, then you should be able to speak and act so that you deal with conflict well.

For example, the following statement is what an assertive group member might say or think before giving an opinion that is different from the opinions of others in the group.

> I understand that within the group there may be a variety of views on this topic; however, I believe that the group would benefit from a consideration of all views before a decision is made. Let us listen to everyone's views and think about their pros and cons before making a decision. My opinion is …

This statement recognises the speaker's right to an opinion; it also recognises the rights of others in the group that may want to have a say, and it recognises that the group would benefit from all ideas being heard before any action is taken. As you become better at being assertive you will not need to speak about the assertive attitude, you will just state your opinion with confidence and respect.

Thinking

Stop here for a moment. Take this opportunity to think about a situation where you might have been more assertive in your interactions with another person. Think about how you did handle the situation. If you had been more assertive, what would you have said or done?

Preventing and dealing with conflict: intercultural competence

Not everyone thinks and acts the same. It is important to remember this when we work in monocultural groups, and even more important when we work in multicultural groups. Cultural misunderstandings can be the cause of some group conflict. However, it is impossible for each of us, in a short time, to fully understand the cultures of the individuals we might work with in a group. We can strive to be more **interculturally competent**, however, and by following some key principles we may be able to avoid some of the misunderstandings that can lead to conflict.

You can become more interculturally competent by:

- valuing diversity
- understanding your own culturally specific attitudes, values and assumptions
- understanding how your actions impact on individuals from other cultures
- using effective interpersonal communication skills such as active listening and assertiveness.

Using effective communication skills early in the life of the group is the best way to prevent and deal with conflict. However, if you are faced with a particularly serious conflict within your group, and your attempts to solve the conflict with respectful open expression and active listening have failed, it is recommended that you ask your tutor for some help.

Preventing and dealing with conflict: moving towards consensus

Preventing the negative outcomes of conflict is just as important as managing conflict so that it contributes positively to the group. It is important for all group members to feel confident to express their opinions. However, when there is a range of different opinions on an issue, groups need to be able to navigate their way towards a consensus. A **consensus** is where all group members consider different ideas and either agree on a preferred option, or agree on a new, more effective option.

A consensus method of conflict resolution and problem-solving takes time and some skill. However, it is well worth the effort. Advice on how to achieve consensus can be found later in this chapter under 'Managing micro processes: making decisions and solving problems'. Other methods of decision-making can be a lot less effective. For example, with a 'majority rule' method, where group members select and vote for the best of a range of conflicting opinions or options, commitment to the outcome can be reduced. With this method a small number (a minority) of group members may not be happy with the final decision and may silently withdraw or become alienated from the decision and the group, or worse still, they may even sabotage attempts to achieve the goal agreed to by other group members.

Social loafing

Another very common problem that can occur within group work is '**social loafing**' (otherwise known as 'freeloading' or 'hitchhiking'). Social loafing is when one or more members of a group fail to contribute fairly towards the group's goals. There are a number of explanations for social loafing, including poor motivation, alienation and laziness.

Table 9.5 Reasons for social loafing

Poor motivation	Some students may not feel very motivated working in groups because they believe their individual contributions will not be evaluated (Karau & Williams, 1993)
Alienation	Some students may disengage from or feel alienated within a group because their initial ideas were rejected and they don't feel their contributions will be appreciated
Laziness	Students who are lazy can get away with it because with group work it is much harder to detect levels of contribution because often other members of the group will compensate for the lack of effort of a few

Social loafing is less likely to occur in group work that requires each group member to submit his or her own individual final response to the assignment after initially working as a group on earlier phases of the task. However, with this kind of group work, social loafing can take the form of collusion. A student may use too much of the work of another student and submit it as his or her own work.

Social loafing and collusion, however, do not have to be an outcome of group work. One method that your lecturer may use to detect social loafing, especially where it is a result of laziness, is the use of peer evaluation.

Avoiding social loafing: peer evaluation
There are two main ways that a lecturer might implement **peer evaluation** within group work.

- *At the end of a project*: each group member submits an evaluation report on each person within the group that can be used by the lecturer to award marks fairly. By using this kind of peer evaluation, social loafers do not unfairly benefit from the efforts of others.

- *During a project*: progressive peer evaluation can be used to intervene early, demonstrating the probable consequences of social loafing on individual marks if members continue to over rely on the efforts of others. This could encourage a social loafer to change his or her behaviour. Early evaluation of this kind can also be useful to uncover other dysfunctional factors that may be at play in the group before the group gets too far into a project.

Go to our website <www.oup.com.au/orc/turner2e> to see an example of a peer evaluation questionnaire that your lecturer might use in your group work.

Avoiding social loafing: encouraging commitment

From the beginning, however, to avoid social loafing and collusion you must ensure that at all times each group member feels that the group's goals are important and that his or her contribution is valued. You can do this by:

- assigning each group member a meaningful task that is clearly important to achieving the group's goal
- as much as possible, ensuring group members get a choice as to which tasks they would prefer to undertake; then they will feel more obliged to the group and more likely to contribute fairly to the outcome (Rothwell, 2004)
- encouraging and supporting all group members, particularly if they are experiencing difficulties
- checking on progress (see section 'Meetings: performing tasks, and monitoring progress').

Meaningful tasks help to keep group members engaged in the group.

If members of your group have felt engaged in the group work and the group has generated some effective outcomes, they are likely to feel more committed to the group and more confident and willing to contribute equitably to a group product or an individual component of a group assignment. Greater commitment and confidence will in most cases also reduce the temptation for collusion.

Lack of leadership

The role of the group leader or coordinator is a very important one. This is especially true for group tasks being undertaken by first-year university or college students. Groups that do not have adequate leadership often face considerable difficulty achieving their objectives.

Leaderless groups often lack:

- direction
- discipline

- structure
- cohesion
- organisation
- a suitable plan for achieving objectives.

It usually takes the direction and guidance of a leader for groups to successfully identify and define the goals of the group as well as effectively allocate and coordinate the tasks needed to achieve the goals. Leaders can also be useful in monitoring interactions within the group and intervening where necessary to facilitate the maintenance of an environment conducive to effective group performance.

Avoiding a leaderless group: choosing a leader

The less experienced you are with working in groups, the more important it is to formally designate a leader for your group. As you become more experienced you may not need to formalise leadership in your group. The more experienced you and your fellow group members become with working in groups, the more likely it will be that leadership functions within the group will be shared.

Choose your leader early to help give your group some direction.

The group leader should be formally designated early in the life of the group, preferably during the forming stage of the group's development. When a leader is chosen early, he or she can help guide the group through the rough storming stage of the group's development. A group leader can be chosen by the group members themselves, or the lecturer. Leaders chosen by the group are likely to be more readily accepted by the group, and go on to successfully lead the group to task completion.

During the group's first meeting, group members can nominate others or themselves and then take a vote to elect the group's choice. This voting approach requires some preparation; in particular, candidates need to have an opportunity to describe to their group their suitability for the role. As part of the 'getting to know you' stage of group formation, group members could be asked to describe their prior experiences with group work and their particular expertise related to the group work task. All group members then have a chance to decide who they would have confidence in as a leader for their group.

Avoiding a leaderless group: leadership functions

As you can imagine, the role of leader is not easy. Not only is the leader responsible for the effective functioning of the group, he or she is also required to participate fully in the group as a regular group member. Balancing leadership functions while participating as an equal in discussions and tasks takes skill. However, if other members of the group share the load by taking on necessary tasks and maintenance roles, the burden on the leader can be reduced. Some of the do's and do nots associated with group leadership are outlined in Table 9.6.

As a consequence of the power that comes with the role of leader, other group members may look to you for guidance. Your behaviour can have both a positive and negative influence on the actions of your fellow group members (for example, arriving and leaving meetings on time, interrupting and supporting). Modelling good group work behaviours (using good behaviours yourself as an example for others) is an important characteristic of good leadership.

Table 9.6 Leadership do's and do nots

Leadership do's	Leadership do nots
As a group leader you need to ensure that: • open and frequent effective communication is maintained • an agreed aim for the group work is established • all group members are given a chance to express their views • mutual respect, understanding and trust are fostered • all group members are committed to the goals of the group • there are clear roles and responsibilities for each participant • participants feel a part of the process and the outcome • group meetings stay on track with established agendas • records are kept of decisions made by the group	As a group leader you need to: • avoid dominating rather than facilitating group process • be careful not to impose your own ideas on other members of the group • avoid having a say, or at least the final say, on everything that is said and done within the group • avoid being the only one to answer questions raised in the group

DO YOU THINK YOU HAVE WHAT IT TAKES TO BE A LEADER?
Complete the Leadership Skills Inventory in the resource kit for lecturers to see if you have leadership tendencies.

Activity

Managing micro processes

Overcoming the challenges that can disrupt group work can take a considerable amount of time and effort. However, if your group follows some of the basic guidelines outlined above you are likely to avoid, or at least reduce the impact that some of the challenges can have on your group. However, these challenges are not the only issues that your group needs to focus its attention on. There are

Manage your group by paying attention to the micro processes.

other matters beyond dealing with conflict, social loafing and leadership that need to be considered.

Micro processes are the administrative and procedural activities needed within a group to create maximum efficiency. Micro processes include:

- managing meetings
- setting up the group
- performing tasks and monitoring progress
- dividing the work
- creating a project timeline
- creating a safe-ideas climate
- creating a productive group
- making decisions and solving problems
- dealing with dysfunctional behaviour
- finalising and pulling the project together.

Paying attention to micro processes and making sure they are managed well can mean the difference between an effective group and a group that is not so effective. Micro processes encompass the general organisation and management of group time and tasks, as well as the additional strategic and behavioural do's and do nots that are useful in overcoming some of the common pitfalls within groups. With micro processes we start from the very beginning.

Meetings: setting up the group

In your early meetings your group is subject to the conditions described in the forming stage of group development. There is likely to be some uncertainty about how to act and what to do. In spite of this, aim to achieve a few basic outcomes that will help you set up an efficient working group. You will probably use two meetings to cover the following goals:

- spend time getting to know your fellow group members
- exchange contact details
- clarify group purpose, goals, objectives, due dates, resources and assessment criteria
- negotiate procedural roles (leader, recorder, technical supporter and diplomat)
- establish a realistic and responsible project time line (see the following section)
- negotiate and decide upon the division of work (see the following section)
- negotiate and decide on a meeting schedule (based on such factors as each member's availability and location)

- decide on the processes to be used in subsequent meetings (for example, processes for decision-making, conflict resolution and dealing with non-working members)
- establish expectations for member behaviour (include expectations about meeting attendance and task completion)
- ensure the 'recorder' takes minutes of the proceedings
- set an agenda (a list of items to be dealt with at a meeting) for your next meeting.

Meetings: performing tasks and monitoring progress

As your group develops, your meetings will be very task orientated. In these meetings, guided by your group leader, your group should aim to follow the procedures below:

- refer to the agenda to note what items are to be addressed in the meeting
- briefly remind yourselves of the decisions made in the previous meeting
- check group progress against plans and the established project timeline
- organise support for any member having difficulty
- establish an agenda for the next meeting
- record the minutes of the meeting
- finish the meeting on time
- evaluate the effectiveness of your meeting.

Dividing the work

Ensuring that group members are assigned an equal distribution of the tasks is an important aspect of the success of a project. However, the **division of work** does not just involve breaking the project up into equal parts. The division of work can have an impact on the level of commitment that a group member feels towards the group, and therefore possibly encourage or discourage social loafing. As outlined earlier in the chapter, in order to encourage commitment, group members need to be assigned tasks that are meaningful and preferably ones they have had some part in choosing. To divide up the work effectively you need to:

- identify and list all necessary tasks and define their significance in terms of the overall project
- be very specific with what the group expects from each member for each task (general comments like 'review the literature' are not specific enough)
- estimate how long the task should take—set deadlines

- negotiate tasks with group members around personal weaknesses, strengths and preferences
- divide the tasks up fairly between members
- provide group support (feedback) for all tasks, whether completed individually or jointly
- review the list at a later point to ensure all tasks have been identified correctly at the start (you may need to renegotiate tasks and deadlines)
- ensure that the group oversees the creation of the complete project (see the following section on 'Finalising and pulling the project together').

If a member of your group leaves part of the way through your project, your group may have to renegotiate the way that work has been divided up. If a member leaves towards the end of the project, and has not contributed very much towards the project by the time they leave, you may have to renegotiate project expectations with your lecturer.

Creating a project timeline

All group projects should be guided by a plan. Once the goals of the group have been determined, and decisions made as to who will do what, the group needs to negotiate a timeline that can guide actions. For it to be effective, the timeline needs to:

- be realistic
- consider all opportunities and constraints (time, resources and skill)
- involve everyone in the decision-making
- align with imposed project deadlines
- build in flexibility.

Our website <www.oup.com.au/orc/turner2e> contains a project timeline sheet that you might like to use to help your group to establish a realistic and practical timeline.

Creating a safe-ideas climate

Effective meetings rely on a safe climate within the group that encourages open expression and testing of ideas. Managing and maintaining a safe-ideas climate relies heavily on the effectiveness of those undertaking the types of group maintenance and task roles outlined earlier in the chapter. Effective engagement of these roles creates and maintains a safe-ideas climate that encourages:

- effective brainstorming processes (all ideas welcome, with evaluation and constructive criticism left until all ideas have been shared)
- contribution and involvement

- respect and valuing of opinions
- support and encouragement of others
- the valuing of different perspectives.

Creating a productive group: making decisions and problem-solving

Good problem-solving and decision-making is the key to the success of the group. Collaborative problem-solving is what group work is about, so if you fail to get problem-solving processes right, then you are likely to end up with an inferior group outcome. Effective problem-solving involves all group members in the following processes:

- defining and clarifying the problem
- gathering all the facts and understanding their relationship to the issue or problem
- thinking about and suggesting possible options and solutions
- considering and comparing the advantages and disadvantages of each option or solution
- selecting the best option
- deciding how to best implement or achieve the chosen option.

When your group gets stuck, confused or off course, the best solution is to:

- identify and acknowledge the process problem (for example, we are stuck, confused or off course) and explore possible reasons
- make explicit the meeting objectives as outlined in the agenda
- acknowledge time constraints
- restate the content problem (ask: 'What are the issues being explored?')
- summarise the progress up to that point
- ask for an indication of agreement or disagreement
- ask for suggestions and alternative views
- take a break.

Dealing with dysfunctional behaviour

It is rare to experience group work that is not disrupted with some kind of dysfunctional behaviour or another. The ways to avoid and to deal with dysfunctional behaviour are to:

- establish expectations about appropriate behaviour (or ground rules) early in the life of the group
- decide early how as a group you will deal with dysfunctional behaviour

- don't make assumptions about an individual's behaviour (for example, don't say: 'It is just because X is lazy')
- avoid personal attacks (don't say 'X is lazy', but say 'X has not yet submitted his or her work')
- tell the person about the problem by clearly describing his or her behaviour and saying what impact it is having on the functioning of the group
- give the individual an opportunity to explain and correct his or her behaviour
- offer support
- if necessary, penalise the member (for example, by revealing the lack of effort in the peer review) but do so in a fair and equitable manner (after all the procedures above have been attempted)
- seek assistance from your tutor if you are unable to deal with the problem
- be prepared to exclude the individual if the behaviour threatens the effectiveness of the group.

Finalising and pulling the project together

Preparing the final product for submission is always difficult. If your group has merely cooperated in the gathering of information and largely been able to undertake separate and distinguishable parts of a project, the task of pulling it all together into one assignment is less difficult.

On the other hand, if you have engaged in a more collaborative process and involved all group members in a full experience of the project elements, the task of presenting one coherent product is more difficult. Depending on how you have divided up the work, and depending on what your final product is expected to look like (essay, report or presentation), you might think about the following tips:

- before anyone begins to finalise elements of the project you need to meet as a group at least once to discuss final direction
- each group member then needs to keep in touch with at least one other member of the group to have that person look over drafts
- before submission, time needs to be put aside for everyone to review all elements of the project to ensure consistency and coherency
- once the group is happy with the different parts of the project, one person should be chosen to integrate the parts into a final product, adding an introduction and an agreed conclusion
- finally, each group member should read the final draft before it is submitted.

Go to our website <www.oup.com.au/orc/turner2e> for more activities on the skills covered in this chapter.

Activity

SUMMARY

Group work involves a number of people working together to achieve a common goal. Group work can be collaborative or cooperative. Working in groups in your study provides you with experiences that result in better educational and professional outcomes. However, in spite of the benefits of group work, it can be very challenging.

Research has shown that groups develop in a typical manner. Development tends to follow four main stages: forming, storming, norming and performing. Within groups individuals undertake different roles. Some roles, for example, procedural roles, are explicit, while others are implicit. Implicit roles include task, maintenance and dysfunctional roles.

At different stages in group development, and while undertaking different roles, groups and participants experience various challenges. Some of these challenges include conflict, social loafing and leadership issues. By ensuring that participants engage in effective communication behaviours, such as assertiveness and active listening, and employ proactive strategies, most significant group challenges can be overcome.

Successful group work also relies on groups following some key guidelines. The micro processes that make up everyday group functioning can also have an impact on the effectiveness of group work. Managing micro processes is an essential element of group work. You can not leave these processes to chance. When you take a formal approach to managing the tasks and interactions within your group you will have a greater chance of success.

GLOSSARY

active listening listening for understanding; messages are heard without distraction and checked for accuracy.

aggressive behaviour communicating without respect for the listener; which can involve speaking loudly and angrily, interrupting others and manipulating the conversation.

assertiveness the expression of your opinions and ideas in an open and respectful manner.

consensus agreement after consideration of different ideas and opinions.

division of work assigning an equal distribution of tasks among group members.

dysfunctional roles individualistic, self-motivated roles that reduce the likelihood of the group achieving its goals.

formal group work work or tasks undertaken by a group that attracts a mark or grade.

forming the first stage of group development, where group members are getting to know each other.

group work work (for example, activities, exercises, tasks, discussions, problem-solving, presentations and projects) undertaken by a number of people all striving towards one primary goal or purpose.

intercultural competence the degree to which a person values diversity, and how aware each is of his or her own culture, and how each person's values and attitudes have an impact on other cultural groups.

maintenance roles roles that are focused on the social aspects of the group. They help to build a cooperative and safe environment for all group members.

micro processes the administrative and procedural activities needed within a group to create maximum efficiency.

norming the third stage of group development, where a group establishes agreement on the ways to move forward to accomplish its goals.

peer evaluation method of evaluation that allows members of a group to assess the quality and effectiveness of their own behaviour as well as that of others in the group.

performing the fourth stage of group development, where a group starts to achieve its stated goals and objectives.

procedural roles pragmatic roles that help the group to achieve its goals.

project timeline a plan of action outlining tasks to be completed and expected deadlines.

roles socially recognised patterns of behaviour.

social loafing the term given to a situation where one or more members of a group fails to contribute fairly towards the group's goals.

storming the second stage of group development, where conflict can emerge about goals and roles.

task roles roles that are focused on achieving specific aspects of the group's goals. Task roles tend to give the group a sense of purpose and accomplishment.

chapter TEN

Presentations

Presentations are one of the most powerful ways of giving information to others. Yet many students experience anxiety when they have to present. You can learn how to manage this form of assessment, even if you feel it is daunting. After all, the very fact that you are a university student means that already you have demonstrated courage and engaged in risks.

This chapter provides a repertoire of strategies allowing you to develop your personal 'comfort zone' so that you can engage effectively in oral presentations. You will find out how to:

- create an informative presentation:
  - organise the delivery of the content
  - write outline points and scripts
  - get to know the presentation
  - get to know the presentation environment
  - attend to delivery
  - practise the presentation
  - cope with anxiety
- give a team presentation
- lead a discussion.

The art of presentations

Oral presentations are one of the most active forms of involvement in learning at university. In presentations you are able to use your voice and your body to help convey your understanding of a topic. Yet, you do not have to become the quintessential performer to be successful. The content is still the main focus; the delivery is merely the means of supporting the content.

A presentation, like all assessment, requires good content. The presentation topic needs to be thoroughly researched, and your ideas conceptualised clearly.

The development of content is crucial, as a lecturer assesses your reading, understanding and interpretation of the topic, as being of equal, if not greater importance, than how you deliver it. A well-researched, thought out and ordered presentation forms a solid foundation for the delivery of your material.

However, presentations do need to be effectively delivered in order to convey the message in the most powerful way possible. Certainly, differences exist within and between disciplines on what is the acceptable delivery style for a presentation. Some disciplines emphasise content, and suggest an almost newsreader approach be adopted. Other disciplines expect a solid display of oral techniques. No matter what style of presentation is expected of you, a presentation has to be delivered so that the audience can understand the material.

The informative presentation

The main type of presentation at university is the informative presentation. It is used when the purpose is the delivery of information, for example, when:

- presenting a report
- providing details and information on a specific topic
- giving a tutorial or seminar paper.

Organising the structure of the presentation

A presentation follows the traditional pattern of organisation of ideas and information, modified slightly because of the oral format. The organisational structure is:

- introduction
- body
- conclusion
- question time.

Introduction

In the introduction the focus or theme of your presentation is strongly and clearly stated. Some background information is included to help the audience understand the topic. An overview of the argument in your presentation is provided to help the audience 'tune in' to the presentation.

Use the introduction to engage the audience in the presentation topic.

The introduction for a presentation also uses techniques to engage the audience in the presentation topic. Aim to help the audience listen to the presentation content by creating interest in the topic.

Begin strongly by using:

- a good quotation
- surprising statistics or information
- a question (see 'Engaging the audience' section later in this chapter).

Body

The body of the presentation conveys all the main points. While these have been referred to briefly in the introduction, in the body they are developed with details, explanations, reasons and other forms of evidence. It is even more important to sequence your information logically in an oral presentation than in a written text. A listener, unlike a reader, cannot go back over some earlier concepts. Thus it is crucial to present your argument in a thoughtful, easy-to-follow format (Anholt, 1994; Reinhart, 2002). If your presentation delivers information in a step-by-step process your audience will follow your ideas.

Any of the structures available for organising information can be used. However, you are most likely to employ the following overall structures:

Ask: Will the audience be able to follow my line of thinking?

- *historical*: information is organised in terms of time
- *project oriented*: information is given in the order: aim, methodology, results, implications
- *cause and effect*: organised as: problem/issue and outcomes/results; and, possibly, implications/solutions.

All ideas and information that come from the literature need to be cited. This is done slightly differently in a presentation than in a written form of assessment.

To acknowledge sources in a presentation:

Acknowledge sources to establish credibility.

- Always use your own words; otherwise you are plagiarising
- Provide citations where appropriate:
  - verbally, in a conversational form, for example, by saying: 'Smith has some interesting ideas about …', or
  - visually, for example, by placing a citation in the lower right-hand corner of a slide
- Use a few quotations and tell the audience what you are doing:
  - verbally, for example, by saying: 'Here are Smith's own words '…', or
  - visually, for example, by having the quotation, with quotation marks and citation, on a slide.

Conclusion

The conclusion is an important part of a presentation. At times, presenters reach this point and simply finish their seminar with no real ending. However, to maintain a strong presentation a good conclusion needs to be made.

A conclusion should contain the following elements:

Conclude strongly.

- a summary of key points
- a concluding statement to the topic (a memorable statement that summarises or encapsulates your whole presentation)

- a future statement giving future projections, possible choices or responses, or likely outcomes (if appropriate)
- a statement of ending clearly acknowledging the end of the presentation and thanking participants.

Question time

Question time follows immediately after the conclusion. It allows members of the audience to clarify their ideas or to make additional comments. The aim is to allow some space for audience participation, but not to let it detract from your presentation. Do not ask the audience questions.

Question time encourages audience involvement.

To conduct question time:

- Ask the audience if there are any questions
- If a number of audience members indicate they wish to ask a question, select one
- Thank the person for the question and, if the whole audience may not have heard it, repeat it
- Provide a good, clear and succinct answer to the whole audience
- If you don't know the answer, say so
- Ask again for a question
- If there are no further questions (wait only about four seconds), thank the audience
- Make a strong concluding statement to your whole presentation
- Stand confidently and accept the applause.

Table 10.1 Managing difficulties in question time

Difficulty	Managing the difficulty
There are no questions	• Ensure you have a question by organising beforehand for a classmate to ask one • Finish the presentation strongly; give a concluding statement and thank the audience
An audience member is asking too many questions, or trying to engage you in a conversation	• Answer the first question clearly • Address the whole audience in your answer • If there is a second question from the same person, answer that, but also say to the person that you are happy to discuss the issue further after the presentation • Select a different audience member to ask a question • If there are no other questions, then conclude the presentation strongly

Organising the delivery of content for a presentation

In giving a presentation, the delivery has to be organised. The main features are:

- timing
- audience engagement
- resources.

Timing

Presentations are organised in terms of time, rather than word count. Often there are penalties imposed if the set time limit is not adhered to. As a guide, plan your presentation so that the introduction is one-sixth of the time; the body two-thirds; and the conclusion the final sixth of the available time. Usually question time is a separate allocation.

Presentations are timed.

The time of delivery depends on your speaking speed. A presentation is spoken more slowly than a conversation. Notice the speaking speed that makes it comfortable for you to listen, and aim for that. To test the timing, speak your presentation as if you were presenting to an audience.

Audience engagement

A presentation is organised to maximise audience understanding of the content. As a first step, determine the nature of the audience, particularly their interests, needs and existing knowledge. At university your audience is generally familiar to you. However, it is useful to also consider the particular demographic features of the audience; for example, age, gender, ethnicity, education background, organisational positions and disabilities. Use the audience analysis to determine your presentation style, language and content.

Maximise audience engagement in the topic.

Next, consider ways to engage the audience in the presentation. Some presentations, for example, delivery of a seminar paper, may minimally use **audience engagement**, while other presentations will make greater use of it. Audience engagement should not dominate the presentation, but be used at key points to focus the audience on the content. To engage the audience:

- give examples
- use anecdotes
- ask questions
- perform role-plays.

The most common form of audience engagement is to provide examples for the main points you are making. Often the knowledge in a presentation is technical and abstract, and hence removed from the direct experience of many students.

Examples make it easy to understand points.

Your examples can come from your own knowledge. If you can show members of the audience that what you are saying is already somewhat familiar to them, they will be able to relate to what you are saying, and so listen and understand better.

Anecdotes add interest to ideas, because they are personal.

You can also provide **anecdotes**, or short personal stories, to illustrate a point. As it is difficult for an audience to listen to complex and abstract academic ideas, you can make your academic point, then add a relevant, short, personal story to aid understanding.

Questions engage the audience in thinking about the topic.

Presentations often employ questions as a means of engaging the audience. The purpose of a question is to focus the audience on the topic, not to test knowledge or to find out information.

A **rhetorical question** allows the audience to answer it mentally. Use words to indicate that your question is rhetorical and therefore not to be answered out loud. For example, 'Have you ever asked yourself: Why do presentations create anxiety?' Or you can ask the question but immediately respond yourself, so that the audience has time only to think of the answer. For example, you could ask the audience: 'Does the university refectory sell halal food?' and immediately answer 'We all know it does not'. While rhetorical questions are a powerful tool for engaging the audience actively in your presentation, they must not be overused. Use only one rhetorical question within a presentation.

Another type of question aims for a response from the audience. You can engage members of an audience by asking them to respond to a question as a means of focusing their attention on your topic. To create this question:

- introduce the question by telling the audience how to respond; for example, 'Put up your hand if you have ever …'
- ask a question that is short, clear and capable of being answered by a simple 'Yes' or 'No' (such as 'Have you ever felt anxious about giving a presentation?')
- link the audience response back into your presentation (for example, 'I see, most of you have experienced some anxiety. This is very common for all presenters. In this presentation I will be showing you some techniques for overcoming your fear.').

Always be careful with how questions are asked. Never ask an individual a question. In some cultures, for example, Aboriginal and Torres Strait Islander cultures, singling out individuals to ask them a question is inappropriate. Also, do not engage an audience member in a debate. Limit the number of questions (perhaps two per presentation) to gain maximum impact from their use. Always remember, even when using questions, that you are presenting to the whole audience.

Role-plays are short scripted acts used to illustrate a point.

Another way to engage an audience is to use **role-plays**. A role-play is a short, relevant play scripted by you and designed to illustrate some point in the presentation. It takes considerable preparation and practice, and usually can only be performed in a group, rather than as an individual, presentation. To make a role-play successful, link it into the presentation with a short introduction, and on its conclusion, remind the audience of how it relates to the presentation.

Resources

Most presentations require some resources. These can include:

- handouts of main points, or questions to consider, or activities to undertake
- whiteboard or blackboard with prepared text
- objects to demonstrate procedures or thinking
- overhead transparencies or PowerPoint slides containing the main points.

All of the resources should be relevant, easily read, well conceptualised and formatted. When using overhead transparencies or PowerPoint slides to show the main points of the presentation use:

- one main point per slide (font size 28 or greater)
- a number of supporting points (indent and use font size 20–26)
- a relevant image, if appropriate.

PowerPoint slides can use colour, animation and sound to add to the effect.

Engaging the audience

Activity

1   You have a presentation topic: My favourite sport.
    a   Prepare a question you could ask the audience, as a means of engaging interest.
    b   Present the audience question to your class, note the response, then use just one sentence to link the response back into your presentation topic.
2   You have the same presentation topic: My favourite sport.
    a   Prepare one main point within the body of the presentation.
    b   Prepare some supporting points.
    c   Prepare an anecdote to illustrate the point.
    d   Present your point, supporting points and anecdote to your class (no introduction or conclusion is necessary).

Writing outline points and scripts

Some presentations are part of an assessment item that includes a written report or seminar paper in the form of an essay. If this is the case, the written assessment section should be completed using all the techniques and the style appropriate to it. The presentation, however, must be spoken to the audience, rather than read, to maximise understanding and interest.

Prepare some written notes to help remember what to say in the presentation, but do so in such a way that you minimise the temptation to read and maximise the chance of speaking directly to the audience. There are two options available:

1   Use an **outline** of points and expand on these as you present.
2   Write out a **presentation script**.

Using an outline allows you to remember the main ideas, and to deliver your presentation in the most natural way possible. As you gain in confidence, you will automatically find yourself using this technique.

If you write a presentation script, use the style of an oral. Change your writing to an 'in the moment' or a 'heightened conversation' style for the specific audience who will be present. Use:

- short sentences
- simple sentence structures
- active, rather than passive, voice
- first and second person pronouns
- simple easy-to-pronounce words (although course terminology needs to be used as well)
- words that have a pleasing sound, as tonal qualities are important in an oral presentation.

Example

Writing and speaking

In an essay format you might write:

This essay focuses on the three stages involved in the production of a successful presentation: planning, preparation and practice.

In outline or point form this is:

A successful presentation needs:

Planning

Preparation

Practice.

In script form this might be:

The three factors for success are: planning, preparation and practice.

When you speak you might say:

- *Today, I am exploring the three 'Ps' needed for a successful presentation: planning, preparation and practice.*

Example

What are the main differences between the styles given above?
Why do we use different styles?

If you were preparing for a presentation, which style would you prefer to use: the outline form or the script form?

Thinking

A script is both your guide for your presentation and a backup should you need it. At times, having a script is more of an emotional safeguard than an actual tool. However, if you choose to rely on the script while presenting, *do not read it.* If you read a presentation it is a *reading* not a presentation. Use the script in a more eloquent manner. Refer to it on an 'as needs' basis, or to give a quotation, or simply to have there in case you lose your train of thought.

How does reading affect listening?
Why does it have this effect?

Thinking

Include in your outline of points or script the ways in which you will engage your audience:

- Indicate where an example or anecdote is to be given, and jot down some key words to remind yourself of what it will be about
- If you are using a question, write it exactly and add a reminder to introduce it and link it back in to the presentation.

Write sufficient content so that the presentation can be delivered in the time available. An essay may be read quickly or at leisure by your lecturer. However, the oral is presented during that one timeframe, during that one session. To check timing, practise delivering your presentation out loud and at an appropriate **pace** for the audience to understand.

Most of your outline or script should be written so that just a glance is sufficient to remind you of your task. Use:

- a large font for ease of reading
- few words for immediate understanding.

Getting to know your presentation

Know your presentation well but do not memorise it.

Once you have written the outline of your presentation points or script, get to know it well by thoroughly learning the content. Use the outline or script as a guide only. Do not memorise exactly. Engage as many of your senses as possible to help the information 'sink into' your mind. Practise it as many times as possible, aiming to link your presentation to all of your senses:

- glance at the outline or script (vision)
- speak it aloud (oral)
- listen to yourself (auditory)
- gesture to add emphasis (tactile).

Perhaps even record yourself speaking. Listen and assess where you need to make changes for a better presentation.

Hooks make it easy to remember content and order.

Another technique is the use of hooks. They make it easy to remember content and order. Connect 'chunks' (meaningful groupings) of related information in the point outline or script to **hooks** (such as a word or a letter). The hooks can be memorised exactly, and the attached information can be understood, rather than memorised. Thus the delivery of the presentation will be complete, but also natural and easy to understand.

Mnemonics are a useful strategy to employ to remember information. Mnemonics use letters as the hook.

Example

Hooks for short items in a list (using PRESENT)

Prepare in advance.

Research and read widely.

Engage the listener's attention.

Start with a strong introduction.

Expand and explain.

Note all main points on handouts or slides.

Thank everyone and ask for final questions.

Hooks attached to chunks of information (using DOT)
D (definition of mentoring)
O (origins of mentoring)
T (types of mentoring)

Example

Using hooks

1   Think of four main points you want to make for the presentation topic: 'My favourite sport'.
2   Develop a suitable hook to remember these points (*Hint*: think of a four-letter word associated with your topic. See if you can attach your information to each of the letters. It may take some thinking).
3   Tell the class which hook you chose.

Activity

Getting to know the presentation environment

Before presenting, familiarise yourself with the practical aspects of the presentation environment. Check:

- the size of the room (this will affect how you use your voice)
- the position of the projector or screen (this will determine where you stand)
- the type of equipment available (this will determine what you can use for resources)
- the effect of lighting (you may need to turn off lights immediately over a screen)
- that you know how to use the equipment (for example, how to place overhead transparencies; how to turn on the sound for a PowerPoint show; how to 'click' on for PowerPoint slides).

Attending to delivery

There are a number of elements that need to be considered when delivering a presentation. At times, even if the content is of a high standard, the presentation may not receive the highest mark because the delivery is poor.

Even if the content of a presentation is of a high standard, it may not receive the highest mark if the delivery is poor.

You can improve delivery by attending to the following:

- voice and speech
- whole body movement
- gestures
- eye contact
- attire
- being a performer
- being a communicator.

Voice and speech

Voice is particularly important in a presentation. Your voice needs to be well modulated, with a pleasant rather than demanding tonal quality. It has to be projected at a volume so that all the audience members can hear without straining. You may have content of the highest calibre, but if your audience cannot hear it, then it becomes pointless and everyone feels frustrated. Vary your voice, so that the content is easy to listen to.

A presentation requires good speech. Enunciate words clearly. Even more importantly, practise pronunciation before you give a presentation. Avoid words you 'stumble over' by selecting simpler words. Ensure your speech is fluent. If you need to think during your presentation use a slight pause, as this is preferable to using verbal utterances such as 'Um', 'OK' or 'Ah', which may convey the misplaced notion that you are unprepared. Speak at a pace suitable for a presentation, which is slower than in a conversation.

Whole body movement

During your presentation keep movement to a minimum.

Enter and leave your presentation with a confident walk, no matter how you feel. During your presentation keep movement to a minimum. If you desire to move for emphasis, then move to a specific location and stop. Constant movement, including swaying, is distracting, and places the focus on the movement rather than the presentation.

Stand confidently when delivering your presentation. Choose a position so the audience can see you easily. It is sometimes tempting to turn your back on the audience to read the PowerPoint or visualiser notes behind you. Do not do this.

Gestures

Gestures can be used to provide emphasis. Use arm movements to show the audience they are included in the presentation or to emphasise a point. However, be cautious with **gestures**: they may be misunderstood by members of the audience (for example, 'thumbs up' may connote a good or a bad idea, depending on culture); or they may seem aggressive (for example, if you point to the audience, or to an audience member, or if you thump on the desk). Use gestures for specific purposes, as too many become a distraction.

Eye contact

It is expected at most Western universities that you maintain eye contact with the audience during an oral presentation. However, many cultures regard this as disrespectful and even insulting. If this is the case for you, 'scan' the room without looking specifically at any one person, or look slightly above the heads of the audience. Be careful not to hide your eyes.

Attire

Dress appropriately for your presentation. Your choice of clothing can enhance or distract from the main points being presented. Do not wear caps, as this prevents the audience seeing your eyes. In most presentations you can dress as you normally would for university, but in some cases you may be required to dress formally (as in marketing presentations).

Your choice of clothing can enhance or distract from your presentation.

Being a performer

To make it easier to deliver the presentation you can play a role. A **performer role** may allow you to become someone other than yourself. You can imagine yourself to be a TV presenter, a sports commentator or an actor. By adopting the mantle of another persona (image of yourself) you can momentarily 'suspend the reality of you'.

Being a communicator

Another technique to make delivery easier is to take the opposite approach. Do not think of yourself as a performer, but as a communicator. The presentation then becomes a familiar activity as the **communicator role** becomes just another way of giving information to others.

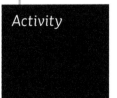

Activity

Practising delivery of a presentation

Practise in pairs (student A and B). Focus on how you deliver the presentation.

1   Student A is to give a one-minute impromptu (no preparation) presentation on the topic: A university degree will lead to a good job.

Student B is to listen to the presentation, and in particular note how the presentation is delivered, then give feedback to Student A, saying what delivery techniques were used well.

2   Reverse the process.

Student B is to give a one-minute impromptu presentation on the topic: Student fees are too high.

Student A is to listen and provide feedback on the delivery techniques that worked well.

3   Both students discuss what parts of their own delivery they thought could have been improved.

Practising the presentation

It's important to practise, practise, practise.

In oral presentations it is important to practise, practise and practise. Practise the presentation out loud, using an appropriate volume and a suitable speed, including gestures and all your techniques for reaching the audience. If you are particularly concerned about speaking to an audience, start by practising in front of inanimate objects such as a piece of furniture; progress to giving your presentation in front of a mirror or a webcam; perhaps give your presentation to a friend; then finally present to your audience.

Coping with anxiety

It is easy to feel anxious while giving a presentation. Oral presentations are an assessable task, so the person who is marking your work is present. While the lecturer is a member of the audience, he or she is also separate from it. The focus for your presentation should be the other students; however, the presence of the lecturer often dominates your mindset, frequently generating anxiety. Anxiety also can occur because students feel vulnerable speaking in front of their peers.

Some anxiety needs to be present; it ensures an edge to your work by forcing you to prepare well and gives an energy to your presentation. However, if anxiety is too great it can detract from your presentation. If this is the case then shift to managing your fear:

- *Reframe the way you think about the oral*: move from 'A presentation is scary' to 'This presentation is only 20 minutes long and I have a lot of material'.
- *Shift focus*: if you are fearful of speaking in front of the audience of your peers and assessor, then shift your focus from how you are feeling.

Refocus on other factors such as the PowerPoint slides, or the ideas in your presentation, or a friend in the audience.

- *Assess the degree of harm that can occur:* assess how often you have failed a presentation; whether your friends have ever abandoned you because you made a mistake; how long you have felt mortified by a mistake.
- *Prepare:* Your fear can indicate specific areas that need attention. If you are afraid of making a mistake, check your information; if you are afraid of mispronouncing words, check pronunciation, practise, and if necessary change to simpler words.

Giving a team presentation

You will give many **team presentations** at university. These require some additional attention so that the presentation is clearly a cohesive team effort. In particular check that:

Team presentations require additional attention.

- content is completely covered
- the content is coherently organised (and not repeated)
- the timing of each section is appropriate
- the strongest speakers are given the introduction and conclusion to present, as this gives the maximum impact for the presentation
- weaker speakers are given support and training
- weaker sections are always balanced by stronger ones
- the presentation is practised as a team presentation.

    To present as a team:

- Introduce the whole team to the audience in the introduction.
- Each team member, after completing his or her section, introduces the following speaker.
- Each new speaker thanks the preceding one for his or her introduction.
- When presenting any opinions or recommendations, speakers refer to the team (for example, 'We believe that ...').
- In the introduction and conclusion, the presentation is summarised as a team effort (for example, 'We will explain ...' or 'We have shown that ...').
- The whole team participates in question time.
- A consistent style is used in presentation visuals (same background, font, formatting, use of imagery and sound).

Activity

Giving a short team presentation

Do this exercise in a group of three. Give a three-minute team presentation on one of the following topics:

1 Chocolate is good for you.
2 Nuclear power should be used to generate electricity.
3 Within this century, humans will be able to live to at least 150 years.
4 Frogs are better pets than lizards.

Decide who will be the first, second and third speakers. Decide how to divide up the presentation. Take ten minutes and prepare the presentation together as a group.

Give the presentation.

Leading a discussion

Sometimes you will be asked to not only present a seminar paper but also to **lead a discussion**. This is a very demanding task, and probably will only be expected of you in later years at university. This type of presentation requires that you have an excellent knowledge of the whole topic area. Usually you present a summary of the main points, lead the discussion, supplying additional information as needed, then conclude the discussion with a good summary of the main points in the topic and the main comments made by the tutorial.

The aim of a discussion is to encourage your classmates to comment on the main issues in the topic

As the aim of a discussion is to help your classmates comment on the main issues in the topic, prepare questions to encourage debate:

- Select the main issues that need to be attended to
- Select the main debates in the literature on the topic
- Select information to encourage discussion
- Prepare some **open questions** that encourage full responses.

Table 10.2 Leading a discussion

Do nots	Do's
Do not assume all students have read the material	Do provide basic information
Do not ask questions: • that test knowledge (e.g. 'What does Smith say about …?') • that are closed (i.e. can be answered by just one word)	Do ask open questions to encourage response (for example, ask 'What do you think of Smith's claim that …?')

Table 10.2 Leading a discussion (*cont.*)

Do nots	Do's
Do not comment on each response	• Do ask your fellow students to comment on the response • Give tips, if necessary, to extend the discussion (e.g., say 'Natalie has made the point that Smith's claim is not backed up by research. Does this mean we should ignore the claim?')
Do not just rely on the students' level of knowledge	Do prepare some knowledge for students (e.g. present two contradictory claims and ask students to comment)

Go to our website <www.oup.com.au/orc/turner2e> for more activities on the skills covered in this chapter.

Activity

SUMMARY

In this chapter we have examined the many aspects of a presentation that make it a distinctly different form of assessment. While the basic structure of any presentation follows the traditional format of introduction, body and conclusion, a presentation also includes a range of other considerations as a means of enhancing its spoken nature. This chapter has also discussed the special requirements of a team presentation and of leading a discussion. Presentations may create some anxiety in students, but with practice they can become an enjoyable, and even a favoured, form of assessment.

GLOSSARY

anecdote a short personal story used to illustrate a point.
audience engagement using techniques to involve the audience in listening to a presentation.
closed questions those that can be answered with a simple word.
communicator role one in which a person sees that his or her primary purpose is to communicate with others.

gesture the use of arm movement to carry meaning.

hook something, such as a letter, that can be used to recall the information that is mentally attached to it.

leading a discussion an assessment item in which a student has to help a tutorial group discuss some topic.

open questions questions that encourage a full response.

outline the presentation of information in dot-point form.

pace the speed at which speech occurs.

performer role undertaken when a person deliberately takes on the behaviours of a performer.

presentation script a presentation written in conversational style as an aid to help in delivering the content.

question time the time after a presentation has ended when the audience is invited to ask questions of the speakers.

rhetorical questions questions that are asked for the sole purpose of making someone think of an answer, but no response is expected.

role-play a short scripted play used to illustrate a point.

team presentation given by a number of people working together to produce the one presentation.

chapter ELEVEN

Examinations

Examinations are the traditional means of testing a student's knowledge. They are used as the sole form of assessment in most countries; for example, in China, Vietnam, Thailand, the Indian subcontinent and in the Middle Eastern countries. In Western universities, however, examinations are usually only part of the assessment process, along with essays, reports and presentations.

In this chapter you will learn:

- why we have examinations
- how to learn throughout the semester
- how to learn in the revision period
- the types of examinations
- how to respond to different questions:
  - multiple-choice
  - true/false
  - fill-in-a-blank
  - short answer
  - case study
  - essay
  - problem solving using calculation
- how to sit for a formal examination:
  - preparation immediately before an examination
  - what to do in perusal time
  - what to do when writing an examination
- what to do if ...
  - you are too sick or troubled to sit for an examination
  - your results are much less than you had expected.

Why examinations?

Students may feel that years of experience in doing examinations have prepared them well. This is not totally true. Most local students are familiar with all the forms of questions used in examinations. However, at university these become more difficult because the level of knowledge being tested increases and, as a result, more advanced examination skills are required.

International students have had a great deal of practice in examinations. Nonetheless, the type of questions, what is being assessed, and how to study are all likely to be different in a Western country. Hence, even with all their skill at sitting examinations in their home countries, international students need to learn additional examination skills.

Examinations have much to offer as an assessment tool. They can test a student's knowledge and memory of course content. In many respects this is a fairer form of assessment than others, as some students cheat in essays and reports by copying or paying someone to write, using too much help or relying on the work of others.

However, examinations do have their own problems as a form of assessment. The greatest difficulty is assessing a student for an entire course on a performance of just two or three hours. In this context, many things can go wrong. Students may be sick or nervous and so underperform. Some domestic and international students also do not have sufficient English skills to write fast enough or even to comprehend questions, thus making the examination not a true test of their knowledge. As well, although examinations test both understanding and memory, the mere fact that this has to be done in a short period means that the test of understanding is incomplete.

There have been a number of solutions to the problems of having just one final examination. The most popular used are:

- a range of assessment items, including an examination
- a range of assessment items with a '**hurdle**' in the final examination (a minimum that must be reached in order to achieve a pass in the course)
- a series of examinations during a course.

Learning throughout the course

Examinations cannot be prepared for at the last moment. They require that you have understood your course content well. This means that learning needs to take place throughout the course.

Learning needs to be continual.

The way assessment is set up in a semester can cause confusion about how to learn. As there is no assessment in the first weeks, students are often lulled into a sense that nothing has to be done. When assignments have to be produced in the middle of the semester they may be equally misled, believing that this is all they are required to focus on.

Nothing could be further from the truth. Learning of course content has to be continually engaged in during the semester.

Aim for deep learning. Ask while learning:

- Why am I learning this?
- What interests me?
- How does this link to what I already know?
- What is considered important and why?
- How could this be useful?

The basic requirement in any course is that you know and understand all the course terminology. All disciplines have a large range of specific terms that are used to describe and explain what is important. You can neither achieve any understanding until you know this terminology, nor can you provide adequate answers to any examination questions unless you can use it. Chapter 2 explains how to learn these.

Know and understand the course terminology.

Some courses are built around your mastering a number of formulae, for example, in courses such as accounting, statistics and economics. It is essential that you know and understand how to use the formulae. Usually tutorials are constructed to give you graded practice in applying the formulae to problems. Make sure you attempt all tutorial problems. If you cannot do any, then seek help from fellow students and the tutor. If you miss a tutorial, make sure you still do the problems and check the answers.

Know and understand how to use all formulae.

Textbooks and lecture notes contain a vast amount of information. One means of helping understanding is to recognise the patterns used in organising the knowledge. If you try to understand only discrete (separate) pieces of information, you will find it an impossible task. A system of organisation provides a meaning structure, and hence makes the information more easily understood.

Recognise and understand the patterns of organising knowledge in your course.

To notice patterns of organisation, focus on the larger structures (the 'big picture'). Organisation is given by systems of headings and subheadings; and is indicated in the introduction. Focus on these as a necessary aspect of learning. Ask yourself: How is this knowledge organised? Draw a concept map of the structure of presentation of the knowledge.

Once the terminology and the overall structure of organisation are familiar, it is easy to focus on the details. Each week set aside time to read the lecture and textbook chapter carefully. Write out your understanding of each section.

Learn and understand specific details.

Check your understanding constantly. If your textbook has questions attached to the chapter you are learning, see if you can answer these. If there are past examination papers, answer the questions on the chapter you are studying. If there are no questions, make up some for yourself, or even ask your tutor for some.

Check your understanding continually.

Learn collaboratively. One way of enhancing learning throughout the semester is to form a study group. Collaborative learning helps motivation and builds knowledge and confidence (see Chapter 9). More importantly perhaps, study groups are often the beginning of a lifelong network of friends and colleagues.

Seek help. When you do not understand, be sure to seek help immediately. In courses such as accounting, statistics and programming that systematically build on prior knowledge, it is essential to understand each step. In other courses the urgency is not as great, yet you should keep up with them to make learning manageable.

You can obtain help from fellow students and your tutor during the tutorial. However, if you require more focused assistance, see your tutor or lecturer during their consultation time.

Focused learning for an examination: revision

Examinations test understanding and memory of course content. Learning for an examination thus involves long-term study, which leads to understanding of the course content, as well as a short-term focus on learning with an emphasis on memorising with understanding the key ideas.

Planning revision

You probably will not be able to study intensively for your examination until most of your assignments have been submitted. Hence, you may only have a short period for revision. Planning is essential to maximise the time available.

Plan your revision:

- Find out examination dates
- Find out what the examination covers
- Find out the type of examination questions and the weightings
- Draw up a realistic revision plan for all your courses.

If you have any examination timetable clashes, contact your university administration immediately. First, clarify your timetable. Check the examination timetable as soon as it comes out. Make sure that there are no clashes (examinations at the same time). If there are, notify the appropriate section of the university immediately. Also check that your examination schedule is manageable under the university rules. All universities have rules that stipulate the minimum time allowable between examinations and the number of examinations that can be done in a 24-hour period. If your timetable does not meet these requirements, you can request that it be changed.

Second, find out what will be covered in the examination. In some courses it will be the entire course, while in others only parts of the course will be covered. Attend to:

- lecturer statements or hints, usually given towards the end of the course and especially in the last lecture

- what has been emphasised during lectures and tutorials
- past papers, especially if your lecturer ran the course in past years.

Next discover what format the examination will take. The type of questions are important, as well as the weighting (the relative marks) for different sections. This will give you an idea of what to learn.

Finally, draw up a realistic revision timetable. As you prepare for a final examination you are like a long distance runner. You are already quite exhausted because of all the assignment work during the semester, yet you need to make an extra effort to pass the examination. Pace yourself.

Make sure you add in time for relaxation and exercise. These are necessary for maintaining motivation and clarity of mind.

Revising

During the revision process, your learning shifts to an emphasis on memorisation (with understanding). If you have understood your course well, this type of memorisation will not be too difficult.

Concentrate on memorisation with understanding in revision.

Techniques to help you memorise:

- Repeat and write
- Develop a mnemonic (for example, a sentence of words whose first letters stand for each of the most important points), memorise, write
- Read the ideas out loud in a dramatic manner, emphasising the main points as though they were characters in a drama; write them
- Draw diagrams, say them, write them
- Move while repeating the main points: walk, dance, kick a ball, then write
- Visualise or draw an image to associate with the main points, say it, write it
- Develop or use photographic memory (create an image in your mind of key pages. Some people can literally 'read' the answers in the examination by having this kind of memory)
- Test yourself by asking questions and seeing if you can answer them. Do this the day after you learn something, and again just before the examination.

Build in support

All students should make sure they enhance the ability of their brain to function at maximum level by:

Build in brain support.

- eating well
- exercising well.

Eat well, as good food allows a steady build-up of glucose, which is the brain's only source of energy. Avoid too many sweets for, although they may give a burst of energy, they will also create a 'crash'—a sudden lowering of energy. Avoid too much coffee; it will 'wake you up', but too much tends to make it difficult to focus.

Exercise is very beneficial for your brain. It increases the action of your heart and lungs, and so adds oxygen to your blood and provides your brain with what it needs to function at its best.

Dealing with stress

Build confidence. Use stress to gain focus.

Examinations are very stressful. While stress can overwhelm students and prevent them from doing anything, it is also a way of creating a focus on what needs to be done. Find techniques to turn stress to your advantage, so that you remain very focused, but also confident. Some techniques are listed below:

- Acknowledge that you feel stressed
- Confirm that you will still try your best, even though you are stressed
- Build in some relaxation and enjoyment every day
- Look carefully at what is the reality behind your stress (How many examinations have you failed? How many marks do you need to pass the course? What has been your level of achievement in the rest of the course? Even if you failed, what is the worst that would happen?)
- Try to catch your mind and body as it goes through its stress pattern (as you become familiar with your mind and body pattern, you can intervene at an early stage so that stress does not build)
- Recognise that most students will pass
- Remind yourself of difficulties you have overcome
- Remind yourself that each day you learn more.

Activity

Coping with stress
Make up a mnemonic for ways to cope with stress. You can reorder the items.

Practising

It is essential to practise answering the types of questions that will appear in your examination. Mostly, your lecturers and tutors will give you a chance to do exercises in writing examination questions, particularly in your first year courses. Take it very seriously, as practice is probably just as important as study.

This is true for all students; however, if you are an international student it is vital, as you do not have experience in the types of answers required.

If you are not given practice in tutorial time, then you must do this yourself. Write answers to questions in previous examination papers, or questions from tutorials, or in the textbook. Ask your tutor to help you judge whether you have the correct answers.

Preparation for particular types of examinations

Special preparation for an open book examination

If you are sitting an open book examination (see the following section 'Types of examinations'), additional preparation needs to be done. Do the revision as expected for any examination. As well, organise the information that you can take into the examination. Mark pages so that significant sections are easy to find; summarise key ideas and information; underline and highlight important points; and create an index of where to find information. Prepare so that you can write high-quality answers.

Special preparation for a take-home examination

To prepare for a take-home examination (see the following section 'Types of examination'), revise and plan as for an open book examination. Also, free up time and space during the examination time to maximise your chance of doing well. Planning and balance are essential to achieve the high-level outcomes expected. Do not devote all the time available to the examination, as you will become unproductive. Equally, do not leave the examination until the last evening. Balance the examination with your other activities.

Reflecting on past examination experiences

Think of your most successful examination.

1   Why did you feel it was most successful?
2   How did you feel before you sat for this examination?
3   How did you study for it?
4   How did you feel when you first looked at the examination paper?
5   How did you feel after the examination?
6   What did you learn from this experience that you could apply to other examinations?

Activity

Types of examinations

All examinations fall under two broad categories: closed book and open book. A **closed book examination** means that you cannot take any material into the examination and therefore you need to rely on your memory in doing it. For an **open book examination** you are permitted to use course material and notes, although sometimes there are a few limitations. You may, for example, be restricted to just one page of notes or just one book.

There are a number of variations in how an examination is conducted. Most are fairly formal and take place at university. Some may be in lecture or tutorial time; others are held in a set examination period. These examinations can be either closed or open book, although closed book is more common. On the other hand, some examinations are very informal. Occasionally, students are given **take-home examinations**. This means a student collects the examination paper at a certain time, then writes his or her answers over a set number of days (in any place). Clearly such examinations are open book.

Courses may use a range of types of examination. The most popular at an undergraduate level are:

- quizzes: short in-class assessment of a limited area of the course
- mid-term examinations: longer assessment, either formal or in-class; usually assessing the first half of a course
- final examinations: usually formal examinations in a set examination period, but can be take-home examinations.

Types of examination questions

Expect examination questions to use different wording from your lecture notes and textbook.

In most disciplines, examination questions require much more than skill in content knowledge. Good skills in reading, as well as the ability to understand what is required as an answer, are needed.

Reading the question

All examinations call on your ability to read and understand the questions. Focus on the structure (especially the number of parts), the instruction words, and the content (the keywords).

Answering the question

There are seven main types of questions used in examinations:

- multiple-choice
- true/false
- fill-in-the-blank

- short answer
- case study
- essay
- problem solving using calculation.

Multiple-choice

Multiple-choice questions are extremely popular in some disciplinary areas, such as marketing. They consist of a question or statement and a number of possible answers. Typically you are given four alternatives to choose from. Your task is to select the most correct answer.

The ability to answer multiple-choice questions comes from a detailed knowledge of the course terminology and content. You also need skills in selection. Multiple-choice questions tend to be written so that all responses have the appearance of being correct, either because they are all closely related to the correct answer, and/or because they are written to look correct through the use of linguistic tricks. Skills in selecting the correct answer are essential.

The aim in multiple-choice questions is to find the best answer: the answer that most comprehensively and correctly answers the question. Selection can be done in three stages.

In multiple-choice, aim to find the best answer.

First, do the questions where the answer is obviously correct. Read the question carefully and think how you would answer it. Only then look through all the possible answers. If one is obvious, choose it. Once you have made a choice it is best not to change. Your first choice is very likely to be correct.

Second, use elimination to find the most likely answer. If you are not certain of an answer, then look more carefully at the list of possible responses. Use a systematic process of elimination to arrive at the best answer:

- eliminate the obviously incorrect answers
- underline any responses that contain the technical terms that you think need to be in the answer
- check each of these carefully for how they are written (see Table 11.1)
- eliminate any response that cannot be true given the way it is written
- select the best choice.

Multiple-choice question
Circle the letter that corresponds to the correct response.

Example

1   Examinations test:
    a   your understanding
    b   your ability to remember all the information in the textbook
    c   your understanding and ability to study well
    d   your ability to remember and understand.

As a final step in selection, guess an answer for those you have no idea about. Do not do this if you are penalised for incorrect answers.

Table 11.1 Systematic checking of multiple-choice responses

Check carefully if a question or possible response has:	Can only be true if:
Logical operators: and, or, not Example: Examinations test memory and understanding Examinations test memory or understanding Examinations test memory but not understanding	These can only be true if: And: both parts are true Or: only one part needs to be true Not: the part containing the 'not' is false, and the remainder is true
Generalisations: all, every, most, often, frequently Example: All examinations test understanding of course content	These can only be true if the response is true for all, not just for some
Limitations: only, never Example: Examinations are never done at home	These can only be true if the response is limited in the manner indicated
Particularising: e.g. a response that links names of theorists to a theory; a name of a theory linked to its description; an indication that this is 'the main' or 'the most'; or a response that specifies a particular time or place Example: Marton and Saljo developed the theory of the strategic approach to learning	These can only be true if the whole of the description is true
Red herrings: these are incorrect or irrelevant responses or parts or responses Example: Examinations are a good test of how you have learned for your course and how many hours you have spent studying	These must be incorrect, as part of them is incorrect or irrelevant
Double negatives: these are questions in which two negatives are used Example: It is not true that Marton and Saljo did not name the two approaches to learning as deep and surface approaches	These are true if both negatives are removed and the remaining positive statement is true

True/false

True/false questions test not only your knowledge of the course content but your ability to understand how logical operators work.

True/false questions present a statement. Your task is to decide if it is true or false. These questions test not only your knowledge of the course content but also your ability to understand how logical operators work. Approach these in exactly the same way as you would a multiple-choice question. In particular, notice those containing negatives (such as never, not) as they create mental confusion. If a question is written in the negative, it is true if the whole statement (with the negative) is true. If a statement has a double negative, ignore the negatives as the question is, in fact, a positive statement. Reword to a positive statement and decide if it is true or false.

A negative true/false question

<u>True or false?</u>

Marton and Saljo did *not* develop the theory of the strategic approach to learning.

Example

A double negative

<u>True or false?</u>

It is *not* the case that Marton and Saljo did *not* develop the theory of the strategic approach to learning.

Example

Is it a fair test of your knowledge to use linguistic tricks in questions?

Thinking

Fill-in-a-blank

A question that asks you to 'fill in the blank' is quite straightforward. Your task is to find the precise, technical term that is needed. These questions are often asked to check your understanding of definitions.

Fill in a blank

The type of question that provides a statement and a number of possible correct answers is called a _____ question.

Example

Short answer

In many examinations you are asked to respond to questions that require a 'short answer'. Usually, this type of question requires a full response, which may take half to one page of writing. They are not strictly speaking 'short'.

The aim of a **short-answer question** is to test your knowledge and understanding of a specific area. Thus your answer must show what you know, and also your ability, not just to memorise and repeat, but to use your knowledge to respond to the question. Normally, 'part marks' are awarded for any sections in a response that are correct.

The aim of a short-answer question is to test your knowledge and understanding of a specific area.

To respond to a short answer question fully:

- define all course terminology in the question
- use your knowledge to fully respond to the question:
  - give full details
  - use course terminology
  - use names of theorists, if appropriate
  - provide examples if possible.

Example

Short answer question

In what way can a short-answer question be seen as requiring both memorisation and understanding of course content?

Case study

A case study is testing your knowledge of course content, and your ability to recognise the content in, and apply it to, a 'real-life' situation.

Sometimes in an examination you are given a short case study, based on a 'real-life' situation connected to some area in your course, and asked a series of questions about it. A case study is testing your knowledge of course content and your ability to recognise the content in, and apply it to, a 'real-life' situation.

To answer **case study questions**, provide a full response using your knowledge of the case and the course. Give appropriate descriptions of the case and link these to course material. Give full explanations and descriptions of the relevant course material and use course terminology with definitions.

Example

Case study question

Mathew had a great first semester at university. He met many new friends while staying in college. In fact, he spent most of each night drinking and listening to music. He also played football with his college, and tennis and rowing with university clubs. The end of semester examinations had come too quickly, although Mathew was not too worried, as he had managed to pass each assignment in his course. The main problem was that Mathew had three examinations in the first week. He decided to devote the night before each of the examinations to study. His first examination was in Marketing. He stayed in his room cramming as much of the textbook as he could.

The next morning he opened his examination paper and found that all of the questions were multiple-choice. 'Great,' he thought. He quickly raced through the test, easily finding the answers by recognising the course terminology in the responses provided. He was so fast he left the examination half an hour early.

When Mathew received his results he was shocked. He had failed Marketing.

Questions

1   What type of question was used in the Marketing examination?
2   What was wrong with Mathew's technique of answering the questions?

Does the claim in the case above *'The main problem was that Mathew had three examinations in the first week'* provide a true assessment of what the 'main problem' is? Why is such information used in case studies?

Essay

Sometimes you are asked to write an essay response to an examination question. This is quite a difficult examination to do, although, as with short answer questions, you receive part marks for any relevant information you use. The **essay question** is a test of your knowledge of the course and of your ability to use that in a particular situation to respond to a question. Your response has to show thoughtful selection of course content and a developed understanding of it. No in-text citations are needed.

The essay question is a test of your knowledge of the course and of your ability to use that to respond to a question.

To respond well in an essay type examination:

- Understand the question well by looking at the structure of the question, the instruction words and the content keyword
- Decide what course content is required as a response
- Plan your response by organising the content so that it addresses the question
- Write in essay format, using an introduction, a body with good paragraphs and a conclusion
- Use course terminology and full descriptions and examples where possible.

Essay examination question
Write a 350-word essay on the following topic.
Examinations cannot test a student's understanding of course content. Discuss.

Problem solving using calculation

For those questions that require you to work out a problem (for example, in accounting or economics or statistics) make sure you:

- understand the question well
- are aware of all the relevant details
- decide on the appropriate formulae
- use the correct facts from the question
- document all your working as partial marks are likely to be given.

Activity

Trying examination questions
Answer each of the examination questions used as examples above.

The examination

Preparing immediately before an examination

If you have any special needs for an examination, these have to be organised some weeks beforehand. If you have a disability, you can apply for support in the examination. Depending on your needs, you can be given any kind of help, from a person to write the examination as you dictate it, to a computer, to extra time or even a different timetable.

All students must find out what can be taken into the examination. Usually you do not need to bring paper for a final examination, but may need to do so for other tests. Some types of electronic equipment are not allowed, especially electronic dictionaries. Often you can take in paper dictionaries; if so, check what kinds are allowed. If paper dictionaries are permitted, then they must be 'clean' (not contain any writing). You will have to take in writing implements and your student ID. Usually you can take in tissues or lollies or a drink.

Immediately before the examination prepare well by:

- revising key points
- getting enough sleep (watch a movie, read a novel, do some exercise, listen to music—anything to help you fall asleep)
- eating a good meal
- reminding yourself that you have prepared well
- arriving at the examination in good time.

Entering the examination room

Just before the examination begins you will be permitted to enter the examination room. Make sure mobile phones are turned off. You will be directed as to where to place your bag and where to sit. Take what you need with you. Place your student ID on the desk, and fill in the attendance form and the front page of your examination booklet (if required). Do not talk. Do not open your examination paper. Wait patiently for instructions.

Perusal time

The **invigilator**, the person who runs the examination session, will formally commence the examination when everyone is seated. A list of instructions is read out about not cheating, not talking and when you are permitted to leave the examination room. Then the invigilator announces the beginning of the examination. Most examinations start with a perusal time of about 10 minutes.

During the **perusal** you can read your examination paper and may be able to make some notes on it. You will never be permitted to write answers in your examination booklet.

Use perusal time to get to know your examination:

- Check how many sections or questions there are
- Check how many questions need to be attempted
- Check weightings
- Allocate times based on the weightings
- Decide what you know best
- Plan the order of answering starting with the ones you know best
- Jot down information (if you are permitted to write):
    - formulae
    - memory aids or general notes
    - notes for particular questions.

Why would you start with what you know best?

Thinking

Writing the examination

The invigilator will announce when the examination proper begins. At this point you start writing in your examination booklet.

For short answer, case study and essay-type questions, write your answers very clearly. Examiners mark papers quite quickly, so make it as easy as possible for them to see that you know the answer. In particular:

Use different techniques to answer different questions.

- plan an answer
- write the question number
- write clearly, and not in a light pencil
- use every second line
- don't worry about grammar or spelling (unless your examiner has specifically indicated these will be checked)
- use course terminology
- provide full answers and include diagrams where appropriate
- if you are not sure of an answer, try to write something, as you may be given part marks
- leave some space to add additional information later.

For multiple-choice, true/false and fill-in-a-blank questions you normally mark your answers on a question sheet. Make sure you:

- know how to indicate your response
- use a good easy-to-read pencil to allow erasure and corrections later
- go through quickly answering those questions that you know
- generally, do not change your first response, as it is likely to be correct
- go through again, looking at the questions you are not sure of, using 'the elimination technique' to help choose the best answer
- go through again and choose any response for multiple-choice and true/false if you have no idea of the answer, unless you are penalised for having an incorrect answer.

For those questions that require calculation you need to show the steps you take to arrive at the answer, so make sure you:

- use a good easy-to-read pencil for erasure and correction
- (perhaps) list the relevant facts on the side to make sure they will be taken into account
- show each step in your working
- calculate carefully and insert numbers in a step-by-step manner
- (where appropriate) name each entry.

Watch the time.

When you finish the examination, check that you have answered all questions and that they are clearly numbered and that the answered questions are listed on the front of the examination booklet. Also read over answers, and make sure that all the relevant information has been included. In general, don't change answers unless you are absolutely certain that what you have written is wrong.

What if ...

You are very sick or troubled

Universities are interested in helping you do the best you can. If you are very ill on the day of the examination, but nevertheless sit for it, you can apply for **special consideration**. You will need a medical certificate. If special consideration is granted, an extra mark, but usually no more, can be given should you require it to gain a higher grade.

If you suddenly find, on the date of the examination, that you are too ill to sit for it or if some extremely serious problem occurs in your family that prevents you from sitting the examination, then immediately find out what you can do. Acquire documentation. If you are ill, obtain a medical certificate that states that in the doctor's opinion you were unfit to sit for the examination. If it is a personal or family crisis, gather relevant proof. Apply for a **deferred examination**. The application usually has to be submitted within a few days of the original examination date. If it is accepted, you will be granted another chance to do the examination at a later time.

Clearly, these privileges are only given for very special circumstances, and most universities place a limit on how many times you can apply for them.

Your results are lower than you expected

When you receive your examination result you may think it is not consistent with the other marks you have received in your course, or with your knowledge of the course, or your own assessment of how well you did. In this case, you can apply to have your examination paper remarked. Sometimes you will need to pay an application fee.

Go to our website <www.oup.com.au/orc/turner2e> for more activities on the skills covered in this chapter.

Activity

SUMMARY

Examinations encourage learning. This chapter has explored how learning occurs in two phases. First, there is learning with an emphasis on understanding that takes place continuously throughout your entire course.

It forms the necessary basis for the second phase of learning. In the short revision period just before the examination there is a shift in learning technique to one where you focus on memorising (with understanding).

Examinations can be stressful. However, by engaging in continual learning, using techniques for creating focus and confidence, and with knowledge of how to respond to different types of questions, you can face your examinations knowing that you will do your best.

GLOSSARY

case study questions those that ask about a short case study requiring you to show knowledge of the case and your course.

closed book examinations those that do not allow you to take any material into the examination.

deferred examination because of special circumstances the examination is set at a later time than that of the normal examination.

essay questions those requiring an essay response in order to test your knowledge of the course and your ability to use that knowledge to respond to a question.

hurdle a minimum in some assessment item that must be reached in order to be eligible to pass in a course.

invigilator a person who runs the examination session.

multiple-choice questions those that consist of a question or statement and a number of possible answers, only one of which is correct.

open book examinations those in which you are permitted to use course material and notes.

perusal the short period immediately before an examination when you are permitted to peruse your examination paper.

short answer questions those requiring a full response, which may take half to one page of writing.

special consideration this is granted if you have a good reason (with documentation) for not performing to your usual level during an examination. Your mark may be raised very slightly.

take-home examination an examination during which a student collects the examination paper at a certain time, then writes his or her answers over a set number of days (in any place).

true/false questions those that present a statement asking you to decide if it is true or false.

chapter TWELVE

Doing Small-scale Exploratory Research Projects

As a university student, you will be required to undertake some research. Initially, your research will probably take the form of small-scale research projects on topics given to you by your tutor or lecturer. As you progress to higher levels of study, your research may become more substantive and independent. While there are some differences between research that is conducted within different disciplines, there are also many similarities.

This chapter aims to introduce:

- different types of research
- the main approaches to research
- key skills required to undertake small-scale research
- the process involved in research
- the notion of scientific rigour
- methods involved in research
- ethical considerations when undertaking research.

What is research? Why do people research? Where do you find evidence of research? Can you think of some examples of research that have affected your life in some way? Have you ever conducted research?

Thinking

What is research?

Reports on **research** are everywhere. For example, whenever you read a newspaper report about the growing rate of obesity, or divorce, or about the effects of global warming, or the effects of alcohol consumption, you are a consumer of research. If you were in Australia on 8 August 2006, you should also have been a participant in a large-scale research project—the national census. As a tertiary student, you have probably written essays and reports in which you have searched for and evaluated the research literature on a particular topic. On another level, whenever you make a decision about which course of study to undertake or which car to buy, your decision will probably be guided by some private, informal research that you have conducted.

Research may be commissioned by an organisation or a government body (for example, to investigate the impact of a wind farm on the migration and breeding patterns of a rare parrot), it may be conducted for academic purposes (for example, to further the development of knowledge on a topic) or it may be conducted to investigate the preferences of a group of people (for example: Which ice cream flavour do primary school-aged children in Australia like? Which political party do their parents plan to vote for in the next federal election?) or to solve a problem (for example: What can be done to improve traffic flow in a dangerous intersection?).

The quality of the research is assessed on the rigour with which it was conducted and the clarity with which it is presented. Typically, in organisations research reports are published as in-house documents (for others in the same organisation) or in scholarly journals, and the members of the audience are usually other experts in the field and decision-makers in organisations. As a student, and a novice researcher, the primary audience for your research is your tutor or lecturer. As you progress to higher levels of study your audience may expand to other experts and professionals in your field.

A newspaper report on the growing rate of obesity will be written for the general audience, and will generally be a summary of a research report outlining the main points without giving the details. Other experts and interested parties will probably read the original research report and evaluate its findings and the methods used by the researchers and perhaps even **replicate** it; that is, use it to conduct a similar study in another setting. Replicating a research study is a common and valid practice as long as the original study is acknowledged using a referencing system. Policy makers may use the findings of the report to formulate new policies on advertising standards for fast-food outlets, while school councillors may use the same findings to instigate changes to the school tuckshop menu.

Thinking

For what purposes do you think the results from the 2006 National Census could be used?

As you can see, research is not an aimless activity that is conducted in a vacuum or one that is conducted for purely academic purposes; it is a purposeful activity and it is conducted in a systematic manner. Research can take many forms; it can be conducted for many purposes in many disparate settings; and it can generate important information upon which many important decisions are made.

How do the media rely on research?

Look through today's newspaper to see how many reports are about research, and how many journalists and commentators cite research to strengthen their report or argument.

This activity should highlight the prevalence of research and its place in our lives, but remember, as a tertiary student you will not be able to rely on newspaper reports for anything more than to make personal decisions and to generate ideas for your academic research. As a tertiary student you will be required to read more scholarly journal articles and books.

So what is research? Research can be defined as the systematic process of gathering information in order to solve a problem or to answer a question. Gill (1996) also gives us a useful working definition of research: 'My interpretation of research is as the process of finding out new information and explicating the associated meanings, thus building new knowledge; or making new connections between existing knowledges' (p. 37).

As a reader of research it is important that you understand what is involved in the research process, as this will enable you to evaluate the quality of others' research. As a researcher it is important that you develop sound research skills so that your research survives the scrutiny of others.

Researchable issues and questions

Research often starts from the recognition of an issue about which there is some disagreement or lack of understanding. Much of what we know and much of what we base our opinions on is the result of someone's research. Some of this research will have been conducted to answer questions about practical issues and to solve practical problems, but some of the research may have been conducted on remote, highly theoretical questions such as the composition of dust-like particles on Mars. Without research we would have very little access to any knowledge beyond our subjective personal experience.

As we have stated earlier, issues can be found in many different contexts. However, not every issue is worth researching and not every issue can be researched. Once you have a question or a problem in which you are interested, you need to assess your ability to do it justice; you need to construct a plan for your research and decide on your methodology and your method.

Research is the systematic process of gathering information in order to solve a problem or to answer a question.

Research methodology is concerned with the chain of association that links the issue to a research question and the research question to an appropriate method by which the question might be resolved. Each research question may require a unique approach and, as a result, as the research question and design are refined, the methods might also be refined. **Research method**, on the other hand, refers just to the 'tools' (such as interviews and case studies) that a researcher uses for gathering and analysing **data**.

Thinking

Reflect on the results of the previous activity. Identify the different settings for the research in the newspaper reports. Identify the possible reasons behind the research questions and the different methods used to gather data.

Thinking

Why do you want to do research? What kinds of questions and problems are you interested in answering? Identify the settings and contexts in which the issues and problems make themselves manifest.

The research process

There are many different types of research; however, they all share the characteristics of being planned and systematic. Many writers about research have attempted to represent the research process diagrammatically in an attempt to show what actually happens when people research. However, as is true of many other human endeavours, while there are some core elements that are present in all research, there is no one best way to conduct research.

Activity

Draw a diagram of the research process
Before you read any further, draw a diagram of the research process as you understand or imagine it.

As we have already said, research is a planned, purposeful and systematic activity, but there are as many different approaches as there are researches and research problems. One possible representation of the research process might include the following steps.

Identify a problem, idea or topic for research

In the early stages of your tertiary studies, the research topic may be given to you by your tutor or lecturer. This is often the case when a student is new to a particular discipline, and the tutor or lecturer wants the students to familiarise him- or herself with a particular topic, but also to practise the skill of researching in preparation for larger research projects.

However, if you are asked to generate a topic, you may be able to follow your interests or you could generate ideas by reading the research of others. Remember that higher-level research is concerned with solving problems or contributing something new to a body of knowledge. It is by reading what others have previously researched that we may find a gap in the body of knowledge that we may be able to fill.

While all work that you submit as a tertiary student has to be your own original work, as a novice researcher you will not be expected to make new earth-shattering discoveries; rather, you will be expected to make judicious use of others' research to guide you in an investigation of an issue or a problem. As you progress to higher levels of study, you will be expected to search the published literature on a topic with the aim of uncovering that gap in the body of knowledge that you may be able to fill.

Brainstorm

Thus, if you have to generate a topic, begin by brainstorming the problem, idea or topic. This process will help you identify the range of possible perspectives from which the broad topic could be approached. This in turn will help you narrow down the topic so that it is manageable within a certain time frame, word limit or, perhaps even, budget.

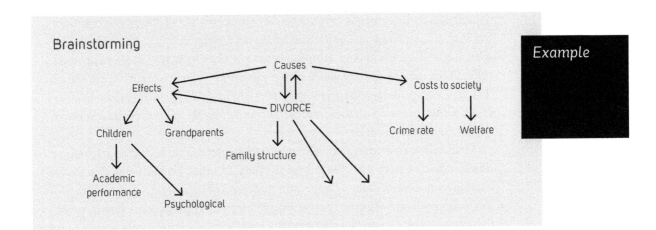

Brainstorming

Example

To brainstorm, write down the broad topic of interest and then consider the topic from as many different perspectives as possible. Do not worry about the details at this stage; the aim is to generate as many ideas as possible.

Narrow down the topic and write the research statement

By the time you reach this stage you should have a good idea about the broad topic and subtopics that you brainstormed. Now, you need to try to write your research statement as succinctly as possible.

Example

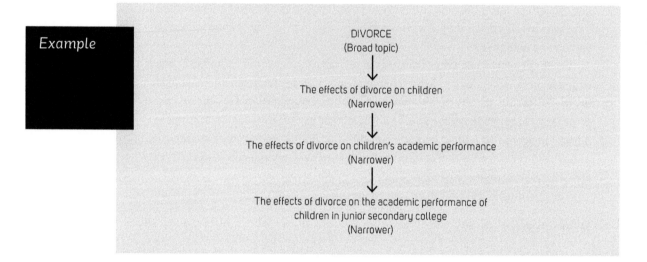

DIVORCE
(Broad topic)

↓

The effects of divorce on children
(Narrower)

↓

The effects of divorce on children's academic performance
(Narrower)

↓

The effects of divorce on the academic performance of
children in junior secondary college
(Narrower)

A researcher may even narrow down the topic further, and focus on a specific age group, gender or socioeconomic group. How the topic is narrowed down will depend on factors such as the question in which the researcher is interested, previous research in the area and the availability of researchable subjects. Your research statement should be succinct, but it must reflect the scope of your study. In other words, it must be short, but contain all the key elements of the study. If, for example, your study focuses on one country, one region, one sociocultural group or any atypical situation, your research statement must reflect this; it must specify which group or country you are focusing on, and in this way acknowledge that there may be significant differences between your study group, in terms of laws, regulations and cultural expectations, and other apparently similar groups.

Your research statement becomes your project title, and it must reflect no more and no less than the research study. In other words, using the above example you cannot claim in your title that you are investigating all children in this category if you are only researching children in a particular region in which there are inadequate family support services for sole-parent families.

Write a focused research statement

1   Select one of the following topics:

   a   drugs

   b   capital punishment

   c   mass media.

2   Brainstorm to find all the perspectives on your chosen topic.

3   Now try writing a focused, manageable research statement. Repeat the process with a topic of particular interest to you.

Literature search and review

As we have suggested earlier, unless you are given a complete research question by your lecturer, you might start thinking about your research topic as a result of reading what others have researched and written on the topic. A literature search and review at this stage is essential in helping you determine whether or not your research is worth doing or to determine which angle to take.

With advancements in information technology it has become increasingly easy to locate information as well as to publish online. However, this brings with it associated problems. In the past, if an author wanted to publish his or her work he or she would send the manuscript or journal article to a publisher, who would then send it to other experts in the area for review. By the time the book, or the journal article, was published the reader could be confident that the book or article had sufficient credibility. While this process is still practised for books and scholarly journals, paper-based and online, there are numerous articles and other kinds of texts available online that are not put through this kind of filtering and cannot thus be considered credible. As a researcher, especially if you wish to be taken seriously, you need to ensure that you access recently published texts and peer-reviewed academic and professional journals.

Once you have searched and reviewed the published literature, and once you have decided on the topic or question for your project, you will need to conduct a more thorough search of the literature and commence a critical review of the literature.

Your research should be informed, but not constrained, by the research of others. The purpose of a literature review is to establish that your research is feasible, that it is worth undertaking and that you have a clear idea about what you are doing. A literature search and review will help you:

- outline key theories in the field
- establish some of the questions that are considered important in this area
- identify questions that have not been adequately answered

- identify disagreements among the findings of previous research studies
- identify methodological faults in previous research
- outline any practical problems that the research may solve
- take up any recommendations for future research.

At times new researchers may be sceptical about finding enough information on their topic. However, once they start searching, the opposite often happens, in that they become swamped with information. The trick is to learn to read strategically by following these steps:

- Follow up references cited in recently published research articles.
- Conduct a search through the university's library database.
- Find a key research study and, using a citation index, see who has cited it (your librarian will be able to advise you how to do this).

Practise the effective reading strategies that you read about in Chapter 3. Read the abstract, the introduction and the conclusion before you decide whether or not the text is likely to be useful to your research. Then read further.

You must also learn to become a critical reader of the research. Ask questions. Does the information in the text match the claims in the title? Is the writer an accepted expert in this area? Are the arguments sound? Do they lead to convincing conclusions? Does the writer present appropriate supporting evidence? How does what this writer say connect with what others say? As you learn more about research methods and methodology, you might also start asking questions about how appropriate they are to the research.

As you read, make clear notes. See the following example of how to set up a notebook. It is important to separate the writer's ideas from your own. It is also vital to record the bibliographic details and to make connections between what various writers say about the same topic.

Example

The effects of divorce on the academic performance of children in junior secondary college.

Brown, J. (2005). *From divorce to divorce*. Sydney, Australia: Synergy Press.

Brown's ideas and quotes	My comments
p. 17 'the children of divorced parents often perform better than average ...'	No supporting evidence. Compare with Read (2004, p. 6); disagrees
p. 26 case study: Jack's academic performance pre and post divorce	This is a good example

Also, as you read, keep asking yourself if and how what you are reading is connected to your research statement. If it becomes clear that it is not connected, do not waste your time. Move on to another, more relevant article.

Remember, as we have stated earlier, research is a process and not every question is researchable. Sometimes, as you gather more evidence and information about a topic, or indeed as you discover the lack of evidence or information, you might find that you need to refine your research statement.

Decide on data collection method

In the next section of this chapter, you will be introduced to two main approaches to research: quantitative and qualitative. Often, these approaches are linked to data collection methods. For example, **quantitative data** are often linked to questionnaires and **qualitative data** to interviews. We argue, however, that the real distinction between the two methods lies in part in how the questionnaire and interview are constructed and in how the data are analysed. As you will read later, if you lean towards the former approach, you will be interested in numerical data (how many, how much) and if you lean towards the latter approach, you will be interested in more in-depth data about how and why. Questionnaires and interviews can both be constructed and analysed to answer both kinds of questions presented by the different approaches.

The term data refers to the information that is collected. Qualitative data can take the form of utterances, observed behaviours and text analysis. Quantitative data can take the form of ranked categories (such as: how many agree, disagree), grades, IQs and income levels.

The type of data collected will be a direct consequence of the chosen research topic and will determine the type of analysis required. A researcher interested in large-scale research will probably work on the assumption that data gathered from large numbers of individuals will provide more reliable information than data gathered from any particular individual. This kind of quantifiable data is regarded as more reliable if conclusions need to be drawn about a significant population.

As we have said earlier, initially you will probably be involved in small-scale research projects. These are likely to lean toward the qualitative approach. The assumption with this sort of research is that the data gathered from an individual or a small group of people can provide a model of the complexity of individual behaviour with greater validity than can the quantifiable data in large-scale research. This kind of research can give us greater insight into complex social situations.

Triangulate

As a researcher it is important to collect data from a variety of different sources. This is called **triangulation**, and it helps the researcher understand the issue from a variety of different, and sometimes competing, perspectives. Often it is just as useful to read the work of those with whom you may disagree as of those with whom you may agree. It is also useful to utilise, whenever possible and appropriate, different research tools or data collection methods. In a subsequent section of this chapter we will outline some of the main approaches to qualitative data collection, including case studies, interviews and questionnaires.

Decide about sources of data

Begin by identifying your **target population**; that is, the larger group about which you want to reach findings. For example, if you wanted to understand how international students in your faculty coped with note taking during lectures, the international students in your faculty would be your target population.

Once you have identified your target population, you will need to consider ways of accessing information about them. In the case of small-scale research projects, you also need to ensure that you will get access to the participants and to any documents that may be confidential or subject to freedom-of-information laws. You also have to give careful consideration to ways of selecting and accessing a sample group. We will consider sampling later in this chapter.

Remember our earlier caution that not all questions are researchable. If you cannot get the information that you need or access a sample group or a case-study participant, you may have to rethink your topic! Furthermore, as a university student, any research involving human beings may be subject to human ethics approval. This includes gaining consent and explaining in plain language the nature and process of the research. We will discuss this in a subsequent section of this chapter.

Choose the sampling technique

Sampling techniques are discussed in the next section. Essentially, if the researcher is interested in answering a question about a large group of people, it is impractical for him or her to research each individual. The sampling process involves choosing from the target population a representative or 'typical' smaller group of individuals to participate in the research. Based on the findings from this smaller group, the researcher should then be able to make **generalisations**, or make statements about the larger group. This is referred to as **probability sampling**.

In some cases it may be legitimate to research a specific group of people, or indeed an individual, to answer a particular question or solve a particular problem that is specific to them. This is referred to as **non-probability sampling** and, as the term suggests, the findings are usually not generalisable.

Gather the information

Like other researchers, you have to ensure that your information-gathering technique is well planned and systematic. If you are conducting interviews with several groups at different times, you need to ensure that your style and your questions are consistent. In some cases the interview may have a semi-fixed structure. This means that the interviewer will have a number of fixed questions that she or he will ask each individual in each group to answer, but will also have some freedom to follow a line of questioning in an unanticipated direction that emerges during the interview.

If you are using questionnaires you need to consider how you will administer them. Will you interview each individual? Will you ask individuals to complete the questionnaire in an environment in which they work or study? Will you post it to them? If you post it, consider how many are likely to commit to responding to the questionnaire and posting it back?

Record the data

As a researcher, you are likely to be swamped with data. Again, it is vital that you are systematic about how you record information. If you conduct interviews, case studies or participant observation, unless you have permission to record the sessions, you will have to write notes as you listen or observe while trying not to be obtrusive. It is essential that on each occasion you set up a notebook in which you record the details of date, location, participants and so on.

While you are listening or observing, you may have a clear idea about the kinds of answers and behaviours that you are looking for, but you may be overwhelmed by unanticipated data that could add to your research. Thus it is important to be focused on what you want to get from the session, but also to be open to possible new directions as well.

Code and analyse the data

When you have collected your data, you should read it several times before you start organising it. Reading it will help you see patterns in the data that will help you categorise it in a meaningful way. Your reading should be focused on answers to your specific questions, but you should also look for emerging issues or ideas that you did not expect. This may reveal new directions for further research.

Example

If you asked a representative group of college students to describe their favourite food, you might get answers such as:

- *Respondent 1:* 'I like pasta. It has to be home made from farm fresh eggs and mixed with semolina flour. My favourite sauce is made from onions, fresh tomatoes, anchovies, a splash of merlot wine and some torn fresh basil. This is topped with shavings of parmesan.'
- *Respondent 2:* 'My favourite food is pizza. I usually prepare my own dough using two eggs and 200 grams of flour, a pinch of salt, some dried yeast and warm water. I knead it and knead it until it's elastic and then I let it rest and rise. I then roll this out, spread some prepared tomato pizza topping on top, add some shredded mozzarella cheese that I buy from the supermarket. I then cook this in my wood-fired oven.'
- *Respondent 3:* 'My favourite food is Atlantic salmon, marinated in a honey mustard sauce and cooked in a wood-fired oven. I serve this with some steamed baby potatoes and slow-roasted cherry tomatoes ...'

With a question like this, you would probably have more respondents. Let us imagine that you interviewed a representative sample of 30 college students.

You would then read and reread the responses for emerging patterns. For instance, from the examples above we can see a pattern forming already. All three mention using tomatoes, so that could be one category, but one mentions using fresh tomatoes, another mentions prepared tomato pizza topping and the third mentions slow-roasted cherry tomatoes. Two mention wood-fired ovens. And two mention cheese, but one is shaved parmesan and the other is shredded mozzarella cheese from the supermarket.

Thinking

Who do you think would be interested in researching the kind of question in this example? How many other possible categories can you identify?

Thinking

Think of some ways in which you might be able to code the information in the last example.

Coding involves reducing the data and representing common categories, if possible, with an abbreviation or a symbol. For example, if you discover that many respondents mention tomatoes, instead of writing tomato time after time you may devise a symbol (such as a simplified diagram of a tomato), and instead of writing cheese you may use an abbreviation (such as 'chz').

Once you have recognised the patterns, you need to consider ways of displaying the data. A recommended way is to present information as a matrix (see the following example). This allows you to view the data and see connections more clearly. The way that you categorise will depend on what you were looking for in your research but, as we stated earlier, you might also find new categories of interest.

Example

Respondent	Type	Toppings/ marinades	How cooked?	Sides
1	Pasta—homemade	Tomato—fresh Cheese • shaved • parmesan Basil		
2	Pizza—homemade	Tomato—bought Cheese—shredded Mozzarella—bought	Wood-fired oven	
3	Fish—salmon	Honey mustard marinade	Wood-fired oven	Baby potatoes—steamed Cherry tomatoes—slow-cooked
... 30				

Write the report

Writing up research is an essential part of the process of learning and communicating effectively with others. This will be the focus of the next chapter.

Quantitative versus qualitative research

There is no one correct way of conducting research. Research methods are intrinsically tied to research questions. However, as a beginning researcher, you will probably encounter the two most common general strategies for conducting research, quantitative and qualitative research. Too often these approaches are presented as competing alternatives. However, most recent research, particularly in the social sciences, will have elements of both.

Rather than seeing them as competing strategies, it may be more useful to regard them as complementing strategies. They both contribute something to our knowledge and understanding.

Quantitative research

As the term suggests, quantitative research is primarily concerned with the collection and analysis of data in numerical form. For example, the quantitative data collected through the 2006 National Census will give the government a snapshot of the population. If, for instance, one of the findings shows that a greater number of people are caring for elderly relatives at home than at the time of the last census, the government may decide to conduct further research into support services for the elderly with the view of reviewing their policies on funding such services. If the results show that an increasing number of people are moving into the outer suburbs of a major city, they may conduct further research into why and into whether or not the infrastructure in that area is adequate.

Example

If a researcher wants to find out how many people are likely to vote for a particular political party in an election, the researcher may select a representative sample of the population and simply ask: 'Which party—Liberal or Labor—will you vote for in the election on Saturday?'

How the researcher selects a representative sample for the research will be discussed in the section on Sampling.

The results that the researcher can hope to yield from this research will be in the form of *how many* respondents answered Liberal and *how many* answered Labor.

The results will not give an indication of *why* the respondents plan to vote for the particular party. This is the realm of qualitative research.

While this kind of information does not give us any insights into the reasons behind the decision, it can be very useful for tracking trends, and it can alert us to the need to conduct some in-depth qualitative research.

If a researcher wants to find out what percentage of the Australian population are numerate (against an accepted measure of numeracy and literacy), the researcher might ask a representative sample of the population, a series of carefully constructed questions such as:

Is 12 per cent of 220:

A   Less than 26
B   More than 26
C   26
D   None of the above

The data would give an indication of *how many* answered the question correctly but it would not give any insights into why the results are such as they are. If the data indicated that the numeracy levels had fallen below an acceptable level, the next step might be to conduct a qualitative study into *why* and then into *how* the problem can be remedied.

Quantitative research has traditionally been regarded as more 'reliable' and 'objective' than qualitative research. However, as we can see in the examples, it can only answer part of the question that we may need to ask. Research into social sciences involves people and people's concerns; their attitudes and experiences cannot be reduced to numbers. While qualitative research is more 'subjective', if conducted with **rigour** it offers deeper insights into human phenomena.

Qualitative research

As we have suggested above, qualitative research is primarily concerned with exploring in more depth and detail the underlying reasons for a phenomenon. It has gained more respect over the last few decades.

Using the previous example, if the data indicated that the numeracy levels had fallen below an acceptable level, the next step might be to conduct a qualitative study into *why* and then into *how* the problem can be remedied.

One approach might be to interview a number of numeracy teachers about their perceptions of the reasons for the falling levels. Another might be to conduct a case study into the numeracy-teaching methodologies at a particular school.

Here is a summary of the differences and similarities between quantitative and qualitative research. Some of the terms will be explained in the next section.

Quantitative	Qualitative
<ul><li>objective</li><li>involves controlled measurement</li><li>creates an 'outsider' perspective</li><li>numerical data</li><li>replicable data</li><li>findings can be generalised</li></ul>	<ul><li>more subjective</li><li>less controlled and more naturalistic</li><li>creates an 'insider' perspective</li><li>holistic data</li><li>deep, real, rich data; less easy to replicate</li><li>findings are less easy to generalise; more cohort and context specific</li></ul>

Scientific rigour

The term **scientific rigour** applies to all research, and not just research into the sciences; it refers to a planned, systematic, thorough and rigorous process of research irrespective of the topic being researched.

Regardless of whether a researcher leans towards the quantitative or the qualitative research strategies, all research has to be conducted and reported with rigour, and it has to be reliable and valid. Rigour in research refers to a process that is conducted, recorded and reported with exactness, precision and detail.

Validity

The validity of the research can be assessed from a number of perspectives. **External validity** can be assessed according to the appropriateness of the generalisabilty of the results. In other words, can the findings be applied to the target population and/or to another similar population?

Internal validity of measurement is concerned about whether or not the methods and approaches that you chose actually measured what you set out to measure. In other words, have you answered the question that you set out to answer?

Reliability

Reliability relates to how well you have carried out the research for your project. A very useful question that you should ask yourself is: 'Would another researcher, looking into the same question in the same setting arrive at the same results (if not the same interpretation)?' The answer should be 'Yes'. To enhance **reliability**, methods, conditions and results of the research must be consistent.

Generalisation

Generalisation relates to how representative your research is of a larger group. In other words, if you are interested in investigating something about a large group of people, you need to ensure that you select a smaller representative group for your research.

Consider, if you carry out a detailed study in a particular setting, will your results be applicable to a similar group in another setting? How will you know? How important is it that they are applicable to a similar group in another setting?

Example

It is important to remember that sometimes it is perfectly acceptable to investigate an issue or a problem that relates to a particular small group of people and does not necessarily have any significance to a larger group. Most commonly, however, researchers will want to make generalisations about a larger target population.

Target population

The target population is the group of people about whom you wish to generalise. For example, you may need to investigate whether or not residents of a particular suburb agree that the main road should be widened. Once you have your question you will need to devise your research tool (for example, a questionnaire). The target population will be all the residents in the suburb. However, as it is unlikely that you will have the time or the resources to administer the questionnaire to each resident, you will need to select a representative sample of the population to whom you will administer the questionnaire.

A target population could be:

- all households in Australia (as in the Australian Census)
- all people over the age of 18
- all state-owned primary schools in Victoria
- all instances of turning on the television and watching a particular television channel in the last week.

Example

Thinking

In your own words, explain the difference between a target population and a sample group. Now read again the explanations that we have offered and see how well the explanations match.

Representative sample

A representative sample is a smaller group, or subset, selected from the target population. If information is obtained from the entire population, such as in the Australian Census, it is not a sample. There are a number of different sampling methods that can be used to ensure that the **representative sample** is indeed 'typical' of the larger population, and that the aims of the research are met. Judicious sampling is the key to any research through which you plan to generalise about a large number of people, because no matter how thoroughly you collect the data, if your sample has not been properly found, your findings will be discredited.

Simple random sampling

Random sampling is also referred to as probability sampling, and it is considered to be the most accurate sampling method. While the word random may imply that the process is arbitrary, or not systematic, the opposite is actually true. **Random sampling** is the process of allocating participants from the larger target population to form part of the sample group in such a way that each member of the population has an equal chance of being selected; in other words, the probability that person A will be selected is equal to the probability that person X will be selected. Random sampling seeks a representative sample through equal probability.

To obtain a random sample, a researcher must first identify an appropriate sampling frame. A **sampling frame** can be a list of all members of a population, or it can be the method of selecting any member of the target population. Commonly used sampling frames include telephone directories, electoral rolls and street directories.

To select randomly, the researcher may use a number of different methods. One method is the lottery system that involves placing the names of each member of the population on slips of paper, placing the slips in a container and drawing them out at random. The researcher could also use a computer-generated list of numbers, with each number corresponding to a member of the target population. These could then be selected randomly by the computer or the researcher. The research may also employ systematic random sampling, in which every 10th or 12th or any other nth case is selected.

Can you think of any other ways of obtaining a random sample? In each case consider the benefits and limitations. For instance, if a researcher uses a telephone book to source participants, the researcher will not have access to the growing numbers of people who exclusively use mobile telephones.

Thinking

When is a representative sample truly representative?

While there are a number of mathematical formulae that can assist the researcher in determining a representative sample size, as a general rule, if the target population to which you wish to generalise is small, then you should include most or even all in your sample group. If the target population is large, you can include a smaller representative sample in your research. In other words, as the population increases, the representative sample size decreases.

Target population	Sample size
10 people	10 people
20 people	19 people
75 people	59 people
100 people	80 people
200 people	132 people
1000 people	278 people
2000 people	322 people
6000 people	326 people
10 000 people	370 people
Source: adapted from Krejcie and Morgan (1970)	

Example

Stratified random sampling

As the name suggests, with random sampling every member of the population has an equal chance of being selected to participate. However, if a researcher wants to find out something more specific about different groups within the target population, the researcher may stratify the population. **Stratified random sampling** involves identifying some of the relevant factors that are present in a population. Some of these factors might be age, sex and socioeconomic status. These factors would then be used to categorise different groups into strata. Once they are identified, the researcher would randomly select a separate representative sample from each stratum.

If you were interested in surveying a representative sample of students at your university about their preferences for a particular computer, you might want to know if there are differences between the preferences of undergraduate and postgraduate students. In this case, you would stratify your group and randomly select a representative sample (the same percentage of participants) from both the undergraduate and postgraduate strata. You would then be able to compare the results between the preferences of undergraduate and postgraduate students.

Purposive sampling

Random sampling may not always be possible, especially when the target population is very large. Also, in some cases random sampling may not be desirable. For example, when researchers wish to learn something about specific groups of members in a population (such as the eldest and the youngest), they may purposefully sample only those particular members. Purposive samples then do not purport to be as representative of the whole population.

There are a number of different **purposive sampling** methods. Maximum variation sampling is one example of this method, and is used when the researcher tries to create a representative sample without sampling at random. The underlying principle is that the researcher deliberately aims to interview a diverse selection of a population. For instance, if the target population were 100 people and the researcher only has the resources to interview 30 people from a wide range of extremes, the researcher may choose to interview the oldest and the youngest, the person who earns most and the person who earns least, and so on, with the aim of finding a representation of the 'average' within the population. Another method involves the selection of participants (such as working mothers) in a non-random manner based on characteristics that are directly relevant to the research question.

Activity

Sampling methods
Conduct some quick research on various sampling methods. Draw up a table and make notes about the uses, the advantages and disadvantages of each method.

Convenience samples

While most research aims to generalise findings to a larger population, there are many valid research studies that aim to uncover something about a particular smaller group of people or an organisation or, as we have suggested earlier, an individual. Furthermore, as a novice researcher you may not have access to information about a larger group or the research skills and resources to conduct a larger study. Under these circumstances, and while you are honing your research skills, you may be able to use convenience or found sampling.

As the term suggests, **convenience sampling** involves surveying those people to whom it is most convenient to get access. Perhaps you have the contact details of this group because they all attended the same graduation ceremony as you, or perhaps you have their details because they are your former clients.

If you use this method of sampling, be aware that you have no way of knowing how representative the sample is. In other words, your findings, the conclusions that you draw and the recommendations that you make will be limited only to the sample group.

Surveys

Surveys provide a snapshot of a given population at a particular point in time; they aim to estimate one or more characteristics of a target population through the thorough investigation of a representative sample. They involve the systematic gathering of information from a representative sample. Surveys are often descriptive, in that they may gather data that will summarise current attitudes to, for example, Australia's involvement in the Iraqi war.

Surveys may be conducted with the aim of establishing causal relationships between a number of different factors, describing attitudes towards enduring issues, or describing the demographic characteristics of a group of people. The methods of data gathering that a researcher chooses will depend on the accessibility of the participants and the volume of possible responses, particularly if the target population is large. The most popular methods of data gathering for surveys are questionnaires and **interviews**.

Questionnaires

Questionnaires remain one of the most widely used tools for gathering data into human phenomena. On the surface it may seem that asking questions about people's attitudes, behaviours, preferences and so on, is a straightforward activity.

Reflect on your experience of answering questionnaires. Were the questions always clearly worded? Were they **open-ended questions** or **closed questions**? Which ones were easier to answer? Did the questions cover the range of responses that you wanted to give? Was the questionnaire too long or not long enough? Were the questions always appropriate, or were some too personal?

Thinking

It is useful to remember your experience of being a respondent to a questionnaire when you are faced with writing a questionnaire as a researcher! Consider the following aspects of using a questionnaire in research.

QUESTIONNAIRES

TYPES OF QUESTIONS

Open-ended

- Respondents are not confined to a particular answer
- As more detailed answers are required, respondents may be more reluctant to commit to answering them
- Difficult to code: more subjective and time consuming
- Bias towards those who express themselves well.

Closed

- Can be pre-coded and easier to analyse
- Can be set up for direct computer input
- Can be limiting
- Can be an 'easy option' for respondents with no opinion
- Can lead respondents towards a particular response.

ADMINISTRATION

Face-to-face

- Researcher can ensure higher completion and return rate
- Researcher can be sure who is responding
- Researcher can clarify the process or questions if necessary
- Can be expensive to bring everyone together.

Mailed

- Anonymity guaranteed
- Can be administered to a larger group
- Requires high commitment from respondents; low return rate
- Inability to identify non-respondents.

Factors influencing the response rate

- If questionnaire is very long, the response rate will be lower
- If there is a cost involved, it will be lower
- If questions are very personal, it may be lower.

Thinking

As you can see from the information in the above example, there are problems associated with questionnaires. Can you think of some ways of overcoming these problems?

WRITING QUESTIONNAIRES

- Avoid questions that are ambiguous.
- Avoid questions that assume specialist or technical knowledge.
- Keep the number of questions to the absolute minimum; a maximum of 15 well-worded questions is recommended.
- Try not to lead your respondents to a particular answer; allow for a range of possible answers.
- Do not ask too many open-ended questions, as they may be too time consuming; as a general rule, if the question can be written as a closed question, it should be.
- Try not to ask sensitive questions early in the questionnaire, as this may affect the quality of the responses overall.

Some types of questions that relate to specific research questions

1 Quantity

In which year did you first arrive in Australia?

2 Category

Have you ever attended a rock concert? (Circle the correct answer)
Yes   No

3 Scale

How would you describe your attitude to compulsory voting? (Circle one of the options below)

Strongly agree
Agree
Neither agree or disagree
Disagree
Strongly disagree

OR

How would you describe your attitude to the news that Australia will start using nuclear power in the near future? (Circle your response.)

Strongly agree	Partly agree	Neither agree nor disagree	Partly disagree	Strongly disagree
x	x	x	x	x

Example

The above examples aim to elicit levels of agreement. However, you can scale questions to elicit levels of satisfaction (for example, on a scale from very satisfied to very dissatisfied), levels of commitment (for example, on a scale or definitely yes to definitely not) and frequency (for example, on a scale from always to never).

4 Multiple-choice

Do you view taxpayers' funds spent on scientific research as any of the following (tick as many as you need to).

An investment
A necessity
A burden
A gamble
None of the above

5 What do you see as the main purpose of education? Please rank the following in order from 1 (for main purpose) downwards.

Personal interest/development
To get a job
Professional development
Social mobility
Improve earning potential
Other (please specify)_____

6 Open-ended

Please comment on any other factors that influence your choices:

_____
_____

Types of demographic questions that can assist the researcher to profile the respondents (while not breaching anonymity and confidentiality)

1   To which age group do you belong? (Please circle)
        Under 20
        21–30
        31–45
        Over 45
2   How long have you lived in Australia?_____
3   Are you currently in full-time paid employment? (Please circle)
YES   NO

Interviewing

Interviews involve questioning or discussing issues with participants. This can be achieved in face-to-face situations or via the telephone or, increasingly, via the internet. Consider the following aspects of interviewing as a technique for gathering data.

INTERVIEWS

ADVANTAGES

- Permit greater depth than a questionnaire
- Allows the researcher to establish rapport and probe
- The researcher can elaborate on and clarify the questions
- Nonverbal cues can be used
- Allows for information to be gathered from groups who are not literate enough to provide written answers.

DISADVANTAGES

- Can be time consuming and costly
- There can be variability between interviews if several interviewers are involved
- There can also be variability between interviews conducted in one context and another, even if the same interviewer is involved
- Respondents may have a range of responses to the interviewer that can affect the quality of their responses (for example, may be too eager to please, may be antagonistic, resentful and so on)
- The interviewer may be biased, may not be skilled, may lead respondents or may display personal qualities that affect the respondents.

TYPES OF INTERVIEW

- May be structured and well defined
- May be partly structured around a set of core questions
- May be unstructured and highly personal.

What do you think are the qualities of a good interviewer? How should an interviewer handle sensitive questions or answers?

Thinking

Case studies

While a survey typically aims to gather information about a large group of people, a **case study** aims to gather detailed information about a smaller group of people, or indeed about an individual. In order to gather this information, the researcher can use one research tool (such as an interview structure) or a number of research tools (for example, interviews, questionnaires and documents).

CASE STUDIES

ADVANTAGES

- Data are drawn from participants' direct experience and therefore regarded as deeply anchored in reality
- Data are 'rich' and 'deep', and as such can illuminate the complexity of human experience
- This richness and depth can be very persuasive
- Although case studies are explorations of specifics, because they typically generate a deeper understanding of a specific issue, some generalisations may be possible.

DISADVANTAGES

- Case studies are usually deeply rooted in their context. It is important to keep reminding oneself about the parameters of the context. In other words, how much of what you gather is atypical and how much may be true in other contexts?
- The complexity of data from a case study can make analysis difficult. As in any complex relationship, the connections between events and other factors may be crucial to the conclusions. As in any other research activity, and as with other data-collection methods, it is important *not* to lose sight of the forest for the trees. In other words, do not get lost in the detail and lose sight of the whole study or main question!

Activity

Case study research activity
Find an example of a case study from which the researcher has generalised, and that has had significance beyond the parameters of its context.

Ethics

Any research involving humans must conform to ethical principles. If you are involved in conducting research as part of a tertiary program, you will be guided, and limited, by the principles for conducting research on humans outlined by the tertiary institution. Some institutions require that all research conforms to these principles; others require that only research that is likely to be published conforms to the principles. You must investigate the policies and procedures in your institution.

In our view, every researcher must try to answer the following questions about any research project:

- Will the research be conducted in an ethical manner? That is, will the participants or subjects from whom data is being collected be treated as they are entitled to be treated by another human being?
- Will the benefit of the research outweigh any potential risk to the participants or subjects?
- What use will be made of the knowledge generated by this research, and to whom will it be provided?

These questions cannot always be easily answered. For this reason tertiary institutions have set up committees that consider all applications for ethical approval to conduct human research.

Ethical guidelines

Conduct a search for guidelines for ethical approval to conduct research on the website for your institution. Now do the same for other institutions. Out of interest, compare and contrast the principles with institutions in another country.

Activity

You will probably find the following principles articulated in the guidelines for ethical conduct of research.

GUIDELINES FOR ETHICAL CONDUCT OF RESEARCH

- Participants/subjects must give their informed consent. This is usually achieved through a Plain Language Statement, a document prepared by the researcher and the supervisor that outlines in 'plain language' the nature and the process of the research and a consent form signed by the participants
- Participants/subjects cannot be coerced to participate
- Researchers cannot withhold from the participants/subject the nature of the research
- Participants/subjects cannot be deceived
- Participants/subjects cannot be led to commit acts that diminish their self-respect
- Researchers cannot violate the participant's/subject's self-determination
- Researchers cannot expose the participants/subjects to physical or mental stress
- Researchers must respect the privacy of each participant/subject
- Researchers must not withhold benefits from participants/subjects
- Researchers must treat all participants/subject with dignity and respect.

As you can see, the job of a researcher is a difficult one. The researcher must try to conduct the research in an ethical manner and respect the rights of the participants or subjects, but must also be mindful of the possibility that the research may lose its substance. In other words, the researcher must balance the rights of the individual with the desire to complete the research.

Activity

What would an ethical researcher do in the following cases?

1 A researcher wants to investigate the financial and organisational structure and the social activities of a political group. In order to get this data, the researcher becomes a member of the group, obtains a position in the organisation, gathers data and then publishes it as an exposé on the group. Is this ethical?
2 A psychology lecturer wants to conduct some research on short-term memory loss. Her students are also required to participate in a research study as part of their course. She advises students in her class that they are required to participate in *her* study or they will not fulfil the requirements of their course. Is this ethical?

Activity

Milgram's research
Conduct a quick search on the internet of Milgram's research in 1963 and subsequent critiques of it. Why was his work widely regarded as unethical? Do you agree with the criticisms?

SUMMARY

This chapter introduced you to research as a systematic process used to gather information for a wide range of purposes. It explored different types of research and focused on the two main approaches, qualitative and quantitative. The major aspects of the research process were described, and the difference between methodology (the philosophical underpinnings) and methods (the tools used to conduct the research) was explained. As a beginning researcher it is useful for you to remember that every research question may require a different set of approaches and tools, and that you need to take time to plan thoroughly, to carry it out systematically and ethically, and to report on it clearly and accurately.

GLOSSARY

case study research aims to gather detailed information about a smaller group of people, or indeed about an individual.

closed questions questions that are precoded so the respondents are confined in their answers to the set of possibilities provided by the researcher.

coding the reduction of data, to be represented with an abbreviation or a symbol.

convenience sampling a survey of those people who are most conveniently accessed.

data the information that is collected.

demographic questions questions not specifically on the topic of the research (such as about age or gender), but can assist the researcher to profile the respondents.

external validity guarantee that the findings can be applied to the target population and/or to another similar population.

generalisation the process of extrapolating from the findings of a sample to a larger group (the target population).

internal validity guarantee that the methods and approaches used actually measure what the researcher sets out to measure.

interviews questioning or discussing issues with participants.

non-probability sampling the use of the findings from research gained from a specific group or individual to solve a problem that is specific to them.

open-ended questions questions that do not confine respondents to a particular answer.

probability sampling (random sampling) research findings gained from a small representative group to generalise about a larger group.

purposive sampling sampling for a particular purpose.

qualitative data data organised in terms of meanings (from an interest in how, why and so on).

quantitative data numerical data (gathered from an interest in how many, how much and so on).

random sampling the allocation of participants from the larger target population to form part of the sample group in such a way that each member of the population has an equal chance of being selected.

reliability the ability to replicate the research: would another researcher looking into the same question in the same setting arrive at the same results, if not the same interpretation?.

replication the ability to conduct a similar study in another setting.

representative sample a sample 'typical' of the larger (target) population.

research the systematic process of gathering information in order to solve a problem or to answer a question.

research method the tool (such as interviews, case studies and so on) that a researcher uses for gathering and analysing data.

research methodology refers to the chain of association that links the issue to a research question and the research question to an appropriate method by which the question might be resolved.

rigour the quality of the research process in terms of how it is conducted, recorded and reports on information with exactness, precision and detail.

sample a smaller group, or subset, selected from the target population.

sampling frame can be a list of all members of a population, or it can be the method of selecting any member of the target population.

scientific rigour the planned, systematic, thorough and rigorous process of research, irrespective of the topic being researched.

stratified random sampling a technique for categorising a population into a number of strata, usually according to demographic variables, that are significant for the research, then randomly selecting a separate representative sample from each stratum.

target population the group of people about whom the researcher wishes to generalise.

triangulation the collection of data about the same phenomenon using different methods, different times and so on, as a means of enhancing accuracy.

chapter THIRTEEN

Writing about Research

Once you have conducted your research, and once you have started to recognise and analyse patterns in your data, you are probably ready to start drafting your report. Like other noble human endeavours, this can be a lonely process and one that involves writing and rewriting. However, without this process, no matter how brilliant the researcher and no matter how enlightening the research, the findings would be of little use to anyone. Conducting the research is only part of the research process. Communicating it effectively makes it meaningful and useful.

This chapter aims to:

- introduce a range of conventions and stylistic features of writing about research
- review the writing process
- help you analyse and meet the needs of your primary audience
- introduce a structure for a research report
- outline the key features of research report sections.

Writing your report

By the time you arrive at the point of writing your research report you should have a solid **literature review**. This was, after all, one of the first steps that you took in the research process, and will form part of your research report. However, you may wish to review it and refine it before you include it in the final draft of your report. The literature review needs to be presented in such a way as to set the contextual and theoretical foundations for your report. This may not have been fully evident when you first conducted the review and began to write it. Now you need to show how it served as the springboard for your research, and you need to refine the language so that it shows the links between what you intended to do and what you have actually done.

By the time you get to this point you should also have a good set of notes that you made during the process of reading for your research and analysing your data. These notes may be rather rough and tentative, but if you examine them carefully you will probably find that there is a pattern in them; some of them are merely descriptive while others may be in the form of summaries and critiques. Just as you looked for patterns in your data, you should start looking for patterns in your notes. This will help you construct an outline for your **research report**.

A research report has clearly organised sections.

Let us begin by considering one possible outline for a research report. We say 'one possible outline or structure' because, while all reports have some common elements, they may also have many differences. The differences arise because each research topic may require slightly different treatment, and different lecturers and university departments may have specific requirements. In all cases, the organisation of key sections should enable you to convey your findings and discussion logically. We will look at the features of some key sections in more detail later in this chapter.

Example

A research report outline

Report sections

Requirements for reports will vary according to the topic of your report, the lecturer's/ tutor's specific requirements and the anticipated response from as well as the anticipated needs of your audience. Below is a guide on what information to include in common sections of reports.

- **Cover (or title) page:** include title of your report, submission date, your name and the names of all team members, the name of the person or organisation for whom the report was prepared; make it look professional
- **Table of contents:** this should reflect all sections of your report; it must show all headings and numbering (first degree and second degree headings) and page numbers
- **Acknowledgments:** it is customary to acknowledge your supervisor (in your case, this will probably be your lecturer or tutor)
- **Statement of ethics approval:** if you were involved in conducting human research, you will most probably have the approval of the ethics committee at your educational institution. It is important to make a statement to this effect at the beginning of your report. You should also attach a copy of the approved application in the Appendices section
- **Abstract:** this is usually written last but appears at the front of your report. It serves as a 'snapshot' of all the main points from all sections of the report. It is written in complete sentences and paragraphs. Aim for approximately half a page in length.

1 Introduction (this is an example of a first degree heading)

1.1 Statement of research topic/question (this is an example of a second degree heading)

The major research question/topic/issue/problem and any embedded minor questions. This needs to be a succinct statement about the main topic of investigation. One or two sentences are sufficient. Any minor, embedded questions can be presented as bulleted points. This was covered in the previous chapter.

1.2 Purpose

Try to express the purpose in one to two sentences. State as concisely as possible the *aim* of your report: Why are you writing it? What is the issue that you are investigating and why? For example, you may write:

The purpose of this report is to investigate the flow of information in the Admissions office at James College and to recommend improvements.

(It is not appropriate to state that you are writing it because it is an assessment piece.)

1.3 Background

The purpose of this section is to bring the reader up to date by *outlining* the history of the topic/problem/situation that you are investigating and linking it to the current situation. The level of detail will depend on your assessment of your primary audience's familiarity with the topic/problem/situation on which you are reporting.

1.4 Scope

This is where you make a statement about the extent of your research. For example, if you studied the communication patterns at a fast-food outlet, the scope should tell the reader whether the study was statewide or conducted within an outlet in a particular suburb; whether it was conducted over a period of one day or one week and so on. If you conducted a survey, you should state the number of respondents.

1.5 Limitations

As a researcher/writer, you do not have unlimited resources. Limitations are those factors that prevent you from, for example, preparing a more comprehensive report. In this section you can make a statement about the time and word limitations, about budgetary limitations and, if appropriate, you can make a statement about your inability to obtain crucial information due to corporate or institutional confidentiality.

(It is inappropriate to comment here on due dates for other assignments and/or the heavy workload that you may have as a student.)

1.6 Methods

This section contains information about the manner in which the information was gathered and analysed. Describe and justify your sampling technique (for example, why did you choose random sampling?) and your sample size (for example, why did you interview 20 people from a population of 150?). Indicate any limitations to your research due to the nature of your sample. Also describe briefly the research instruments used (such as the questionnaire, interview and so on) and the procedures followed.

2 Literature review

In this section you present your review of literature on this issue. This will have served as the theoretical foundation for your study. Now you need to present it to your readers in a way that will set the theoretical context for them.

3 Findings

(This section may have a more informative title and it may have subsections—be guided by your topic and your lecturer or tutor.)

This is the start of the 'body' of your report (*do not* use the heading 'The Body'). In this section you simply present data or facts. You can use combinations of tables, graphs and other visuals. Examples, descriptions or explanations can be included, but *do not* enter into a discussion, interpretation or analysis here.

4 Discussion

(May have subsections and more informative headings—be guided by your topic and your lecturer or tutor.)

In this section you need to discuss the implications of your research, examine underlying causes of any problems and generally comment on, analyse and interpret the data or facts presented in the Findings section. Remember to make links to theory (show how you interpret the results from within the theoretical framework of your literature review) and to use a referencing system. Discuss the validity (see Chapter 11) of your research.

5 Conclusion

The aim of a conclusion is to make a statement or statements about the major issues or problems presented in the report. Each conclusion is tailored to the purpose of the report. If the report aims to solve problems, a conclusion will consist of a statement of major problems—causes, effects and solutions. A conclusion in an informative report may reiterate main ideas presented in the report. This section must not contain any new information.

6 Recommendation

(May not be necessary; be guided by your topic and your lecturer or tutor.)

This section should be a 'call for action', and it must be clearly linked to your findings and discussion. It may also be a call for further research into an aspect of your topic, issue or problem. Present your recommendations in order of priority and use the wording and layout as follows:

It is recommended that:

- All students follow these guidelines
- All students proofread their work
- Further research is undertaken into ...

List of references and/or bibliography

- List of references: an alphabetical list of all sources cited in the report.
- Bibliography: an alphabetical list of all sources cited in the report (as per List of references) *as well as* all texts consulted (but *not used or cited*) when preparing for the report.

Appendix

Include any additional information for your readers' information. Attach any information that, if included in the body of the report, would interfere with the 'flow' of information in the report.

General presentation guidelines

- Use normal Arial or Times New Roman, 12-point font for text
- Use bold 14-point font for main headings and 12-point font for subheadings
- Do not go beyond third level headings
- Use double spacing
- Aim for a detached, objective tone—use more passive constructions. Do not personalise (do not use 'I' or 'We')
- Do not use fancy fonts and borders—aim for a professional presentation
- Edit and proofread your work.

Is the above outline suitable for your topic? Why or why not?

Activity

Consult with your lecturer or tutor, then list the main headings and subheadings of the report that you plan to write. Keep the entire outline in mind as you start drafting under the main headings and subheadings. However, allow for some flexibility in your outline. As you progress you may wish to add, delete or rearrange the sequence of the sections. Also remember, although it is presented at the very beginning of the report, the abstract is usually the last section to be written. Why do you think this is?

Let us now look more closely at some key considerations when preparing student research reports.

- The purpose of the report as an assessment piece is to assess your knowledge of the research process and the extent of your knowledge of the topic, issue or problem. The purpose of your report as a research study may be to solve a problem or illuminate an issue.

- Because your research study is conducted within the specific context of an academic environment, your report must also meet specific academic requirements: you must reference the work of others; you must acknowledge the work of others; and you must adopt an appropriate academic style. It is always advisable to check with your tutor or lecturer for any specific requirements that they may have.

Thinking

What are some features of an academic style of writing?

Academic writing usually has an objective, 'detached' tone, that is, a tone devoid of any personal reference, with a style that avoids humour and emotion.

Activity

Writing styles

1 Imagine that you have the task of teaching a person from a country without kangaroos what a kangaroo looks like, what it eats, how it reproduces, how it moves and about its anatomical features and so on. What kind of information would you include? What kind of language would you use?

2 Now imagine that you have to write a poem about a kangaroo. How would the kind of information that you present change? How would the language and the tone change?

3 Conduct a quick online research activity to locate a scientific report or an encyclopaedia entry on the bald eagle. Now locate a poem or a piece of creative prose about an eagle. What are some of the features of the different kinds of writing?

We would suggest that in the first instance you would use very precise information about the kangaroo's anatomical features (such as the average length of the tail, the duration of the gestation period and the skeletal structure), and about its habitat and so on. In the second instance you might use more emotive language to describe its relationship to human beings, its funny way of getting about and so on.

You must also decide on the right level of use of disciplinary language, often referred to as 'jargon'.

Thinking

What is disciplinary language? Can you think of some examples? Why do people use disciplinary language? When is it inappropriate to use disciplinary language?

Disciplinary language has its place. Often people working in the same field develop a form of shorthand for explaining complex concepts. This has the effect of making their communication within their community more efficient. For instance, a group of computer technicians may communicate quite effortlessly using terms such as CPU and RAM. However, many experts forget that people outside their community do not have the same expertise. For this reason, you need to consider how familiar your primary audience is likely to be with your specialised terminology.

Some of your data may be numerical and may need to be presented in the form of tables and graphs. You need to decide the best way of communicating your data to your reader. This may involve combining written and visual information.

The primary audience

With the exception of the kind of writing that you do in your diary or when you are writing a shopping list for yourself, you write for an audience. Sometimes you will have a definite idea about who this audience is but, more often than not, you will have to imagine them so that you can adapt what you need to communicate to their needs.

As you begin your first draft consider the following issues. Who are your primary readers? While a diverse audience may read your report over time, your report will have a primary readership. This is the group of readers you need to identify and write for. Consider the following:

- Who are they? What is their education level? What is their level of familiarity with your topic/issue/problem? Why are they likely to be interested in this research report? Of course, for most of you, this will be one of the first research projects that you have undertaken and reported on. Therefore, your primary readers will be your lecturers or tutors and your peers. In other words, you will initially probably pitch your writing at a tertiary-educated audience with some specialist knowledge of the topic.
- What do they expect from this kind of report in terms of overall report structure and quality of information?
- What do your readers expect to know about you, your background as a researcher and your qualifications to undertake and present this research on this topic, issue or problem?
- What kind, and how much, common knowledge can you assume? In other words, are they likely to share disciplinary knowledge about the topic, in which case you can bypass some of the fundamentals, or are they likely

to be decision-makers from different disciplines for whom you will need to include some more introductory information?

- Will they be familiar with the discipline or subject-specific vocabulary and specialised terminology, or will you have to include a glossary of terms?

Thinking

Let us consider a topic such as the central processing unit (CPU) of a computer. Imagine that you were asked to write a report on how the CPU works, aimed at the following groups:

1   A group of 16-year-old high school students in an inner suburb of Melbourne
2   A group of retirees in a word-processing class in the University of the Third Age
3   A group of unemployed people in their early 50s who are retraining in preparation for entering the workplace.

- In each case, how would the presentation of your information be different? Why? Now, reflect in the same way about how you will prepare your report for your primary audience.

Features of report sections

Now let us consider some key sections in your report in more detail. It is important to remember that your lecturer or tutor may have specific guidelines, and that you should always allow those to override yours if there is a difference.

The abstract

The abstract provides a summary of the report.

The **abstract** appears at the very beginning of the report. Research can be very complex, and the job of the writer is to make the job of navigating the report easier for the reader. The abstract sets the scene for the readers. It serves as an overview of all the main issues, arguments and findings that are presented in the report. It helps to focus attention on the specific context for the research, and it signals which issues are considered most important.

It is the shortest section (as a general rule, approximately 150–250 words) and, although it appears at the beginning, it is usually the last section to be written. This is because, as a snapshot of the report, it must include information that appears in the conclusion, and the conclusion is not (*and should not be*) reached, and therefore not written, until the end of the process.

The introduction

The introduction helps the reader understand the aim of the research and any limitations in its production.

The introduction usually comprises a number of subsections (see earlier example). Usually, this section follows the abstract. As is suggested by the word, its aim is to introduce the reader to the research project. In this section you need to outline for your reader the kind of research that you are conducting, the context of this research, the purpose of your research (*above the obvious purpose of completing an assessment piece*), the methods that you have employed and why you have done so, and the limitations on you as the researcher.

The writing must be as succinct as possible, but it must represent fully the main aspects of the project.

Methods

The methods section, as the term suggests, is where the researcher sets out in more detail the methods that were used to gather data. If you were involved in human research, other researchers will be interested in whether or not your research is replicable. That is, would another researcher interested in the same issue and using the same methods be able to collect the same data (*even if she or he ends up with different interpretations and conclusions*)? Other researchers will want to know what you did, why you did it, how you did it, to whom you did it and how many you did it to. You will need to justify your decisions and choices.

The method section outlines how the research was conducted and how the data was analysed.

Remember to maintain an objective, academic tone, and avoid personal references and personal pronouns (avoid using 'I' and 'we').

One approach to writing this section is to identify the target population, describe and justify the sampling procedure, describe and justify the instruments that you used (such as an interview or questionnaire), and outline the specific procedures for collecting the data.

Another important aspect of this section is the explanation of the data-analysis process (for example, did you use a particular statistical package or a specific measurement scale?). Your readers will be interested in how you arrived at your conclusions, irrespective of whether they plan to replicate your study or not. Provide an overview and justification of the analysis procedure that you used.

The literature review

In the last chapter we foreshadowed the need to conduct a review of the literature. We also gave you a few tips on how to approach it. In this section, we need to expand on this topic and discuss more fully how you might approach writing it. Let us begin by reviewing what a literature review is.

The literature review provides an overview of the literature as a means of showing the need for the particular research being undertaken.

The literature review is an account of what has already been published on a topic, subject, issue or problem. The version that you finally present in your report should not be representative of all that you could find on this topic but rather, it should include only the most relevant material that you have found on the topic. In other words, during your search you may have located 100 journal articles on the broad research topic, but perhaps only 30 of those articles are directly related to your specific topic.

The articles and books that you consult and review must be written by accredited scholars and researchers and should be peer reviewed. This allows us to assume some credibility about the researchers. Just because something is published on the internet does not mean that it is credible and widely respected as a piece of research.

The purpose of a literature review is to convey to your readers the knowledge and ideas that have already been established on a topic. Another purpose is to establish the strengths and weaknesses of the knowledge and the ideas.

A literature review does include summaries of articles or chapters or books but it must go beyond this. It is not a series of discrete pieces on individual texts that you have reviewed. It is an integrated, cohesive piece of discursive prose that comments critically on, and that draws connections between, the texts that you have selected (irrespective of whether they agree or disagree with each other). Furthermore, it must draw connections between the selected texts and your research topic.

Here are more important points about a literature review:

- Aim to organise the literature review around themes connected with your research question.
- As far as your supervisor, lecturer or tutor is concerned, the literature review allows you to demonstrate your ability to:
  - understand the literature
  - identify relevant journal articles and books
  - critically appraise the research of others.
- A literature review must have the following features:
  - It must be related directly to your research topic.
  - It should identify areas of controversy between researchers.
  - It must synthesise, or bring together, results into a discussion of what is and what needs to be discovered.
  - It should pose questions for further research in the area.

To help write a good literature review consider the following:

- Identify and never lose sight of the problem or research question that you want your literature review to help define.
- Are you searching for theories or/and for methodological approaches?
- Where are you likely to find the information that you are seeking? In academic journals, in government publications or in books?
- How effective are your research skills? Do you need to brush up on your electronic database search skills? Your librarian should be able to assist.
- How effectively are you analysing the literature? Are you merely summarising or can you see connections between various texts and your research topic?

- Are you engaging with research that conflicts with your own findings? Are you taking into account the possibility that other perspectives may be valid and may inform the direction of your discussion?
- How effectively are other writers whose work you are reviewing formulating their arguments? Could they have approached the topic from another perspective?
- How thoroughly have the other writers evaluated the literature relevant to the topic? Does their writing demonstrate the skills that we have identified as being important?
- How sound is their methodology? Do they identify their target group, their sample size and sampling procedure? Do they explain why they chose the instrument for data collection? Do they explain their data analysis procedure?
- Are the arguments well presented in a logical sequence? Do the conclusions follow from the premises, or the findings presented in their article or book?
- Who do you think the articles are written for? Try to identify the primary audience. What kind of evidence will you look for in the writing to help you establish this?
- Does the writer maintain a scholarly, objective tone?
- Does this book or article relate to the specific question that you are investigating? How?

How you organise a literature review is dependent on the aims of your research, the type of material that you research (such as journals, books, electronic journals, marketing brochures and video recordings) or topic(s) that you research. You may structure your literature review in a number of ways, including:

- by themes or topics (if the topic is complex and multilayered with multiple themes)
- in chronological order (if it is important to show the development of a theory or body of knowledge over time)
- by order of relevance
- comparing and contrasting (for example, with contentious issues, a juxtaposition of opposing views may be informative for the reader)
- using a funnel structure (moving from general to specific issues).

Findings or results

In the **findings section** (results section) you may need to combine verbal and visual communication to convey the complete message. The verbal component

Support findings from quantitative data with graphics (such as tables and figures).

will typically form the greater part of your report. Visuals can illuminate, support, enhance, extend and confirm what you write.

What kinds of data are best represented visually? Reflect on the various report sections in your outline. In which section might you find more visuals? What kinds of visuals are available to you? What are some strengths and limitations of different kinds of visuals?

As we have stated earlier, you will probably need to combine visual and verbal communication. Visuals, if well constructed and presented, have the potential for enhancing comprehension of complex information. Furthermore, quantitative data takes a numerical form, and needs to be presented in the form of tables, charts and graphs.

Visuals can provide a summary or an overview of a complex phenomenon that may otherwise take many words to explain. For example, consider what kind of information a diagram can communicate about the human body in comparison with just a verbal report on the body. Then consider how well a combination of visual and verbal information may work.

Visuals can reveal trends and patterns embedded in your data that may otherwise remain buried in masses of words and numbers.

Support findings from qualitative data with quotations.

Findings from qualitative data need to be presented with a rich description. Whether you are reporting on the findings from an open question in your questionnaire or from an interview, give quotations from the data to support the claims you are making. Do not provide the name of the respondent.

In some reports, it may be appropriate to combine findings and discussion, but as a general rule we recommend that they are kept separate. Your findings should be just that: a presentation of the data that you have found as a result of a methodical research process. This data can be presented visually and described verbally. Often when inexperienced writers attempt to combine the presentation of their findings with a discussion of those findings, they run the risk of confusing the 'hard evidence' and their interpretation of that evidence. Remember, different people can analyse the same findings, the same data, and make different interpretations and reach different conclusions.

We have just recommended that you present the findings in this section and avoid a discussion of those findings. However, we recommend that you describe the findings. What do you see as the difference between discussing something and describing it?

Discussion or description?

- This chair is made from Tasmanian ash. It has four legs. Each leg is 50 cm in height and 4 cm in width. It has a high back (70 cm in height, 30 cm in width) and a 30 × 30 × 15 cm cushioned seat. It is upholstered in black velvet.
- This chair is much better than the ones in the kitchen. It is much more comfortable because it has a cushioned seat. The ones in the kitchen are just moulded plastic and very cold to the touch. This one is also more appealing to look at because of its timber finish and black velvet upholstery.

The first example is a description of a chair. It aims to give the reader an idea of its physical appearance and its structure. The second example is more of a discussion, as it compares one chair with others and offers opinions about its comfort and appeal. Any two people could look at the same chairs and offer different opinions, but the height of the legs, the size of the cushioned seat and so on are measurable and verifiable.

Similarly, when you describe a chart or a graph in your report, the information must be verifiable. Later, in your discussion section, you will be able to present an opinion, an interpretation of the data in the chart or the graph.

Discussion

In the **discussion section**, link your data to the body of knowledge on the topic by engaging in academic discussion with the writings of others. This means that you link your findings and literature review and show the relationships between them. This may mean that you need to present arguments in support of your interpretation and arguments in conflict with your interpretation. The purpose of the latter is twofold: on the one hand you show your readers that you have read widely and that you are aware of, and have seriously considered, divergent views; on the other hand it gives you an opportunity to refute those views, through a clear line of argument, in order to strengthen yours.

In the discussion section evaluate and interpret your results.

Consider the following questions:

- *How* are your findings similar to or different from the findings of previous researchers?
- *Why* are they similar or different?
- *How well* does your research meet your stated purpose for the research? Why or why not?

In this section, refer your reader back to the findings section and to relevant graphs and tables. Also comment on the validity of your results (see Chapter 11).

The conclusion

Use the conclusion to link all parts of the report together.

In the conclusion, draw the research together into a coherent whole. The conclusions must be drawn only from the evidence presented in your report, so do not include any new information here. Consider also the following questions:

- What knowledge has been gained as a result of this research?
- What, if anything, should be done better next time?
- Was it worth the effort? Why? Why not?
- How should this research be followed up?

Proofread your report.

You may have finished the conclusion, but this does not necessarily mean that you have finished the project. Every writer must learn to proofread for typographical and spelling errors, logical development of arguments and logical presentation of information. It is good idea to proofread for one type of error at a time and then to give it to someone else to proofread. Another reader will almost always pick up errors that you have missed, but they may also pick up ambiguities in your discussion and so on.

Activity

Reading a research article

Go to Appendix E for some exercises related to reading a research article.

Activity

Go to our website <www.oup.com.au/orc/turner2e> for more activities on the skills covered in this chapter.

SUMMARY

In this chapter you have been introduced to some of the main features of a research report and the most important steps in writing it, including the need to understand your audience and to write from a reader's perspective. As a final point, before you begin to research you have to read and critically evaluate a large number of texts. Take this opportunity to learn how to write well from the most effective of these.

GLOSSARY

abstract an overview of all the main issues, arguments and findings that are presented in a research report.

discussion section the part of a research report that links the findings to the literature review and comments upon them.

findings section the part of a research report that presents findings but does not comment upon them.

literature review an account of what has already been published on a topic, subject, issue or problem, and is organised to reveal the connections between the selected texts and the research topic.

research report a document that presents the entire research process in an organised manner.

APPENDIX A

Basic Guidelines for Writing Citations and Reference List Items (APA 6th)

The guide can be used to help in both electronic and manual creation of reference list items. Use it to:

- check the correctness of reference list items downloaded from databases or generated by reference management software
- select the appropriate fields to complete when using reference management software
- follow the instructions for each field when manually creating a reference list item or an in-text citation.

Table 1 shows citations and reference list items for the basic form of the most common source types.

Table 2 gives information about how to deal with variations to the content in a number of fields in reference list items (authors, publication dates, titles and subtitles, editions, page numbers, editors, place of publication, publisher, electronic locator information).

Table 3 outlines how to manage variations in in-text citation components (author, date, specific place identifier)

Table 4 indicates what to do when citations to the same source are repeated in a text.

Table 1 Citations and reference list items for different source types (basic forms)

Note: Only one way of writing a citation is shown. See Chapter 5 for how to write the citation with the author's name as part of the text.

Book (printed)
First in-text citation Use: (Family name of author, year, p. X) e.g. (Greetham, 2001, p. 30) **Reference list item** Family name of author, Initial. Initial. (Year of publication). *Title of book*. Place of publication: Publisher. **Example** Greetham, B. (2001). *How to write better essays*. Basingstoke, England: Palgrave.

ebook

First in-text citation
Use: (Family name of author, year, p. X)

e.g.
(Shaw, 2001, p. 20)

Reference list item
Family name of author, Initial. Initial. (Year of publication). *Title of book* [Name of Software version]. doi: XXXXXXXX OR Retrieved from URL

Example
Shaw, M. C. (2001). *Engineering problem solving: a classical perspective* [Adobe Reader version]. Retrieved from http://knovel.com/

Note:
As the book exists both in a printed and an ebook form, indicate the software used to generate the electronic version [Adobe Reader version]. If the book only exists as an ebook the name of the software is not required.
If there is a DOI use that instead of the URL.
Use the URL for the site from which the book was downloaded (domain or host name is sufficient) or the full URL if it is short.

Chapter (or section) in an edited book (printed)

First in-text citation
Use: (Family name of author, year, p. X)

e.g.
(Thomlison, 1996, p. 91)

Reference list item
Family name of author, Initial. Initial. (Year of publication). Title of chapter. In Initial. Initial. Editor's family name (Ed.), *Title of the book* (pp. first–last page numbers of chapter or section). Place of publication: Publisher.

Example
Thomlison, T. Dean. (1996). Intercultural listening. In M. Purdy & D. Borisoff (Eds.), *Listening in everyday life* (pp. 79–120). New York, NY: University Press of America.

Journal article with DOI (digital object identifier)

First in-text citation
Use: (Family name of author, year, p. X)

e.g.
(Ellery, 2008, p. 509)

Reference list item
Family name of author, Initial. Initial. (Year of publication). Title of article. *Title of Journal*, volume(issue), first–last page numbers of article. doi: XXXXXXXX

Example

Ellery, K. (2008). Undergraduate plagiarism: A pedagogical perspective. *Assessment & Evaluation in Higher Education, 33*(5), 507–516. doi: 10.1080/02602930701698918

Note:
Always include the volume, in italics.
Use issue number (in parentheses and in roman upright font immediately after) if the volume is not paginated continuously.
Students are usually required to provide both volume and issue.

Journal article accessed electronically without DOI

First in-text citation

Use: (Family name of author, year, p. X)

e.g.
(Wong, 2004, p. 161)

Reference list item

Family name of author, Initial. Initial. (Year of publication). Title of article. *Title of Journal, volume*(issue), first–last page numbers. Retrieved from the URL of the Journal homepage OR the URL for the site used to download the article

Example Journal homepage URL

Wong, J. K.-K. (2004). Are the learning styles of Asian international students culturally or contextually based? *International Education Journal, 4*, 154–166. Retrieved from http://ehlt.flinders.edu.au/education/iej

Example download site URL

Wong, J. K.-K. (2004). Are the learning styles of Asian international students culturally or contextually based? *International Education Journal, 4*, 154–166. Retrieved from www.informit.com.au

Note:
The APA Manual requires the URL for the Journal homepage. However, using the URL for the site from which the article was downloaded is generally acceptable. See Chapter 5.

Journal article accessed as a printed copy with no DOI

First in-text citation

Use: (Family name of author, year, p. X)

e.g.
(Auer & Krupar, 2001, p. 430)

Reference list item

Family name of author, Initial. Initial. (Year of publication). Title of article. *Title of Journal, volume*(issue), first–last page numbers.

Example

Auer, N. J., & Krupar, E. M. (2001). Mouse click plagiarism: The role of technology in plagiarism and the librarian's role in combating it. *Library Trends, 49*, 415–433.

Conference paper formally published in conference proceedings and accessed electronically

First in-text citation
Use: (Family name of author, year, p. X) OR if there are no page numbers (Family name of author, year, para. X)

e.g.
(Sanson, 2009, para. 6)

Reference list item
Family name of author, Initial. Initial. (Year of conference). Title of paper. In Initial. Initial. Family name of editor (Ed.), *Title of the conference proceedings* (pp. first–last page numbers of paper, if available). Place of publication: Publisher if available. doi OR Retrieved from URL

Example
Sanson, M. (2009). Preparing tomorrow's lawyers today: Graduate attributes in first year law. In J. Thomas (Ed.) *First Year in Higher Education Conference*. Brisbane, Australia: QUT Publications.Retrieved from www.fyhe.com.au

Conference paper not formally published in conference proceedings and accessed electronically

First in-text citation
Use: (Family name of author, year, p. X) OR if there are no page numbers (Family name of author, year, para. X)

e.g.
(Hsu, 2004, para. 4)

Reference list item
Family name of author, Initial. Initial. (Year of conference, month of conference). *Title of paper*. Paper presented at Title of Conference, Location. doi OR Retrieved from URL

Example
Hsu, J. Y. (2004, June). *Reading, writing, and reading-writing in the second language classroom: A balanced curriculum*. Paper presented at the Annual International Conference on English Teaching and Learning in the Republic of China, Taichung, Taiwan. Retrieved from www.eric.ed.gov

Note:
When the conference paper is not formally published as part of a book or in a journal, give the year and month of the conference as the publication date for the reference list item only.

Report from an organisation (government, company or institution) when the author is different from the organisation

First in-text citation
Use: (Family name of author, year, p. X)

e.g.
(Bradley, 2008, p. X)

Reference list item
Family name of author, Initial. Initial. (year). *Title of report* (report number if available). Place of publication: Publisher. OR Retrieved from Name of Organisation website: URL

Example
Bradley, D. (2008). *Review of Australian higher education: Final report.* Retrieved from the Australian Government, Department of Education, Employment and Workplace Relations website: www.deewr.gov.au/highereducation/review/pages/reviewofaustralianhighereducationreport.aspx

Report from an organisation (government, company or institution) when the author is the organisation

First in-text citation
Use: (Name of Organisation [abbreviation if available], year, p. X)

e.g.
(Australian Bureau of Statistics [ABS], 2010, p. 2)

Reference list item
Name of Organisation. (year). *Title of report* (report number if available). Place of publication: Author. OR Retrieved from URL

Example
Australian Bureau of Statistics. (2010). *Australian social trends—international comparisons* (No. 4102.0). Retrieved from www.abs.gov.au/socialtrends

Note:
When the author and the publisher are the same use the word 'Author' for the Publisher.

Web material from an organisation (government, company, institution)

First in-text citation
Use: (Family name of author, year, p. X) OR if no page numbers (Family name of author, year, para. X)

e.g.
(Liu, 2006, para. X)

Reference list item
Family name of author, Initial. Initial. (Year of publication if available; if not use: n.d.). *Title of web page.* Retrieved from Name of Organisation website: URL

Example
Liu, C. (2006). *Meeting the challenges of Chinese import demand.* Retrieved from BHP Billiton website: www.bhpbilliton.com/bbContentRepository/ chinasteamcoalsummit06.pdf

Note:
If there is no author for the web page use the name of the organisation that produced the web page in the author field and omit the organisation name in the URL field.

Artwork

First in-text citation
Use: (Family name of artist, year)

e.g.
(Bancroft, 1995)

Viewed electronically

Reference list item
Family name of Artist, Initial. Initial. (year). *Title of artwork* [Type of artwork]. Retrieved from URL

Example
Bancroft, B. (1995). *Black sister family* [Painting]. Retrieved from www.artgallery.nsw.gov.au/collection

Viewed at a gallery
Family name of Artist, Initial. Initial. (year). *Title of artwork* [Type of artwork]. City of viewing, Country: Name of gallery.

Example
Bancroft, B. (1995). *Black sister family* [Painting]. Sydney, Australia: Art Gallery of NSW.

Note:
Advice on how to cite artworks is provided on the APA Style Blog (2010).
Indicate the type of artwork in square brackets immediately after the title.
If an artwork is viewed in a text, use the style for the relevant source type.

Film

First in-text citation
Information to identify the item (year)

e.g.
Inception (2010) produced and directed by Nolan ...

Reference list item
Family name of producer, Initial. Initial. (Producer), & Family name of director, Initial. Initial. (Director). (year). *Title of the picture* [Motion picture]. Country of origin: Studio.

Example
Nolan, C. (Producer), & Nolan, C. (Director). (2010). *Inception* [Motion picture]. United States: Warner Bros.

Secondary sources (i.e. citing and referencing information from a source you have not read but found in another source)

First in-text citation
(Author of the idea or information as cited in Author of the source read, year of the source read, p. X)

e.g.
(Chow as cited in Nield, 2004, p. 191)

Reference list item
Provide a reference list item for the source that was read

Nield, K. (2004).Questioning the myth of the Chinese learner. *International Journal of Contemporary Hospitality Management, 16*, 189–196.

Note:
As you advance in your degree you will be expected to find the original source and read and cite that.

Table 2 Reference list item fields—variations

Author (reference list item field)	
One author	Family name of author, Initial. Initial. e.g. Shaw, M. C. (2001). ...
Two authors	Family name of first author, Initial. Initial., & Family name of second author, Initial. Initial. e.g. Volet, S., & Renshaw, P. (1996). ... *Note:* *Always keep the authors of a source in the same order as found on the source.*
Three, four or five authors	Family name of first author, Initial. Initial., Family name of second author, Initial. Initial, ..., & Family name of final author, Initial. Initial. e.g. Turner, K., Ireland, L., Krenus, B., & Pointon, L. (2011). ... *Note:* *Always keep the authors of a source in the same order as found on the source.*
Organisation (Group) as an author (for example government department, company, institution, organisation)	Full name of the Organisation e.g. International Labour Office. (1997). ... *Note:* *In an electronic copy, if the organisation is both the author and publisher, omit the organisation name before the URL and instead use: Retrieved from URL* *In a printed copy if the organisation is both the author and the publisher, use 'Author' in place of the publisher's name.*

No identified author	*When a title of a chapter, article or web page takes the place of the author in the author field, use roman (upright) font: Title* e.g. Find websites. (n. d.). ... *When a title of a journal, magazine, newspaper, book or report takes the place of the author in the author field, use italics: Title* e.g. *The Australian.* (2011, January 2). ...
Date of publication (reference list item field)	
Date of publication—most sources e.g. books, articles, reports, web pages, audiovisual material, art, data sets etc.	(year) e.g. (2001)
Date of publication—daily or weekly periodical (e.g. newspaper, magazine)	(year, month day) e.g. Wilson, N. (2007, January 26). Costs, prices take some shine off BHP. *The Australian*, p. 21.
Date of publication—no date	(n.d.) e.g. Fallon, F. (n.d.). ... *Note: 'n.d.' is an abbreviation for 'no date'.*
Title (reference list item field)	
Title of article or chapter or section of a larger document (i.e. title of an embedded source)	Title of article, chapter or section: Subtitle e.g. The impact of paid work on the academic performance of students: A case study from the University of Canberra *Note:* *Title is in roman (upright) font.* *First word, all proper names and the first word of the subtitle are capitalised.*
Title of a book, ebook, report (i.e. title of a stand-alone source)	*Title of book, ebook, report: Subtitle* e.g. *Listening in everyday life: A personal and professional approach* *Note:* *Title is italicised.* *First word, all proper names and the first word of the subtitle are capitalised.*

Title of a journal	Title of Journal
	e.g. International Journal of Contemporary Hospitality Management
	Note: Title is in italics. All significant words are capitalised.
Editions (reference list item field)	
Revised, second or later edition	Revised edition use: (Rev. ed.).
	2nd or later edition use: (2nd ed.). OR (3rd ed.) OR (Xth ed.) in parentheses immediately after the title.
	e.g. Hay, I., Bochner, D., & Dungey, C. (2006). Making the grade: A guide to successful communication and study (3rd ed.). Melbourne, Australia: Oxford University Press.
Page numbers (reference list item field)	
Page numbers for an article in a journal	first–last page numbers
	e.g. 507–516
Page numbers for a chapter or section of a book	(pp. first–last page numbers for the chapter or section)
	e.g. (pp. 79–120)
Editor (reference list item field)	
One editor	Initial. Initial. Family name of editor (Ed.).
	e.g. J. Thomas (Ed.)
	Note: Initials precede the family name. If there are two initials use them, if not, use one. Include (Ed.) as an abbreviation for 'Editor'.
Two editors	Initial. Initial. Family name of editor & Initial. Initial. Family name of editor (Eds.).
	e.g. M. Purdy & D. Borisoff (Eds.)

Three, four or five editors	Initial. Initial. Family name of first editor, Initial. Initial. Family name of second editor, ..., & Initial. Initial. Family name of final editor (Eds.), e.g. F. Marton, D. Hounsell, & N. Entwhistle (Eds.)
Place of publication (reference list item field)	
Place of publication	If the place of publication is outside the USA use: City, Country: e.g. London, England: If the 'Place of publication' is in the USA use: City, State abbreviated: e.g. Boston, MA: *Note:* *It is usually acceptable for students to always use:* City, Country:
Publisher (reference list item field)	
Publisher	Publisher's name. Omit any non-essential details e.g. 'Publishers' or 'Co.' or 'Inc'. Include 'Books' or 'Press'. e.g. for John Benjamins Pub. Co. use: John Benjamins e.g. for Oxford University Press use: Oxford University Press
Electronic locator information (reference list item field)	
DOI (digital object identifier) present	USE: doi: XXXXXXXXXXXXXXXXXXXX e.g. doi:10.1080/02602930701698918
No DOI	Use: URL e.g. Retrieved from www.informit.com.au *Note:* *The rules for which URL, or how much of a URL to use, or what to include before the URL, depends on the source type.*

Table 3 First in-text citations—variations

Variation	First in-text citation
Author (in-text citations)	
One author	In parentheses: (Family name of author, year, p. X) e.g. (Shaw, 2001, p. 20) OR In text: Family name of author (year, p. X) e.g. Shaw (2001, p. 20) ...
Two authors	In parentheses: (Family name of author & Family name of author, year, p. X) e.g. (Volet & Renshaw, 1996, p. X) OR In text: Family name of author and Family name of author (year, p. X) e.g. Volet and Renshaw (1996, p. X) ...
Three, four or five authors	In parentheses: Family name of first author, Family name of second author, ..., & Family name of final author, year, p. X) e.g. (Turner, Ireland, Krenus, & Pointon, 2011, p. X) OR In text use: Family name of first author, Family name of second author, ..., and Family name of final author (year, p. X) ... e.g. Turner, Ireland, Krenus, and Pointon (2011, p. X)
Organisation (Group) as an author (for example government department, company, institution, organisation)	If not abbreviated use: Name of organisation e.g. (Monash University, 2010, p. X) If normally abbreviated use: Name of Organisation [abbreviation] e.g. (International Labour Office [ILO], 1997, p. X)

Variation	First in-text citation
No author	For a chapter, article or web page with no author, use: ("Title", year, p. X) e.g. ("Find websites", n.d., para. X) OR for journals, magazines, newspapers, books and reports with no author use: (*Title*, year, para. X) e.g. (*The Australian*, 2012, p. 2) *Note: The abbreviation 'n.d.' is used when there is no date for the publication.*
Date (in-text citations)	
Date for books, articles, ebooks, reports etc.	Use: (Family name of author, year, p. X) e.g. (Wong, 2004, p. 161)
Date for daily or weekly periodical (e.g. newspaper, magazine)	Use: (Family name of author, year, p. X) e.g. (Wilson, 2007, p. 21) *Note: The reference list item supplies the specific date but the in-text citation need only provide the year.*
No date	Use; (Family name of author, n.d., p. X) e.g. (Fallon, n.d., p. X) *Note: 'n.d.' is an abbreviation for 'no date'.*
Specific place (in-text citations)	
Indicating a specific place when page numbers are present	Use: (Family name of author, date, p. X e.g. (Shaw, 2001, p. 20).
Indicating a specific place when there are no page numbers	Short document: (Family name, year, para. X) e.g. (Smith, 2001, para. 4) OR Longer document with headings: (Family name, year, Heading title section, para. X)

Variation	First in-text citation
	e.g. (Hsu, Recommendations for future research section, para. 2) OR Long document with Chapters and headings: (Family name of author, year, Chapter title, Heading name section, para. X) e.g. (Shaw, 2001, Chapter 1, Engineering education section, para. 2) *Note:* *If the section name is long it may be shortened. If this is done use double inverted commas around the shortened title.*
Citing a secondary source	
Citing a claim found cited in another source (a secondary citation)	(Family name of the author of the claim as cited in Family name of the author of the source read, year, p. X) e.g. (Chow as cited in Nield, 2004, p. 92) *Note: The year and page number refer to the source in which the claim is cited i.e. the source read.*

Table 4 Repetition of citations in a text

Number or types of authors	First citation	Subsequent citations
One or two authors	Use: (Family name of first author, date, p. X) or (Family name of first author & Family name of second author, year, p. X) e.g. (Greetham, 2001, p. X) OR (Volet & Renshaw, 1996, p. X)	Use: the same information as in the first citation e.g. (Greetham, 2001, p. X) OR (Volet & Renshaw, 1996, p. X)
Three, four or five authors	Use: (Family name of first author, Family name of second author, ..., & Family name of final author, date, p. X) e.g. (Hay, Bochner, & Dungey, 2006, p. X)	Use: (Family name of first author et al., year, p. X) e.g. (Hay et al., 2006, p. X)
Organisation (Government department, company, institution, or organisation) which is not normally abbreviated	Use: (Name of organisation, date, p. X) e.g. (Monash University, 2010, p. X).	Use: same as for the first citation e.g. (Monash University, 2010, p. X).
Organisation (Government department, company, institution, or organisation) which is normally abbreviated	Use: (Name of organisation [abbreviation], date, p. X) e.g. (International Labour Office [ILO], 1997, p. X)	Use: (abbreviation, date, p. X) e.g. (ILO, 1997, p. X)

Note: Developed from *Publication Manual of the American Psychological Association* (6th ed.), by The American Psychological Association, 2010, Washington, DC: Author.

APPENDIX B

Additional Exercises for Chapter 5:
Writing reference list items for a variety of
source types

Write a reference list item for each of the following. Start by noticing the type
of source. Then select the required information and format it according to APA
6th rules. Check the 'Reference list guide' in Appendix A for how to deal with that
type of source and also any variations.

Note: As far as possible, the bibliographic information is presented as you
would find it in a library catalogue or database.

1   Mouse click plagiarism: The role of technology in plagiarism and the
    librarian's role in combating it. Nicole J Auer, Ellen M Krupar. Library
    Trends. Urbana: Winter 2001. Vol. 49, Iss. 3; p. 415, 18 pgs. Retrieved from
    Academic Search Premier database: www.web.ebscohost.com

2   VOICES FROM CHINESE STUDENTS: PROFESSORS' USE OF ENGLISH
    AFFECTS ACADEMIC LISTENING Jinyan Huang. College Student Journal.
    Mobile: Jun 2004. Vol. 38, Iss. 2; p. 212, 11 pgs. Retrieved from ProQuest:
    www.proquest.com

3   Title: Making the grade: a guide to successful communication and study/Iain
    Hay, Dianne Bochner, Carol Dungey.
        Edition: 3rd edition.
        Publication: 2006. South Melbourne, Vic. Oxford University Press

4   A Chapter titled 'Studying in a Second Language: the experiences of
    Chinese students in Canada' written by John R. Kirby, Rosamund A.
    Woodhouse and Yamin Ma. The chapter is in a book with the following
    bibliographic details: Title: The Chinese learner: cultural, psychological
    and contextual influences/edited by David A. Watkins and John B. Biggs.
    The book was published in Hong Kong by the Comparative Education
    Research Centre and in Melbourne, Victoria for the Australian Council for
    Educational Research, in 1996.

5   Article title: 'Land and Discover! A Case Study Investigating the Cultural
    Context of Plagiarism'. It is written by Neera Handa and Clare Power. The
    article was published in the *Journal of University Teaching and Learning
    Practice*, Vol. 2 Issue 3b in 2005 and was retrieved from: http://ro.uow.edu.
    au/jutlp/vol2/iss3/8

6   Article title: Plagiarism instruction online: assessing undergraduate
    students' ability to avoid plagiarism
        Author: Pamela A. Jackson
        Journal title: *College & Research Libraries*, 2006
        Retrieved from ProQuest database: http://proquest.umi.com

7   Title: Evidence, argument and social responsibility: *first-year* students'
    experiences of information literacy when researching an essay
        Author: Lupton, Mandy
        Source: Higher Education Research & Development; Nov2008, Vol. 27
        Issue 4, p 399–414, 16p
        DOI: 10.1080/07294360802406858

8   Title: Developing academic persistence in first year tertiary students:
    a case study.
        Personal Author: Huntly H; Donovan J
        Author Affiliation: University of Western Australia; Central Queensland
        University
        Source: Studies in Learning, Evaluation, Innovation and Development;
        v.6 n.1 p.1–14; May 2009
        Uniform Resource Identifier: http://sleid.cqu.edu.au/include/getdoc.php?
        id=804&article=242&mode=pdf
        Last Revision Date: 24 Aug 2009
        Document Number: 175720

9   Article title: Plagiarism instruction online: assessing undergraduate
    students' ability to avoid plagiarism
        Author: Pamela A. Jackson
        Journal title: *College & Research Libraries*, 2006
        Retrieved: from the American Library Association website: http://web2.
        ala.org/ala/acrl/acrlpubs/crljournal/backissues2006a/septembera/
        jackson06.pdf
        DOI: 10.1108/00907320510597408

10 Article title: 'Embedding plagiarism education in the assessment
    process'. It was published in 2006 by Ruth Barrett from the University
    of Hertfordshire, UK and James Malcolm also from the University of
    Hertfordshire, UK. It was published in the International Journal for
    Educational Integrity Volume 2, Number 1 and retrieved from the
    International Journal of Educational Integrity website: www.ojs.unisa.edu.
    au/index.php/IJEI/article/viewFile/23/18

11 Title of webpage: Language and Learning Online. It is part of Monash
    University Learning Support website and was accessed at the following URL
    www.monash.edu.au/lls/llonline/study/index.xml

APPENDIX C
Case Study Exercise

QUESTION 1: WRITING AN ANALYSIS AND DISCUSSION OF A CASE STUDY PROBLEM

i   Read the following short case study. The problem it is examining is lack of time management.

ii Select all the information related to Margaret's lack of time management as described in the case study. Consider: What evidence is there that Margaret has not managed her time well? What are the possible causes of her poor time management? What are the effects of her poor time management?

iii Read the extract written by Byrd and MacDonald (2005), after the case study.

iv What have Byrd and MacDonald (2005) found about time management that is relevant to the problem in the case study?

v   Write a well-developed paragraph in which you fully describe the problem of lack of time management in this specific case, and then link it to what the literature (the extract supplied) has found out about the lack of time management. Remember: Do not use citations when you describe the case; do use citations when you use the literature.

Case study: Timed out

Margaret raced into her tutor's office. 'Sorry I'm late', she said breathlessly, 'I had to stay longer at my job. They needed me because another staff member rang in sick.'

'How can I help?' said Lesley, glancing at the pile of essays on her desk, 'but, first, just to let you know, we now only have five minutes before my next student appointment.'

Margaret placed her bag on the floor and pulled out her essay. 'Lesley, I wanted to know why I did so poorly. I only got 5 out of 20. Usually, at high school, I did well in my classes.'

Lesley glanced over the essay. 'Well, you have only read two sources. You have only written 1000 words. It was meant to be well researched and 1500 words in length.'

Margaret thought of how tired she'd been after writing her assignment. Her friend Pam had helped when she'd heard that the essay had to be written in one day. She'd given her copies of the two sources and even made dinner. That made doing the essay possible. Still she had had to work non-stop. She'd read the sources quickly, skimming and scanning for relevant information. Then she'd stayed up all night writing the assignment and finished just in time for her tutorial at 8.30 a.m. on Monday morning.

'But I thought I wrote well,' groaned Margaret.

'Yes, your language is quite good. In fact, just looking at how you have expressed yourself, I'd say you were quite a clever student. It looks like you did not spend enough time on the essay,' suggested Lesley. 'Sorry Margaret, my next student is here now. I'll see you next week in the tutorial. We can talk about this again.'

Margaret stood up and left, almost too tired to care.

Extract

Below is an extract (in italics) from an article by Byrd and MacDonald (2005, p. 29).

Time management is a skill that all of the participants noted as critical for college readiness. Participants indicated the importance of this skill when discussing time needed for studying outside class and course-load requirements while trying to manage priorities for work and family. The theme of time management elicited a range of responses. Two participants pointed to a lack of time and difficulty with time management as the biggest obstacles to doing well in college, while other students related time management skills and multitasking abilities as a strength contributing to readiness for college-level work. Six participants spoke of having strong time management skills and related this strength to life experiences, especially work related experiences, and to being older.

APPENDIX D
Reading and Understanding a Research Article

QUESTION 1

Read the extract (in italics) and answer the questions.

The extract is from an article by McKenzie and Schweitzer (2001, p. 24).

EXTRACT

This prospective study will examine the relationship between academic, psychosocial [psychological and social], cognitive [thinking], and demographic variables, and the academic performance of first year Australian university students. The variables are based on factors identified in previous research as being important predictors of academic performance. Academic performance is based on the first semester GPA of students. The aim of the study is to identify the variables within each of the four factors that affect academic performance, with a view to develop a model which could be used to identify students at risk of academic problems. Based on previous research, several hypotheses are proposed.

METHOD

Participants

A sample of 197 first year university students from the Faculties of Science (n = 149) and Information Technology (n = 48) in a large urban commuter-based university (p. 26) consented to participate in the study.

Procedure

The purpose of the study was explained to students in lecture time four to eight weeks prior to the end of semester examinations ... The return rate was over 65% for the Science students but there was a poor response rate for the Information Technology (IT) students.

a What is a literature review?
b The section of the literature review above is outlining the research focus. Which variables are the authors studying? What is a variable? How do you think the authors decided to use these particular variables?
c Examine the Method section 'Participants'. Describe the sampling technique the authors use. Would this sample enable the authors to extend their findings to all students at their university? Explain your answer.

d   Examine the Method section 'Procedure'. What is a response rate? Which group of students had a poor response rate? The study found that the average GPA (Grade Point Average) for the IT students in the sample was quite different from the average GPA for all IT students. Why do you think this might have happened?

QUESTION 2

Read the extract (in italics) and answer the questions.

The extract below is an article by Krause and Coates (2008, p. 495).

EXTRACT

Survey Methodology

One of the notable strengths of the first-year studies is that they provide statistical estimates which are relevant across numerous Australian universities. In 2004, the First Year Experience (p. 496) Questionnaire (FYEQ) was mailed to a 25% random sample of first-year commencing undergraduate students, stratified by 11 defined broad fields of education, chosen from each of 13 participating public universities in Australia. The project asked institutions to select campus-based students who were first-time entrants to higher education enrolled in bachelor, associate degree or undergraduate award programs. The sample included domestic and international students enrolled in full-time study.

a   Describe the sampling method used by the researchers. What is the advantage of using this?
b   The sampling included domestic and international students. Why do you think the researchers specifically sought out these two groups of students?

QUESTION 3

Read the extract (in italics) and answer the questions.
The extract is by Thompson (2003, p. 263).

EXTRACT

DATA ON STUDENT USAGE OF THE INTERNET

Students in each of the surveys consistently rated their [web] searching skills quite favourably, with the overwhelming majority reporting their skills as good, above average, or even excellent (Lubans, 1999). One must question the reliability of these responses, as the capacity for students to accurately assess their own skills is highly subject to their own perceptions. A more meaningful way to collect data on students' Internet skills would be for faculty and professional academic librarians to assess the information students are actually finding and using for references ...

a   Does the author of this extract believe that Lubans's findings are correct? Give a reason for your answer.

b   From what section of the article do you think this extract comes? Select your answer from one of the following: Literature review; Method; Results; Discussion. Explain your answer.

c   Given the information in this extract, how would you expect the author to find information about internet skills in her research?

BIBLIOGRAPHY

Ainley, M. (2004, November). *What do we know about student motivation and engagement?* Paper presented at the Australian Association for Research in Education International Education Research Conference, Melbourne. Retrieved from www.aare.edu.au/04pap/ain04760.pdf

The American Psychological Association. (2001), *Publication manual of the American Psychological Association* (6th ed.). Washington, DC.: Author.

Andrusyszyn, M., & Davie, L. (1997). Facilitating reflection through interactive journal writing in an online graduate course: A qualitative study. *Journal of Distance Education/Revue de l'enseignement à distance 12.1/2.* Retrieved from www.ebscohost.com

Anholt, R. (2005). *Dazzle 'em with style: The art of oral scientific presentation* (2nd ed.). Oxford, England: Elsevier Academic Press.

APA Style Blog (2010, April 1). There's an art to it. Retrieved from http://blog.apastyle.org/apastyle/2010/04/theres-an-art-to-it.html

Applegate, C., & Daly, A. (2005). The impact of paid work on the academic performance of students: A case study from the University of Canberra. *Centre for Labour Market Research (CLMR) Discussion Paper Series (05/1).* Retrieved from Curtin University of Technology, Curtin Business School, Centre for Labour Market Research website: www.business.curtin.edu.au/files/05_1.pdf

Armbruster, B. (2000). Taking notes from lectures. In R. F. & D. C. Caverly (Eds.), *Handbook of college reading and study strategy research* (pp. 175–199). Mahwah, NJ: Lawrence Erlbaum Associates.

Auer, N. J., & Krupar, E. M. (2001). Mouse click plagiarism: The role of technology in plagiarism and the librarian's role in combating it. *Library Trends, 49,* 415–433. Retrieved from www.press.jhu.edu/journals/library_trends

Australian Government. Department of Finance and Administration. (n.d.). *Annual report 2002–2003.* Retrieved from www.finance.gov.au/publications/annual-reports/annualreport02-03/index.html

Australian Government. Department of Industry, Tourism, and Resources. (2005). *Annual report 2004–2005.* Retrieved from www.industry.gov.au/annualreport/04_05/index.html

Baik, C., & Greig, J. (2009). Improving the academic outcomes of undergraduate ESL students: The case for discipline-based academic skills programs. *Higher Education Research & Development, 28*(4), 401–416. doi: 10.1080/07294360903067005

Barrass, R. (2002). *Study! A guide to effective learning, revision and examination technique* (2nd ed.). London, England: Routledge.

Barrett, R., & Malcolm, J. (2005). *Embedding plagiarism education in the assessment process.* Paper presented at the 2nd Asia-Pacific Educational Integrity Conference, Educational Integrity: Values in Teaching, Learning & Research, University of Newcastle, Australia. Retrieved from www.ojs.unisa.edu.au/index.php/IJEI

Beall, H. & Trimbur, J. (2000). *A short guide to writing about chemistry* (2nd ed.). Toronto, Canada: Longman.

Bell, J. (2003). Statistics anxiety: The non-traditional student. *Education, 124,* 157–162. Retrieved from www.proquest.com

Benzie, H. J. (2010). Graduating as a 'native speaker': International students and English language proficiency in higher education. *Higher Education Research & Development,* 29(4), 447–459. doi: 10.1080/07294361003598824

Biber, D. & Gray, B. (2010). Challenging stereotypes about academic writing: Complexity, elaboration, explicitness. *Journal of English for Academic Purposes* 9(1), 2–20. doi: 10.1016/j.jeap.2010.01.001

Biggs, J. (2003). *Teaching for quality learning at university* (2nd ed.). Buckingham, UK: The Society for Research into Higher Education & Open University Press.

Biggs, J. (Ed.). (1991). *Teaching for learning: The view from cognitive psychology.* Hawthorn: The Australian Council for Educational Research.

Birrell, B. (2006). Implications of low English standards among overseas students at Australian universities. *People and Place,* 14(4), 53–64. Retrieved from http://elecpress.monash.edu.au/pnp

Boekaerts, M. (2001). Context sensitivity: Activated motivational beliefs, current concerns and emotional arousal. In S. Volet & S. Järvelä (Eds.), *Motivation in learning contexts: Theoretical advances and methodological implications* (pp. 17–31). Amersterdam, The Netherlands: Pergamon.

Borchers, T. (1999). *Small group communication.* Retrieved from Allyn & Bacon, Communication Studies website: www.abacon.com/commstudies/groups/roles.html

Bowden, J., & Marton, F. (2004). *The university of learning.* London, UK: RoutledgeFalmer.

Brookfield, S. (1998). Critically reflective practice. *Journal of Continuing Education in the Health Professions,* 18, 197–205. doi: 10.1002/chp.1340180402

Buck, G. (2001). *Assessing listening.* Cambridge, UK: Cambridge University Press. doi:10.1017/CBO9780511732959

Burns, T., & Sinfield, S. (2003). *Essential study skills: The complete guide to success at university.* London, UK: Sage.

Buzzan, T. (2005). *The ultimate book of mind maps.* London, UK: Thorsons.

Byrd, K. L., & MacDonald, G. (2005). Defining college readiness from the inside out: First-generation college student perspectives. *Community College Review,* 33, 22–39. doi: 10.1177/009155210503300102

Chu, C.-N. (1992). *Thick face black heart: The warrior philosophy for conquering the challenges of business and life.* Beaverton, OR: AMC Publishing.

Chanock, K. (2007). What academic language and learning advisers bring to the scholarship of teaching and learning: problems and possibilities for dialogue with the disciplines. *Higher Education Research & Development,* 26, 269–280. doi: 10.1080/07294360701494294

Clanchy, J., & Ballard, B. (1997). *Essay writing for students: A practical guide* (3rd ed.). Melbourne, Australia: Addison Wesley Longman.

Coakley, C., & Wolvin, A. (1996). Listening in the educational environment. In M. Purdy & D. Borisoff. (Eds.), *Listening in everyday life: A personal and professional approach* (pp. 179–212). New York, NY: University Press of America.

Comfort, J. (1995). *Effective presentations.* Oxford, England: Oxford University Press.

Cooper, G. (2003). *The intelligent student's guide to learning at university.* Altona, Australia: Common Ground Publishing.

Cottrell, S. (2003). *The study skills handbook* (2nd ed.). Basingstoke, UK: Palgrave Macmillan.

Coxhead, A. (2000). A new Academic Word List. *TESOL Quarterly, 34*(2), 213–238. doi: 10.2307/3587951

Crewe, W. J. (1990). The illogic of logical connectives. *ELT Journal, 44*(4), 316–325. doi: 10.1093/elt/44.4.316

Crisp, D. T. (2004). Plagiarism and the reputation of the university: How to distribute effort between educating students on attribution and rigorous detection of cheating? *AUQA Occasional Publication.* Retrieved from www.auqa.edu.au/auqf/pastfora/2004/program/papers/Crisp.pdf

Davies, M. (2004). BYU-BNC: The British National Corpus. Retrieved from: http://corpus.byu.edu/bnc

Davis, B. G. (1993). *Collaborative learning: Group work and study teams.* Retrieved from University of California, Berkeley, Office of Educational Development website: http://teaching.berkeley.edu/bgd/collaborative.html

Davis, L., & McKay, S. (1996). *Structures and strategies. An introduction to academic writing.* Melbourne, Australia: Macmillan Education.

Denscombe, M. (2003). *The good research guide: For small scale social research projects* (2nd ed.). Maidenhead, England: Open University Press.

DeVito, J. A. (2004). *The interpersonal communication book* (10th ed.). Boston, MA: Pearson.

Diaz-Gilbert, M. (2005). Writing skills of advanced pharmacy practice experience students whose first or best language is not English. *American Journal of Pharmaceutical Education, 69,* Article 101. Retrieved from www.ajpe.org/aj6905/aj6905101/aj6905101.pdf

DiBattista, D., & Gosse, L. (2006). Test anxiety and the immediate feedback assessment technique. *The Journal of Experimental Education, 74,* 311–328. Retrieved from www.tandf.co.uk

Drucker, P. F. (1977). *Management.* London, England: Pan Books.

Dundes, L. (2001). Small group debates: Fostering critical thinking in oral presentations with maximum class involvement. *Teaching Sociology, 29,* 237–243. doi: 10.2307/1318721

Easton, G. (1992). *Learning from case studies* (2nd ed.). New York, NY: Prentice Hall.

EndNote. Bibliographies made easy. (n.d.). Retrieved from Thomson Reuters website: www.endnote.com

Exam preparation: Frequently asked questions. (n.d.). Retrieved from Edith Cowan University, Learning Advisors website: www.ecu.edu.au/student/student-learning/exam_preparation_faq.html

Feinberg, J. (2009). *Wordle.* Available at www.wordle.net

Find Websites. (n.d.). Retrieved from Berkeley University, Library website: www.lib.berkeley.edu/Help/search.html

Flowerdew, J. (1994). *Academic listening: Research perspectives.* Cambridge, England: Cambridge University Press.

Flowerdew, J. & Li, Y. L. (2007). Language re-use among Chinese apprentice scientists writing for publication. *Applied Linguistics, 28*(3), 440–465. doi: 10.1093/applin/amm031

Francis, G. (1994). Labelling discourse: An aspect of nominal-group lexical cohesion. In M. Coulthard (Ed.), *Advances in written text analysis.* (pp. 83–101). London, England: Routledge.

Gilquin, G. & Paquot, M. (2008). Too chatty: Learner academic writing and register variation. *English Text Construction 1*(1), 41–61. doi: 10/1075/pp. 41–60

Glesne, C., & Peshkin, A. (1992). *Becoming qualitative researchers.* London, England: Longman.

Goodale, M. (1998). *Professional presentations.* Cambridge, England: Cambridge University Press.

Greetham, B. (2001). *How to write better essays.* Basingstoke, UK: Palgrave.

Griffith University. (2008). *Institutional framework for promoting academic integrity among students.* Retrieved from Griffith University Policy Library website: www62.gu.edu.au/policylibrary.nsf/binders/03ee5c37f0926a0e4a25736f0063eaea?opendocument

Hall, D., & Birkerts, S. (1998). *Writing well* (9th ed.). New York, NY: Longman.

Hamilton, D. (1999). *Passing exams: A guide for maximum success and minimum stress.* London, England: Cassell.

Hancioglu, N., Neufeld, S., & Eldridge, J. (2008). Through the looking glass and into the land of lexico-grammar. *English for Specific Purposes, 27,* 459–479. doi: 10.1016/j.esp.2008.08.001

Handa, N. (2007). Proving, improving and (dis)approving internationalisation of higher education. In P. L. Jeffreys (Ed. & Compiler), *International Education Research Conference.* Conference conducted by the Australian Association for Research in Education, Fremantle, Australia. Retrieved from www.aare.edu.au/07pap/han07418.pdf

Handa, N., & Power, C. (2005). Land and discover! A case study investigating the cultural context of plagiarism. *Journal of University Teaching and Learning Practice, 3,* 64–84. Retrieved from http://jutlp.uow.edu.au/2005_v02_i03b/pdf/handa_006.pdf

Hay, I., Bochner, D., & Dungey, C. (2002). *Making the grade: A guide to successful communication and study* (2nd ed.). Melbourne: Oxford University Press.

Haywood, S. (n.d.). *Academic Word List Highlighter.* Available from www.nottingham.ac.uk/~alzsh3/acvocab/awlhighlighter.htm

Heaton-Shrestha, C., May, S., & Burke, L. (2009). Student retention in higher education: What role for virtual learning environments? *Journal of Further & Higher Education, 33*(1), 83–92. doi: 10.1080/03098770802645189

Howard, R. M. (1995). Plagiarisms, authorships, and the academic death penalty. *College English, 57,* 788–807. doi: 10.2307/378403

Huang, J. (2004). Voices from Chinese students: Professors' use of English affects academic listening. *College Student Journal, 38,* 212–223.

Hubbs, D. L., & Brand, C. F. (2005). The paper mirror: Understanding reflective journaling. *The Journal of Experiential Education, 28,* 60–71. Retrieved from www.aee.org

Hughes, B. M. (2005). Study, examinations, and stress: Blood pressure assessments in college students. *Educational Review, 57,* 21–36. doi:10.1080/0013191042000274169

Hui, L. (2005). Chinese cultural schema of education: Implications for communication between Chinese students and Australian educators. *Issues in Educational Research, 15,* 17–36. Retrieved from www.iier.org.au

Hunt, S. (2003). Encouraging student involvement: An approach to teaching communication. *Communication Studies, 54,* 133–136. Retrieved from www.tandf.co.uk

Jackson, P. (2009, September 25). What to use—the full document URL or home page URL? [Blog post]. Retrieved from the APA Style website: http://blog.apastyle.org/apastyle/2009/09/what-to-usethe-full-document-url-or-home-page-url.html

Jackson, P. A. (2005). Incoming international students and the library: A survey. *Reference Services Review, 33,* 197–209. doi: 10.1108/00907320510597408

Johnson, D., Johnson, R., & Holubec, E. (1998). *Cooperation in the classroom.* Edina, MN. Interaction Book Company.

Johnson, M. (1999). *Archaeological theory: An introduction.* Oxford, UK: Blackwell.

Jones, B., & Frydenberg, E. (2000). Coping with transition: A case for providing resources to first year university students. *Australian Journal of Guidance and Counselling, 10,* 81–93. Retrieved from www.australianacademicpress.com.au

Jung, E. H. (2003). The role of discourse signalling cues in second language listening comprehension. *The Modern Language Journal, 87,* 562–577. doi: 10.1111/1540-4781.00208

Kahn, N. (1998). *More learning in less time* (5th ed.). Gwynedd Valley, PA: Ways-to-Books.

Karau, S. J., & Williams, K. D. (1993). Social loafing: A meta-analytic review and theoretical integration. *Journal of Personality and Social Psychology, 65,* 681–706. doi: 10.1037/0022-3514.65.4.681

Kayfetz, J., & Stice, R. (1987). *Academically speaking.* Boston, MA: Heinle & Heinle.

Kearns, H., & Gardiner, M. (2007). Is time well spent? The relationship between time management behaviours, perceived effectiveness and work-related morale and distress in a university context. *Higher Education Research & Development, 26,* 235–247. doi:10.1080/07294360701310839

Krause, K.-L., & Coates, H. (2008). Students' engagement in first-year university. *Assessment & Evaluation in Higher Education, 33,* 493–505. doi: 10.1080/02602930701698892

Larcombe, W., & Malkin, I. (2008). Identifying students likely to benefit from language support in first-year Law. *Higher Education Research & Development, 27(4),* 319–329. doi: 10.1080/07294360802406791

Lashley, C., & Best, W. (2001). *12 steps to study success.* London, England: Continuum.

Lea, M., & Street, B. (1998). Student writing in higher education: An academic literacies approach. *Studies in Higher Education, 23(2),* 157–173. doi: 10.1080/03075079812331380364

The Learning Centre (n.d.). Writing a case study report in engineering. Retrieved from University of New South Wales, The Learning Centre website: www.lc.unsw.edu.au/case_study/index.htm

Learning Support. (n.d.). *Sample report.* Retrieved from Monash University, Language Learning Online website: www.monash.edu.au/lls/llonline/writing/general/report/1.xml

Lebauer, S. (1999). *Learn to listen, listen to learn: Academic listening and note-taking.* New York, NY: Pearson ESL.

Lillis, T., & Turner, J. (2001). Student writing in higher education: Contemporary confusion, traditional concerns. *Teaching in Higher Education, 6(1),* 57–68. doi: 10.1080/13562510020029608

Lynch, T. (1983). *Study listening.* Cambridge, England: Cambridge University Press.

Lynch, T., & Anderson, K. (1992). *Study speaking.* Cambridge, England: Cambridge University Press.

McCarthy, P., & Hatcher, C. (2002). *Speaking persuasively: The essential guide to dynamic presentations and speeches* (2nd ed.). Crows Nest, NSW, Australia: Allen & Unwin.

McIlroy, D. (2003). *Studying @ university: How to be a successful student.* London, England: Sage.

McKenzie, K., & Schweitzer, R. (2001). Who succeeds at university? Factors predicting academic performance in first year Australian university students. *Higher Education Research & Development, 20,* 21–33. doi:10.1080/07924360120043621

Making exam anxiety work for you (n.d.). Retrieved from University of South Australia website: www.unisanet.unisa.edu.au/control examanxiety

Marriott, P., Edwards, J. R., & Mellett, H. (2004). *Introduction to accounting* (3rd ed.). London, England: Sage.

Martin, M. (1997). Emotional and cognitive effects of examination proximity in female and male students. *Oxford Review of Education, 23,* 479–487. doi: 10.1080/0305498970230404

Marton, F., & Saljo, R. (1984). Approaches to learning. In F. Marton, D. Hounsell, & N. Entwhistle (Eds.), *The experience of learning* (pp. 39–58). Edinburgh, Scotland: Scottish Academic Press.

Marton, F., Dall'Alba, G., & Beaty, E. (1993). Conceptions of learning. *International Journal of Educational Research, 19,* 277–300. Retrieved from www.elsevier.com

Mathony, M., & Poulis, A. (2004, November–December). Strengthening the nexus between teaching and learning through increased attention to feedback to students: A research-led teaching approach. In P. L. Jeffery (Compiler), *Australian Association for Research in Education Conference Papers,* Melbourne, Australia. Retrieved from www.aare.edu.au

Maxwell, J.A. (1996). *Qualitative research design.* Thousand Oaks, CA: Sage.

Meece, J., Anderman, E., & Anderman, E. (2006). Structures and goals of educational settings. *Annual Review of Psychology, 57,* 487–502. doi: 10.1146/annurev.psych.56.091103.070258

Misra, R., & McKean, M. (2000). College students' academic stress and its relation to their anxiety, time management, and leisure satisfaction. *American Journal of Health Studies, 16,* 41–52. Retrieved from www.va-ajhs.com

The National Committee of Enquiry into Higher Education. (1997). *Report of the national committee.* Retrieved from www.leeds.ac.uk/educol/ncihe

Neuman, W. L. (2006). *Social research methods* (6th ed.) Boston, MA: Allyn & Bacon.

Nield, K. (2004). Questioning the myth of the Chinese learner. *International Journal of Contemporary Hospitality Management, 16,* 189–196. doi:10.1108/09596110410531186

Nisbett, R. (2003). *The geography of thought: How Asians and Westerners think differently— and why.* London, England: Nicholas Brealey.

Nonis, S. A., & Hudson, G. I. (2006). Academic performance of college students: Influence of time spent studying and working. *Journal of Education for Business, 81,* 151–159. doi: 10.3200/JOEB.81.3.151-159

Novak, J. (2002). Meaningful learning: The essential factor for conceptual change in limited or appropriate propositional hierarchies (liphs) leading to empowerment of learners. *Science Education, 86,* 548–571. doi: 10.1002/sce.10032

Novak, J. D., & Cañas, A. J. (2006). *The theory underlying concept maps and how to construct them* [Technical Report IHMC CmapTools 2006–01]. Retrieved from Florida Institute for Human and Machine Cognition website: http://cmap.ihmc .us/publications/researchpapers/theorycmaps/theoryunderlyingconcept maps.htm

Ostler, S. (1987). English in parallels: A comparison of English and Arabic prose. In U. Connor & R. Kaplan (Eds.). *Writing across languages: Analyses of L2 texts*. (pp. 169–184). Reading, MA: Addison-Wesley.

Owl Online Writing Lab. (n.d.). Getting started with your report. Retrieved from Purdue University, The Owl at Purdue website: http://owl.english.purdue.edu/workshops/ hypertext/reportW/index.html

Page, S., Farrington, S., & DiGregorio, K. (1999, July). Promoting academic success through valuing and supporting diversity amongst Indigenous students in a block mode health science program. Paper presented at HERDSA Annual International Conference, Melbourne, Australia. Retrieved from the HERDSA website: www.herdsa.org.au/wp-content/uploads/conference/1999/pdf/Page.PDF

Payne, B. K., & Monk-Turner, E. (2006). Students' perceptions of group projects. The role of race, age and slacking. *College Student Journal, 40*(1), 132–139. Retrieved from web.ebscohost.com

Problem solving exams. (n.d.). Retrieved from The University of Melbourne, Language and Learning Skills Unit website: www.courseworks.unimelb.edu.au/ researchandwriting/problemsolvingexams.php

Problem solving techniques (n.d.). Retrieved from www.mindtools.com/pages/main/ newMN_TMC.htm

Purdy, M. (1996a). Intrapersonal and interpersonal listening: Self listening and conscious action. In M. Purdy & D. Borisoff (Eds.), *Listening in everyday life: A personal and professional approach* (pp. 21–54). New York, NY: University Press of America.

Purdy, M. (1996b). What is listening. In M. Purdy & D. Borisoff (Eds.). *Listening in everyday life: A personal and professional approach* (pp. 1–20). New York, NY: University Press of America.

Ramsay, S., Barker, M., & Jones, E. (1999). Academic adjustment and learning processes: A comparison of international and local students in first-year university. *Higher Education Research & Development, 18*(1), 129–144. doi: 10.1080/0729436990180110

Randall, K., Hoppes, S., & Bender, D. (2008). Developing an honor statement for university students in graduate professional programs. *Journal of Allied Health, 37*, 121–124. Retrieved from http://findarticles.com

Redman, P. (2001). *Good essay writing: A social sciences guide* (2nd ed.). Milton Keynes, UK: Open University with Sage.

Reinhart, S. (2002). *Giving academic presentations*. Ann Arbor MI: University of Michigan Press.

Rendle-Short, J. (2005). Managing the transitions between talk and silence in the academic monologue. *Research on Language and Social Interaction, 38*, 179–218. doi: 10.1207/s15327973rlsi3802_3

Rignall, M. & Furneaux, C. (1997). *English for academic study series: Speaking*. London, England: Prentice Hall.

Roig, M. (1997). Can undergraduate students determine whether text has been plagiarized? *The Psychological Record, 47*, 113–123. Retrieved from http://thepsychologicalrecord.siuc.edu

Rose, D., Lui-Chivizhe, L., McKnight, A., & Smith, A. (2003). Scaffolding academic reading and writing at the Koori Centre. *Australian Journal of Indigenous Education, 32*, 41–49. Retrieved from www.uq.edu.au/atsis/ajie/docs/2003324149.pdf

Rost, M. (2002). Listening. In R. Carter & D. Nunan (Eds.), *The Cambridge guide to teaching English to speakers of other languages* (pp. 7–13). Retrieved from http://assets.cambridge.org

Rothwell, J.D. (2004). *In the company of others: Communicating in small groups.* New York, NY: McGraw-Hill.

Scanlon, P. M., & Neumann, D. R. (2002). Internet plagiarism among college students. *Journal of College Student Development, 43*, 374–386. Retrieved from www.jcsdonline.org

Scollon, R. (1995). Plagiarism and ideology: Identity in intercultural discourse. *Language in Society, 24*, 1–28. doi: 10.1017/S0047404500018388

Siler, T. (1996). *Think like a genius.* New York, NY: Bantam Books.

Silva, T., & Leki, I. (2004). Family matters: The influence of applied linguistics and composition studies on second language writing studies: Past, present, and future. *The Modern Language Journal, 88*(i), 1–13. doi: 10.1111/j.0026-7902.2004.00215.x

Silvey, D. (2005). *The reader's voice: Developing your understanding and enjoyment of college reading.* New York, NY: Pearson/Longman.

Simpson, O. (2008). Motivating learners in open and distance learning: Do we need a new theory of learner support? *Open Learning, 23*(3), 159–170. doi: 10.1080/02680510802419979

Şirin, A., & Güzel, A. (2006). The relationship between learning styles and problem solving skills among college students. *Educational Sciences: Theory & Practice, 6*(1), 255–264. Retrieved from http://web.ebscohost.com

Smith, D., Campbell, J., & Brooker, R. (1999). The impact of students' approaches to essay writing on the quality of their essays. *Assessment and Evaluation in Higher Education, 24*(3), 327–338. doi: 10.1080/0260293990240306

Soto, J. G., Anand, S., & McGee, E. (2004). Plagiarism avoidance: An empirical study examining teaching strategies. *Journal of College Science Teaching, 33*, 42–48. Retrieved from www.nsta.org/college

Style manual: for authors, editors and printers (6th ed.) [Revised by Snooks & Co.]. (2002). Milton, Queensland, Australia: John Wiley & Sons.

SWOT Analysis: Discover new opportunities: Manage and eliminate threats (n.d.). Retrieved from www.mindtools.com/pages/article/newTMC_05.htm

Taillefer, G. (2005). Reading for academic purposes: The literacy practices of British, French and Spanish Law and Economics students as background for study abroad. *Journal of Research in Reading, 28*(4), 435-451. doi:10.1111/j.1467-9817.2005.00283.x

Tang, E. & Ng, C. (1995). A study on the use of connectives in ESL students' writing. *Perspectives, 7*(2). 105–122. Retrieved from www.google.com.au

Thomlison, T. Dean. (1996). Intercultural listening. In M. Purdy & D. Borisoff (Eds.), *Listening in everyday life* (pp. 79–120). New York, NY: University Press of America.

Thompson, C. (2003). Information illiterate or lazy: How college students use the web for research. *Portal: Libraries and the Academy, 3*, 259–268. doi: 10.1353/pla.2003.0047

Todd, T., & Eveline, J. (2004). *Report on the review of the gender pay gap in Western Australia.* Retrieved from www.commerce.wa.gov.au/labourrelatios/PDF/Publications/Gender_Pay_Final_Rep.pdf

Toohey, S. (1999). *Designing courses for Higher Education.* Buckingham, UK: The Society for Research into Higher Education and Open University Press.

Trueman, M., & Hartley, J. (1996). A comparison between the time-management skills and academic performance of mature and traditional-entry university students. *Higher Education, 32*, 199–215. doi: 10.1007/BF00138396

Tuckman, B. W. (1965). Developmental sequence in small groups. *Psychological Bulletin, 63*, 384–399. doi: 10.1037/h0022100

Turner, H. & Williams, R. L. (2007). Vocabulary development and performance on multiple-choice exams in large entry-level courses. *Journal of College Reading and Learning, 37*(2), 64-81. Retrieved from www.eric.ed.gov

Verderber, R. F., & Verderber, K. S. (2003). *The challenge of effective speaking.* Melbourne, Australia: Thomson.

Volet, S., & Renshaw, P. (1996). Chinese students at an Australian university: Adaptability and continuity. In D. Watkins & J. B. Biggs (Eds.), *The Chinese learner: Cultural, psychological and contextual influences* (pp. 205–220). Hong Kong, China: Comparative Education Research Centre.

Vygotsky, L. (1978). *Mind in society: The development of higher psychological processes.* Cambridge, MA: Harvard University Press.

Wiersma, W. (1991). *Research methods in education* (5th ed.). Boston, MA: Allyn & Bacon.

Winckel, A., & Hart, B. (2002). *Style guide for engineering students* (4th ed.) [Revised and updated by M. Behrend & B. Kokkinn]. Retrieved from the University of South Australia Flexible Learning Centre website: www.unisa.edu.au/ame/research/doc/ReportWritingStyleGuideforEngineer.pdf

Wong, J. K.-K. (2004). Are the learning styles of Asian international students culturally or contextually based? *International Education Journal, 4*, 154–166. Retrieved from http://ehlt.flinders.edu.au/education/iej

Yeo, S. (2007). First-year university science and engineering students' understanding of plagiarism. *Higher Education Research & Development, 26*, 199–216. doi: 10.1080/07294360701310813

INDEX

Page references in **bold** indicate definitions.

Printed in Australia
19 Sep 2017
647104